ICEMAN

Brenda Fowler was born in Iowa in 1963. She holds a B.A. in journalism and international relations from the University of Wisconsin at Madison and an M.A. in humanities from the University of Chicago. As a Vienna-based contributor to the *New York Times*, she covered Central Europe and the discovery of the Iceman. Her work has also appeared in the *New York Times*, the *New York Times Magazine*, and *Lingua Franca*. She lives in Chicago.

ICEMAN

UNCOVERING THE LIFE AND TIMES
OF A PREHISTORIC MAN
FOUND IN AN ALPINE GLACIER

BRENDA FOWLER

PAN BOOKS

First published 2000 by Random House

First published in Great Britain 2001 by Macmillan

This edition published with a new epilogue 2002 by Pan Books
an imprint of Pan Macmillan Ltd
Pan Macmillan, 20 New Wharf Road, London N1 9RR
Basingstoke and Oxford
Associated companies throughout the world
www.panmacmillan.com

ISBN 0 330 48177 0

1 3 5 7 9 8 6 4 2

A CIP catalogue record for this book is available from
the British Library.

Printed and bound in Great Britain by
Mackays of Chatham plc, Chatham, Kent

For Mom and Dad

A primary cause for the poverty of the sciences
is their presumption of wealth. It's not their goal
to open the way for boundless wisdom,
but to set a limit on boundless error.

—BERTOLT BRECHT, *Life of Galileo*

He gave his life for tourism.

—STEVE MARTIN, "King Tut"

A NOTE ON SOURCES

Much of the information in this work comes from interviews, usually multiple and often conducted in person, with these people from September 1991 to the present.

Walter Ambach, Gert Ammann, Otto Appenzeller, Arthur Aufderheide, Bernardino Bagolini, Lawrence Barfield, Thomas Bereuter, Wolfram Bernhard, Sigmar Bortenschlager, Don Brothwell, Simon Buteux, Raúl J. Cano, Luigi Capasso, Silvano Dal Ben, Lorenzo Dal Ri, Raffaele C. De Marinis, Stefan Dietrich, Markus Egg, Henning Engeln, Katharine Everett, Angelika Fleckinger, Angelo Fossati, Othmar Gaber, Armin Gatterer, Roswitha Goedecker-Ciolek, Ivo Greiter, Geoffrey Grime, Willy Groenman–Van Waateringe, Renate Guggenberg, Sonia Guillén, Helmut Hager, Hans Haid, Oliva Handt, Michael Heim, Rainer Henn, Tim Holden, Rainer Hölzl, Bruno Hosp, Andrew K. G. Jones, Werner Kofler, Anton Koler, Walter Leitner, Andreas Lippert, Roman Lukasser, Dean L. Mann, Reinhold Messner, Hans Moser, Elisabetta Mottes, William A. Murphy, Jr., Manfred Neubauer, Helmut Niederkofler, Werner Nosko, Hans Nothdurfter, Walter Oberhuber, Klaus Oeggl, Svante Pääbo, Gernot Patzelt, Harm Paulsen, Annaluisa Pedrotti, Alois Pirpamer, Markus Pirpamer, Werner Platzer, Reinhold Pöder,

Johan Reinhard, Christian Reiter, Franco Rollo, Walter Romussi, Elsebet Sander-Jøergensen, Dieter Schäfer, Hatto Schmidt, Tillmann Scholl, Horst Seidler, Charlotte Sengthaler, Erika Simon, Helmut Simon, Torstein Sjøvold, Gernhard Sperl, Konrad Spindler, Anne Stone, Friedrich Tiefenbrunner, Hans Unterdorfer, Eddy van der Velden, Robert Wallner, David Weaver, Jürgen Weiner, Ned Woodall, Elisabeth Rastbichler-Zissernig, Dieter zur Nedden.

CONTENTS

PROLOGUE

NO ROOM
IN THE HELICOPTER

All weekend long, Professor Konrad Spindler had been casually following the story in the local media. According to the first report, on September 21, 1991, two hikers had stumbled upon a body melting out of a glacier deep in Austria's Ötztal Alps, near the Italian border. That was not far from the University of Innsbruck, where Spindler, an archaeologist, had served for the previous three years as chair of the small Department of Pre- and Early History. Apparently, someone had slipped into a crevasse in a glacier and died there before help arrived. In such cases, decades could pass before the corpse resurfaced at the glacier's melting edge. Occasionally, it could even take a century.

The recovery scenes were uncommonly grisly. Since the body is composed mainly of water, one locked inside a glacier can take on the properties of ice itself. As gravity pulls the glacier down a mountain, the frozen corpse deforms, stretches, and snaps like a rubber band. Glacier corpses can shatter into pieces or stretch out thin, like an image in a fun-house mirror. If the corpse is sealed off from air, it usually converts into adipocere, a waxlike substance that sometimes looks like crumbling Styrofoam and has a terrible stench. Often, by the time they melt out of the ice, these poor souls are no longer recognizable. Only through dental records or identity cards can authorities hope to learn who they are.

By Monday, reports confirmed that this particular corpse was different. According to the local newspaper, it was intact and remarkably well preserved.[1] It also appeared to be rather old. The world-famous mountaineer Reinhold Messner had happened by the scene and reported that the corpse held a metal ax in its hand and wore shoes like those of the Eskimos. He conjectured that it might be five hundred years old. That dating caught Spindler's eye, since he knew that human corpses evaded the natural decay process only in highly unusual circumstances. The bogs of northern Europe had yielded a few ancient corpses, one of which, the famed Lindow Man of Britain, was an astounding three millennia old. Here and there around the world, a few other naturally preserved bodies had come to light. But Spindler had never before heard of a body of archaeological interest emerging from a glacier.

The article's precise description of artifacts found with the body suggested that people had touched or even removed them. If so, that would be a blow for archaeology, since the relationship of artifacts to each other and to the ground in which they are deposited is critical to an understanding of them. As Spindler knew well from decades of patient labor in the field, a model archaeological excavation requires the careful sifting of each layer of dirt; every find, no matter how small, must be catalogued and whisked into a safe place. Progress was slow, and the spoils usually meager. Important information about the deposition of artifacts could be erased by a gust of wind.

The corpse was said to have already been delivered to the University of Innsbruck's Institute of Forensic Medicine, which also housed the medical examiner's office. Resolving to find out what was going on, Spindler picked up the phone and dialed.[2]

Recently, Spindler had started a minidepartment in medieval and historical archaeology at the university, where a fifteenth-century corpse would fit right in. The case also appealed to his varied interests. Spindler had written on a wide range of topics, from the Celts to twentieth-century pottery. Though he lived and worked in the Austrian province of Tyrol, he was a German by birth and had worked there for years. In the 1970s he had excavated a Bronze Age site in Germany known as Magdalenenberg, and he had a reputation as an ambitious researcher. In his short tenure at Innsbruck, Spindler had won the respect of his colleagues, but he was not chummy with them. He was a big man, age fifty-two, with a deliberate walk and an inscrutable frown, which lent him instant authority.

Like most archaeologists, he toiled in relative anonymity. He had nothing to do with the small clique of human origin archaeologists, like the Leakeys, who jet around the world, dig things up in secret African locations, and call press conferences to announce spectacular discoveries. The local media rarely paid any attention to the minor archaeological discoveries made in Tyrol province. The harsh mountainous landscape had been considered uninhabitable until about four thousand years ago, and the region contained no spectacular ancient monuments like the royal tombs of Egypt. Spindler's department consisted of just a handful of professors. Funding even their modest excavations was difficult, and they had only minimal conservation facilities. Spindler's new emphasis on the medieval world, by which time Tyrol was quite important, thus made sense. Students needed experience in the field, and there was plenty from that period to find.

When his call reached the office of the medical examiner, Spindler was connected to Dr. Rainer Henn, the head of the institute. No, Henn told Spindler, the corpse was not yet in Innsbruck and, no, he couldn't comment on rumors that it was several hundred years old. He was, however, leaving shortly to fly to the scene in a government helicopter. When Spindler inquired whether he might come along in case the find turned out to be of archaeological importance, Henn said that was impossible. The helicopter was not large enough. But he reassured Spindler that if anything about this glacier corpse was of potential interest to an archaeologist, he would be sure to let him know.

All Monday morning, the state-run radio station gave updates on the imminent recovery in its regular hourly reports. In Spindler's department, housed in a multistory building on the banks of the river Inn in downtown Innsbruck, the halls were quiet. Summer break was not yet over, and he was the only professor not away on vacation or at an excavation. By the afternoon, Spindler had still heard nothing from Henn. His working day over, Spindler got in his old Mercedes and drove home to the small village outside Innsbruck where he lived with his wife and their young children.

Back in his Innsbruck office, the phone was ringing.

ICEMAN

CHAPTER 1

THE FIRST TO SEE IT

U P AHEAD, still some two hours away, the snow-covered Similaun rose like a huge white sail against the cloudless Alpine sky. The last time Helmut and Erika Simon had stood on this spot, ten years earlier, the trail through the snow to the summit had been easy to pick out. But this summer had been unusually warm, nearly all the snow at this altitude had melted, and the trail had vanished amid the jumble of ice pockets and jagged gray schist that formed the backbone of the Tyrolean Alps. On their previous trip, they had turned around here and headed back down the mountain. But this time, despite the wind they had battled all day, Helmut was determined to reach the summit of the 11,808-foot Similaun.

After strapping crampons on their boots, they prepared to cross the Niederjochferner, a massive glacier, the surface of which had the consistency of refrozen crushed ice. The glacier was melting, and the runoff water had bored a network of tiny tunnels and canals into its surface. As they stepped onto the glistening ice, the Simons could hear water gurgling and dripping as it moved through the glacier.

It was Wednesday, September 18, 1991. Their day had begun six hours earlier and about 3,600 feet lower in the tiny village of Vernagt in Italy's Schnalstal. Vernagt consisted of a few pretty farmhouses and small inns, clustered around the sunny side of a man-made lake. At the crack of dawn, the Simons had pulled on their backpacks for a long day's hike. The route, which led up a steep valley, over the glacier, and up the snowy mountain's flanks to the summit, demanded stamina but no special climbing equipment. Every summer day, a dozen or more tourists reached the peak, one in a chain along the Austrian-Italian border. For the Simons, frequent visitors to the Schnalstal mountains, the path was tolerably challenging.

Both in their early fifties, the Simons were practical hikers who had spent the first few days of this vacation on shorter hikes, trying to acclimatize themselves to the high altitude and getting their office legs in shape. They were from Nuremberg, Germany, where Helmut, a cheery man with a bulldog's gait, worked as the custodian of the public library and Erika, a slight and solemn figure, put in her time at the local newspaper's personnel department. For a while, the going was smooth, and they fell into a nice rhythm of small steps across the crunchy expanse of the glacier, which flowed down the northern side of the mountain into Austria's Ötztal. Suddenly, they drew to a halt.

Two yards ahead, the ice was split by a chasm that ran as far as they could see in both directions and was wide enough to swallow a person. Together the couple inched forward cautiously for a closer look into the wondrous abyss. The solid ice walls of the plunging crevasse were hues of gray, brown, and white and shone like opal or were swirled like some precious, dark marble. How deep it was, or where it led, the Simons could not fathom.

Climbing lore was filled with tales of menacing crevasses obscured by snow cover, and the Simons had heard their share. A hiker who inadvertently walked onto snow concealing a crevasse could break through and plunge into the ice. Sometimes, the snow would then fall in and bury the hiker alive. If the victim survived the fall, it might be almost impossible to claw out of the icy trench. Trapped hikers could then die of hypothermia. The risk was real, which was why people who ventured over snow-covered glaciers were supposed to rope up together in a line. If one fell through, then the others could try to pull him out.

Since this crevasse was visible, it was not really a problem, although the Simons had to walk parallel to it for several yards before the gap narrowed enough for them to be able to step across it. Again, they turned toward the summit. But they soon ran into another fissure and then another. Somehow they had entered a maze of crevasses. Again and again, they were forced to take long detours, looking for places to cross.

When they finally reached the rocky ridge that led up to the summit of the Similaun, Helmut glanced at his watch. It had taken them nearly three hours to get to this point when it should have taken only two, and now the sun was halfway down in the western sky. He realized that they might not have enough daylight left to make it back down the mountain. Erika wouldn't like it, but Helmut knew they could always get a bunk in the drafty old Similaun *Hütte*, a rustic Alpine lodge where they had rested for a few hours over lunch on the way up the mountain, and then descend in the morning.

As they finally approached the summit, a younger couple overtook them. Minutes later, the four were crowded around the rocky cone of the summit, breathing hard and surveying the Alps of Italy and Austria. If you knew how to stand, you could get one foot in both countries, since the border ran right along the ridge. Helmut asked the other couple to take a picture of him and Erika next to the wooden cross that marked the highest point of the summit. After a short rest, all four set off back toward the Similaun lodge. By the time they arrived, it was nearly 6 P.M., and the first stars were already sparkling in the pale evening sky.

Accessible only by foot over mountain trails, the timbered, three-story lodge was situated well above the tree line in the nook of a pass over the main Alpine ridge, a stone's throw from the Austrian border. The cramped bunk rooms had no running water, and the toilet was outside. Anyone who had to visit it in the middle of the night faced a miserable dash along the edge of a cliff, guided only by a dim bulb hanging over the door. The Simons, who had nothing but the sweaty clothes on their backs, were not prepared to spend the night away from their cozy bed-and-breakfast in the valley, but Helmut persuaded his wife it was too dark to risk the descent. Anyway, as alpine lodges went, the century-old *Hütte* had a lot of character. They could get a hearty meal here, plenty of Italian red wine, and awaken with the sun.

The next morning, Helmut rose quickly and went outside to check the weather. The sky was radiant. He stood for a while looking at the sun illuminating the mighty snowcap on a mountain range to the west. The night before, the couple he and Erika had met at the summit had invited them on a climb up the nearby Finail Peak. He knew Erika's first priority was to hurry down the mountain and into a hot shower. But on such a day, and with such good company, he knew he would be able to convince her to make a go at another summit.

After breakfast, the Simons and their new friends started on the trail to the Finail Peak, which closely followed the main Alpine ridge. The landscape was lunar in its bleakness. The reddish gray stone that formed the ridge was gradually crumbling away, and the result was an endless sea of uneven rock slabs. Some of these boulders balanced precariously for centuries before finally crashing down on one side or the other of the ridge. Occasionally the trail traversed a field of snow over ice embedded in the broken rock. At this altitude, far above the tree line, real soil was nonexistent. Even at the peak of summer, only a few weedy sprouts found places to plant themselves amid the heaps of stone. Walking demanded strict attention, since a misplaced step could send a person hurtling against a rough boulder or careening down a slope.

Shortly after noon, the happy group reached the summit. Toward Italy, they looked down on a boulder-strewn and treeless landscape that merged gradually with the pine forests and then ended in a burst of emerald green and marine blue. These were the pastures and artificial lake at Vernagt. The view into Austria was not nearly as inviting. Though the decline was more gradual, the slopes were draped in deep snow and ice. To the northeast, more craggy Ötztal mountains, like choppy waves on a stormy sea, extended to the horizon.

As exciting as the panorama was, no one wanted to linger on the narrow ledge, where they were buffeted by gusts coming up from the Schnalstal. The two couples exchanged addresses and then quit the summit. Since the Austrians were headed into the Ötztal, the couples' paths soon diverged, and they paused to say warm goodbyes.

The younger couple headed down the rocky slope and the Simons turned to canvass the landscape ahead for a marker that would get them on the trail to the lodge. Erika spotted a pile of rocks with a stick coming out the top about one hundred yards away, and the couple began hiking toward it. Known colloquially as a *Steinmanndl,* or "little stone man," in German, such man-made markers were stacked up every so often, and occasionally planted with a stick, to guide tourists along sections of Alpine trails. A minute later, they reached a low ridge of rock that formed a wall around a long trench. The floor of the trench was filled with meltwater, ice, and snow. To circumvent the water, they proceeded to one side, moving along the inside of the trench, over snow and rock. Helmut was walking in the lead when he suddenly caught sight of something dark against the white snow. Just a half hour earlier he had been outraged to see broken glass from a champagne bottle on the summit of the Finail. At first he thought it was just more trash, and he silently cursed the lazy tourist who had done it. But his wife's next words came in the same instant in which he, too, recognized what he was seeing.

"Look, it's a person!" Erika exclaimed.

Aghast, they halted, steps from a human body stuck in the ice. Instinctively, they veered from the macabre scene and scrambled up four or five steps onto a ledge in the low ridge that nearly enveloped the trench. In the next instant, Helmut sprinted back to try to recall the Austrian couple. After some eighty yards he stopped, yelling their names against the wind. He scanned the landscape below but, seeing no one, he turned and dashed back to Erika, who was still standing speechless on the ledge above the body. Helmut's heart pounded.

There, protruding from a solid bed of ice, was a torso, face down. Not a hair remained on the head. The shoulders and upper back were naked. The skin was brown and stretched so tautly across the back and shoulders that the ribs were visible. It looked emaciated. A dozen ideas flickered through their minds. They wondered who it could be and what had happened. Since the shoulders were so narrow, Erika decided it must be the corpse of a woman.

The face appeared to rest on a cushion of slush and ice. Clumps of dark stringy material underneath the chin reminded Erika of seaweed on a beach. On the back of the head was a circular break in the skin. It looked like a wound, but the Simons did not think too much about it or even wonder why the skin was still intact. They did not have much to compare this to.

Helmut started removing his camera from its case, but Erika protested and admonished him for even thinking of taking a photograph. It was the height of disrespect to make an image of a dead person, she said.

But Helmut insisted. If this were his relative, he would want to know exactly what had happened. Still on the ledge several feet above the corpse, he crouched and aimed his camera. Then, thinking better, he pushed the telephoto button, the lens glided out, and he snapped the picture. He could have taken another, but he thought one was enough.*

Emboldened, Helmut then descended into the trench for a closer look at the corpse. Erika stayed glued to the ledge. Not far from the head, Helmut noticed something lying on the ice, and he stooped to pick it up. It was a flattened bundle wrapped in white birch bark and apparently tied up with leather laces. As he turned it in his hands, he noted how fragile and soggy it was. To Erika it looked like something a bird might have carried up. Helmut had no idea what it could be or even whether it was anything at all. After another moment's contemplation, he tossed it aside.

Nearby was a piece of a blue rubber ski clip, the kind he himself had used a decade earlier to bind his skis together. Helmut did not really consider whether this object had belonged to the person whose corpse now lay here in front of them. The Simons did not speak much. Neither did they touch the corpse. Moments earlier, they had been chatting merrily with their young friends, and now, abruptly, they had stumbled upon a death. Something terrible had happened to this person, and they realized that the same thing could happen to them. They were awed, and a little intimidated, by the appearance of death on this beautiful day.

After several minutes, Helmut climbed back onto the ledge, and the couple stood a moment in contemplation. They were still an

---

*Less than a week later, when this photograph of the corpse's head was published around the world, it was usually called the "last picture" on the roll of film. Indeed, it was the thirty-sixth frame on a thirty-six-frame roll. However, Helmut Simon eked out one last photo—the thirty-seventh—of his wife back at the Similaun lodge later that day.

hour from the lodge. Together, they walked toward the *Stein-manndl*, noted the relation of the marker to the corpse, and then departed for the lodge.

Soon, they encountered a lone hiker coming toward them, and they greeted each other as they passed. A few steps further on, the Simons stopped and turned to watch the man's path. He seemed to stay on the main track, so they guessed he would not happen upon the corpse. Helmut briefly considered whether they should even report what they had seen. The plans for the rest of their vacation might be ruined if they had to spend time in a police station, filling out reports or serving as witnesses. Without resolving the issue, they continued on toward the lodge.

Markus Pirpamer, the spirited young caretaker of the Similaun *Hütte,* was tidying up the kitchen when the Simons walked in. Oddly, the couple thought later, they had not reflected on their morbid discovery much on the hike back, and Helmut had almost forgotten about it. He ordered his usual beer, as well as an orange juice for Erika. Then she gave her husband a nudge. "Is anyone missing from around here?" he asked.

Markus, a sinewy twenty-six-year-old with a handsome, lined face that belied a summer spent outdoors, remembered the Simons from the evening before. He shook his head. "No," he drawled with growing curiosity.

Helmut then got right to the point. "We just came across a corpse melting out of ice," he said.

The news galvanized Pirpamer. His father, Alois, was the head of the volunteer Alpine rescue squad in Vent, the tiny village just down the mountain in Austria, so Markus had grown up hearing tragic stories about people's battles against mountains and ice. He himself had once become dangerously disoriented while trying to reach his *Hütte* during a snowstorm. He knew death haunted these mountains, but this was the first time that it had confronted him on his watch.

He expertly quizzed the Simons on the corpse's location and assured them that he would handle everything. The Simons wandered outside with their drinks and joined some other hikers at a sunny

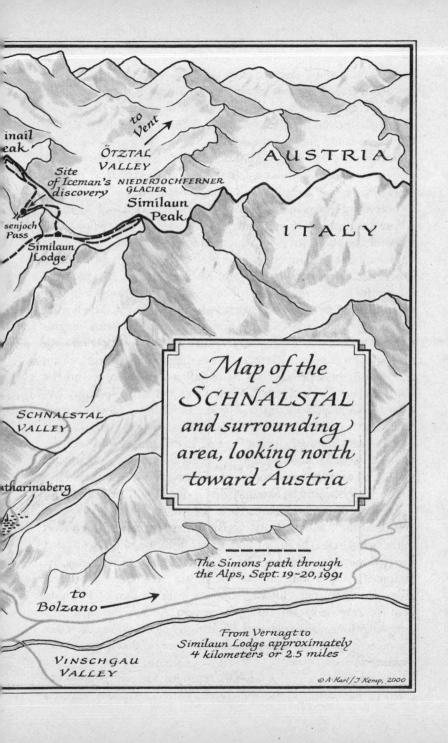

to Vent

ÖTZTAL VALLEY

AUSTRIA

inail eak

Site of Iceman's discovery

NIEDERJOCHFERNER GLACIER

Similaun Peak

ITALY

senjoch Pass

Similaun Lodge

SCHNALSTAL VALLEY

atharinaberg

Map of the SCHNALSTAL *and surrounding area, looking north toward Austria*

to Bolzano

The Simons' path through the Alps, Sept. 19–20, 1991

From Vernagt to Similaun Lodge approximately 4 kilometers or 2.5 miles

VINSCHGAU VALLEY

© A·Karl / J·Kemp, 2000

table. Soon Markus emerged from the lodge with a pair of binoculars and marched Helmut to a spot with a view of the Finail Peak. From there, Helmut once again explained the location of the find, noting the proximity of the unusual *Steinmanndl* and stick. The binoculars could not pick the site out.

Back inside the lodge, Markus telephoned his father, who ran the Hotel Post and its popular tavern in Vent. Alois kept close tabs on news in the village and the surrounding mountains, but he could recall no missing persons from recent years. His guess was that the corpse was probably that of some unlucky tourist. They would have to notify the authorities—the question was *which ones.*

Helmut Simon's directions were not precise enough for even the experienced Pirpamers to determine where the corpse lay relative to the border between Italy's province of South Tyrol (known in Italian as Alto Adige) and the Austrian province of Tyrol. The border had an ugly and painful history, but in an era of European integration and openness, the locals barely paid it any heed. People on both sides spoke a dialect of German, made their livings off agriculture and tourism, built their houses out of timber and stucco, and ate the same kinds of foods. Though Markus was a German-speaking Tyrolean, his Similaun *Hütte* stood on Italian territory. Alois was from Vent, but his wife was from the Schnalstal, as was Markus's girlfriend. Every summer, hikers from all over Europe, and well beyond, crossed that border without ever having to show a document.

Alois advised his son to inform the police in both countries. They had maps and would be able to figure it out from their offices.

Markus called the gendarmerie in Sölden, an Austrian town near Vent, and the carabinieri, Italy's paramilitary branch of the police, in the Schnalstal. The impression he got from the officials was that the retrieval would happen that day, so he went outside to ask the Simons to hang around until the helicopter arrived. At first, the Simons agreed to wait. But after an hour, with no sign of an imminent recovery operation, they grew restless. Already they had been gone a day longer than planned. So, after giving the young caretaker the name of their bed-and-breakfast, they set off down the mountain into the Schnalstal.

The burden of responsibility now transferred to him, Markus decided he had better locate the corpse. With his kitchen helper, a young Bosnian, he headed for the site. Markus knew the *Stein-manndl* with the stick was close to a pass called the Hauslabjoch. After an hour's hike and five minutes' scan of the terrain, the two spotted the brown corpse sticking out of ice at one end of a long, shallow trench. Markus had passed by here more times than he could count, and he had never seen so little ice and snow in the trench.

The young men approached tentatively. The corpse looked exactly as Helmut Simon had described it. It seemed to be almost standing up in the ice, and was naked as far as they could see. Like the Simons, Markus noted what looked like a bad wound on the back of the head.

Suddenly, he spotted something else. There, on the rocky ledge where the Simons had stood, was another object. He took a step forward and unhesitatingly picked it off the rocks. It looked like an ax. The wooden handle was smooth and weathered. The tawny metal blade, barely broader than a hammerhead, was inserted into a beaklike notch in the handle and then bound in with a strip of leather. That style of hafting looked old-fashioned, and both young men examined it closely. Neither recalled ever having seen a tool exactly like it before.

Markus now noticed that the rocks where he had found the ax were plastered with tangled string and bunches of what looked like the fur of a chamois, a goatlike animal that had been hunted to extinction in this part of the Alps. That meant the fur must be rather old. Scattered among the string and fur were a few weathered boards and sticks. Markus thought it was strange that the German couple had not mentioned these things to him, especially the ax. He wondered whether they could have missed them. As he set the ax back on the reddish rocks, he noticed that it became well camouflaged.

Lots of things were. The further they looked, the more they found. Leaning up against the ledge was a long wooden stick with a very neatly whittled surface. Its lower end disappeared into solid ice at the bottom of the trench. On the slushy ice near the corpse's head, Markus also spotted the birch-bark object Helmut had picked up and tossed to the side. It appeared to be stuffed with wet hay.

Markus realized that all this wood must have been carried up from a lower altitude, since no trees grew here. He assumed these were all the belongings of the person whose body was now stuck in the ice. The discoveries were quite exciting, if somewhat troubling. He was sure this was no one he had known. He guessed that this accident had occurred some time ago, probably before he was born. After scavenging around the site for a half hour, he and the Bosnian cook returned to the lodge.

Markus's report of a corpse had set off little flurries of activity in the normally sleepy offices of Alpine law enforcement. The Italian carabinieri who staffed the tiny station in the Schnalstal were not supposed to handle mountain accidents. Technically, such incidents were the responsibility of the Alpine Aid Unit, a branch of the Customs Guard, located in another building just one hundred yards away. But work was a little slow, so the carabinieri decided to check the map themselves to see whether the site was in Italy or Austria. No official map of the border area was available, so the men consulted the map of the Alpine Club, the one normally used by tourists. The carabinieri saw it was a close call, but they decided the site was Austria's, and they took no further action on the matter that day.

Meanwhile, over the mountain border in Sölden, Austrian gendarmes, as one branch of the country's law enforcement was known, had been poring over the same Alpine Club map. They, too, had concluded that the site was in their country. That meant someone was going to have to go up there and bring the corpse down. By law, all mountain accidents had to be investigated by Alpine gendarmes, who had special training in, among other things, rescuing people from glacier crevasses and avalanches. But no Alpine gendarme was on duty that day in Sölden, so the commander called up Anton Koler, a regional inspector based sixty miles away in the town of Imst, at the mouth of the Ötztal.

In Koler's nine years on the job, there had been more than two hundred mountain accidents annually in his district, and the figure kept rising every year. Usually the accidents were minor: skiers breaking their legs or hikers getting lost. Glacier corpses turned up rarely. But over the last century, in a trend not yet well understood, the Alpine glaciers had been melting slowly, and this summer's melt had been extreme in some places. Across Austria, five other bodies had already been recovered from glaciers this season, and all were presumed or known to be crevasse accidents.[1] Just three weeks ago, Koler had recovered the remains of a Viennese couple who had disappeared one summer day in 1934. He had seen by the style of their hiking clothes and leather boots that they had been in the ice a long time. There had even been a twisted pair of wire-frame glasses found among the bodies.

Technically, Koler could have told the commander to have Alois Pirpamer extricate the corpse and bring it down the mountain, but he knew using a government helicopter would make the job faster and easier. An Alpine gendarme would have to fill out a report at some point anyway, so Koler ordered a helicopter for the following morning. He would do the recovery himself.

Back in Sölden, the commander had been looking through the station's files for active reports of missing persons. When the search turned up nothing, he drove up the valley to the Hotel Post. Alois Pirpamer and his wife recalled that an Italian music professor had left on a hike from the Schöne Aussicht lodge in 1938 and never arrived at his intended destination. The commander noted this and spoke once again by phone with Markus Pirpamer, who was still at the Similaun lodge, a five-hour hike away. That evening, the station in Sölden sent out the following teletype report, which was later released to the media.

alpine incident =
corpse found at hauslabjoch (niederjochferner) - advance report on 19th september 1991 around 12:00 p.m. climbers coming down from the finail summit found a partially melted-out corpse in the vicinity of the hauslabjoch (a little below it) on the niederjochferner. it is practically standing up in the ice. only head and shoulder areas are sticking out of the ice. the caretaker of the similaun Hütte, markus pirpamer reported this to the gp [gendarmerie post] in soelden. He himself was on the site this afternoon. based on the equipment it is a mountain accident that happened many years ago. in vent it was learned that since the year 1938 a music professor from verona named capsoni, who was on the way from the schoene aussicht via the hauslabjoch to the

similaun Hütte is still missing. the recovery of the corpse will follow as far as can be seen on 9-20-1991. a further report will be
submitted.[2]

Early on the afternoon of Friday, September 20, an Austrian government helicopter touched down on the Hauslabjoch. Anton
Koler climbed out and greeted Markus Pirpamer, who was on hand
to show the craft where to land. Without much ceremony, the two
men, who already knew each other, walked into the trench. Markus
pointed out the body in the ice.

Koler saw right away that this was no ordinary glacier corpse. It
was in one piece and had no obvious stench. But Koler had encountered death in many different ways in his line of work, and the
fact that this glacier corpse was somewhat unusual did not really
concern him. His first task was to document the site in case it turned
out to be the scene of a crime. His hunch was that it was not. Apart
from the body, the main evidence was the ax, fur, string, and wood
scattered atop the rock ledge above the corpse. Pirpamer had already picked up and examined these items, but Koler did not seem
bothered that the evidence had been disturbed. In fact, he had to
move the ax a little to get it to show up in a photograph against the
camouflaging rock. This was not exactly pristine detective work, but
he did not consider it too important in this case. If this were clearly
the scene of a murder, the inspector might have taken dozens of
photographs. But he now took only two: one of the evidence on the
ledge, and the other of the emaciated corpse.

To aid in the extrication, he had brought along a little gadget his
station had recently acquired. It was a small, pistol-like jackhammer
that was supposed to be very effective at blasting away ice. He
switched it on, and, without delay since the skies did not look
promising, he set to chiseling away the ice. It was tough work.
Markus soon offered to chip in, though he had never operated such
a tool before.

As they hammered the ice away, slowly revealing more of the
corpse's upper body, they noticed that it appeared to be draped over
a boulder. The left arm reached over to the right, crossing under the
chin, while the right one extended out and then down into the ice.

It did not look like a very comfortable position. But by this point the two men were thinking mainly of their own comfort. The further they dug, the deeper in ice, slush, and melted water they had to work.

Koler lay on his stomach on the ice, almost up to his shoulder in icy water and slush, and aimed the miniature jackhammer at the ice. He could not see exactly where the tip of the hammer was striking, and a few times he felt the machine drive into the corpse itself. Shreds of dried flesh rose to the surface of the water. But he was not worried about the damage. Recovering a body was never pretty. He wanted to finish the job as efficiently as possible, but the work was tougher than he had anticipated.

Less than an hour after they had started, with the corpse still packed in ice up to the hips, the tool ran out of compressed air. Koler did not have a refill. Moreover, the weather, which in the high Alps could change within minutes, had turned threatening. The rest would have to be finished later. Koler was mildly annoyed. He had flown up here at considerable expense, and now he was not going to be able to finish the job. He radioed the helicopter, which had retreated to a lower altitude, and took one more picture of the corpse. The two men had made progress. The top of the corpse's buttocks was now visible, as were the sides of the chest, all the way up to the head. Only the legs were still entirely buried in the dark ice. The damage from the jackhammer was also clearly visible, especially around the left hip. The stringy flesh was ripped out down to the bone.

While working over the corpse, Markus had noticed several rows of black marks on the corpse's back. They ran parallel to the spine and looked to him like burns or even brands. He was not sure what to make of them or the round break in the skin on the back of the head. Koler was operating on the assumption that if this was the scene of a crime, it must have happened a long time ago, probably in the previous century. He did not know who this might be, but considering that strange ax, he doubted it was the Italian music professor. The helicopter soon arrived, and Koler told Markus that the recovery would be resumed the next day. Markus then picked up the ax and set it inside the helicopter.

Back in Vent, Alois Pirpamer, a few gendarmes from Sölden, and the local undertaker, who had been expecting a corpse, had gathered in the tavern of the Hotel Post to await the helicopter. They all knew each other and were joking and exchanging bits of news at Alois's regular table when they heard the rotors of the helicopter coming down through the rocky valley. Stepping outside, they watched it approach and noticed that no body bag was tied on beneath the craft. Alois wondered what had gone wrong. Koler climbed out of the helicopter and explained the situation to the other gendarmes and the undertaker, who had driven thirty miles up the valley to meet this corpse. According to Austrian law, only licensed undertakers were permitted to transport the dead along roadways. The day's trip might have been a bust, but the undertaker could still be confident that there was some business to be done here.

The ax was taken to the station in Sölden. The commander was impressed by its easy, balanced swing. Curious about what kind of metal the blade was made of, he took out his car key and scratched through the dull brown surface. It was bright and orange, so the commander concluded that it must be copper. Unfortunately, he was not aware that copper axes had not been produced since the Stone Age. But he did think he should treat this piece of evidence with some care. He lined a box with old newspaper, bedded the ax inside, and then carried it downstairs to the air-raid shelter for safekeeping.

Several hours later, the gendarmes in Sölden received a call from a German-speaking carabiniere in the Schnalstal who informed them that he had just located the grave of the Italian music professor. The body on the Hauslabjoch, therefore, must belong to someone else. He also concurred that the corpse was on Austrian territory. With little ado, the case had officially landed in the lap of the Austrians.

CHAPTER 2

A DIFFICULT RECOVERY

ON SATURDAY, SEPTEMBER 21, Reinhold Messner awoke in the Weisskugel lodge, several miles west of the site of the discovery. Messner, the world's most accomplished mountain climber and a household name in Europe, was on day eleven of his highly publicized forty-one-day tour of South Tyrolean peaks. If all went well, he and his climbing partner, Hans Kammerlander, would reach the Similaun lodge sometime that afternoon. Over breakfast that morning, Messner was paging through the local newspaper, *Dolomiten,* when a brief article caught his eye.

CORPSE DISCOVERY ON TYROLEAN GLACIER

Innsbruck (APA)—The mortal remains of an unknown alpinist were discovered Thursday afternoon on the Niederjochferner in the locality of Sölden. The identity of the corpse, which had been lying in the ice for several decades, could not at first be clarified.[1]

Yet another little human tragedy in the mountains, Messner thought sadly, before turning the page. As the only man alive who had climbed all fourteen of the world's highest peaks, including Mount Everest solo, Messner was intimately familiar with the dangers inherent in mountain climbing. His own brother had frozen to death on a mountain, and he had lost several other friends to

storms, avalanches, and falls. Whether by sheer luck or informed in-
solence, Messner was still alive. Even now, at the age of forty-seven,
he could not give up climbing.

By all accounts, Messner, whose abundant chestnut curls and un-
tamed beard made him look like an aging hippie, was the best
climber who had ever lived. Over the years he had learned that he
could use his reputation to profit not only himself but also those
causes he cared about. Messner wrote and lectured extensively on
his climbing adventures and the people and places he encountered
along the way. Environmental issues were his pet concern, and he
spoke out urgently on the need to protect the remote mountainous
areas of the earth such as those in South Tyrol. He despised how the
cable-car lines and ski runs had now branded the Alps' forests of
pine and fir.

Once a Swiss newspaper had played an elaborate joke on Messner
by setting up a newspaper stand high on the Matterhorn, the country's most important mountain, just before Messner was scheduled
to pass by on a hike. The prank had all of Europe in stitches, but
Messner himself was only slightly amused. He really did believe that
the Alps were sacred.

In recent years, he had turned to a more explicitly political cause.
He identified himself ethnically as a German-speaking Tyrolean, but
he also spoke fluent Italian and strongly supported South Tyrol's
autonomous status within the Italian state. He had little patience for
those who looked back nostalgically to the time before the end of
World War I when South Tyrol was united with the northern part
of Tyrol under the Austrian Habsburgs. He believed South Tyrol
should develop its own unique identity, and this message had found
resonance among the province's German-speaking youth. Part of
the point of Messner's tour of South Tyrolean peaks was to draw attention to the region's own history and traditions. He had invited
various experts to meet him at lodges along his route for informal
discussions on topics such as sacred prehistoric sites and the eco-
nomics of shepherding. When the tour was over, he would write up
his experiences in a book. Like a Jacques Cousteau of the mountains, Messner had become famous through his singular exploits
and rich by knowing how to publicize them. The media were constantly tuned in to Reinhold Messner.

To those who knew mountains, like the Pirpamers, the man was a living legend. They were honored that he was planning to stay in their lodge, even if they were somewhat preoccupied with the corpse on the Hauslabjoch. Alois, whose rangy stride and sparkling blue eyes had been passed down to his son, was scheduled to lead a group of hikers from the lodge to the Similaun summit the same afternoon as Messner's arrival. He had hiked up from Vent the day before and spent the evening in conversation with Markus, who recounted how he and Koler had tried to free the corpse from the ice earlier that day. After breakfast the next morning, Alois headed for the Hauslabjoch. He found the corpse easily and spent a good while poking around, examining the bits and pieces lying on the rocks. He thought he recognized the carved wooden branch frozen in the ice as a type of walking stick carried in the Alps years ago. People had used them when crossing glaciers to test the snow ahead for crevasses.

When he got back to the lodge, he asked his son to cover the corpse as quickly as possible. The Pirpamers depended on tourism for their livelihood, and a dead hiker sticking out of a bed of ice was not exactly a good promotion for their region. Soon after receiving a call from a gendarme in Sölden who said no helicopter was free to do the recovery that day, Markus and another lodge employee set off for the site with a black plastic trash bag.

The day was warm again and a lot of water and slush had accumulated around the corpse, which was still frozen to the boulder below. The two tried sweeping it away, but it flowed back stubbornly. By now, Markus was quite comfortable around the corpse, and he no longer paid much attention to the little scraps of leather, string, and other bits of material that floated by as he carried out his task. The main thing, he thought, was to keep the corpse cold, to prevent it from spoiling. Toward this end, he put a little slush on the body, covered the whole thing with the black plastic, and weighted it down with stones and bigger chunks of ice. He took a few steps back and examined his handiwork. Now the grave was barely noticeable amid the white snow, gray ice, and rock.

Markus had just turned to head back to the lodge when he noticed a flat piece of birch bark lying loose on some rocks just outside the trench. He stopped to pick it up. The delicate, oval-shaped object was the size of his hand and had evenly spaced holes around the edge. Someone must have cut it like that, Markus thought, remembering the birch-bark object he had seen lying near the corpse. Somehow it had been broken into lots of little pieces in the last several days. Markus decided to spare this perfect little piece by bringing it along with him to the lodge.

Soon after his return, Hans and Gerlinde Haid arrived at the lodge from the Ötztal, where they lived in a picturesque old farmhouse. He was a folklorist who had written several books on Alpine life, and she studied folk music. Both knew a great deal about the history of the region. Recently he had published a book in which he claimed to have discovered several prehistoric sites of worship in the uppermost reaches of the Ötztal, not far from the Similaun lodge. His books sold well, but academics barely paid them heed. He was convinced that the connections between the Schnalstal and Ötztal went back millennia, but the University of Innsbruck's professional archaeologists had found very little to back this up. Haid knew that he and Messner shared an audience, so he had gladly accepted the Alpinist's invitation to meet up during his tour. The topic would be traditional ties between the two valleys.

Markus Pirpamer had not mentioned the corpse to many of his guests, but he knew who the Haids were and that they might have something to say about it. As the Haids listened eagerly, Markus told them about the discovery and showed them the piece of birch bark he had found there. When he mentioned the ax, Hans Haid's curiosity soared. He grilled Markus on the shape of the blade and the way it was hafted. He thought the artifact Markus described sounded quite old and might even be relevant to the history of the area. He wanted to see the ax and was disappointed to learn that it had already been taken down the mountain. The couple decided to wait for Messner before rushing off to take a look at the corpse.

Before long, the great climber and his partner arrived with a local guide. Their path from the Weisskugel lodge had taken them within yards of the concealed corpse, but a light snow had been falling on the Hauslabjoch, and they had not noticed it. When the Haids told the men about the odd discovery, Messner remembered reading about it that morning in the paper. But only when Markus and Haid mentioned the ax and drew a picture of it did he become intrigued.

Like Haid, Messner knew something about ax technology. [In the early 1970s he had visited Papua New Guinea and seen people making and using stone axes.] Provided that Markus's account was correct, the tool might be a rather important find. They all agreed to go see the corpse for themselves.

Messner and his two companions arrived at the Hauslabjoch first, easily located the plastic, and pulled it away. For a moment or two, the three men stood together in silence around the body. Messner felt a rush of sympathy for this desperate figure. The posture of the body, with the two arms stretched out to the right, suggested that the man—he assumed it was a man—had lain down on this large rock in exhaustion. He noted immediately that the corpse was astonishingly well preserved.

Peering through a foot of water that covered the corpse from the waist down, growing deeper toward the feet, Messner observed that the legs were wrapped in what looked like leather bands sewn together. Even the rows of seams were visible through the water. They saw a shoe on the right foot, which seemed to be lying atop the left one, and noticed grass sticking out along the top of the shoe around the ankle. Messner knew that Lapps near the Arctic Circle stuffed their shoes with grass for insulation, and he assumed that this individual had been doing the same thing.

Messner was starting to think that this was an important archaeological find. He would not have been surprised if the corpse was at least several hundred years old, though he could not fathom how the grass in the shoes had lasted so long. The stringlike stuff on the rocky ledge added to his confusion. He did not know when string was invented, but this looked like the extra-thick variety he remembered from his childhood. Yet the blue rubber ski clip nearby looked newer. Somehow it did not fit together.

Kammerlander, meanwhile, had found a stick on the ledge near the string and fur and was using it to hack away some of the ice around the corpse's legs to see what else was down there. The guide, too, was prying at the corpse. Messner knew it wasn't a good idea to poke around like that, but he did not try to stop them. They were grown men, responsible for their own actions.

In any case, the two men soon realized the work was going nowhere. The corpse was stuck too deeply in the ice. They might, however, be able to get a look at the face. Messner knelt down on the ice in front of the corpse and lowered his head. Kammerlander grasped the back of the cold, moist head and tried to pull it up. Normally, a corpse's neck would have bent back slightly. But this neck was frozen stiff, and the head just barely tilted back. Messner couldn't get his own head low enough to see into the man's eyes. But he did notice a woven grass mat on the rock under the corpse's chest. He guessed the man had probably spread it across the boulder before he had lain down.

Searching the area around the site, the men also noticed fragments of birch bark smeared into the slush and snow near the corpse. They could not make anything at all out of the pieces. For a while, they turned their attention to digging out the long whittled branch, which they concluded was a walking stick, but this, too, proved unsuccessful. Despite the thaw in the trench, the ice was obstinate.

Messner's group had been at the site for at least fifteen minutes before Hans Haid arrived. Gerlinde was still somewhere behind him. As soon as Haid saw the corpse, he was convinced it was an important find. He suspected the round wound on the back of the head was from a trephination, an operation in which a hole is cut into the skull so the brain can be removed. Skeletons from several prehistoric cultures displayed such holes. By the time Haid's wife arrived, Messner's group was preparing to leave. Together, the climbers re-covered the corpse before setting off for the lodge. But these strange artifacts had proved too tempting. Unbeknown to the others, one of the five left the site with a small souvenir.

Back at the *Hütte,* talk of the strange corpse continued through the afternoon and early evening. Pirpamer said the authorities knew about the find and were planning to come get it the next day. Still, Messner reported the find to his expedition manager, who had arrived while they were away, and he asked him to alert authorities in South Tyrol when he went down the mountain the next day.

In the meantime, Messner himself had no intention of keeping silent about it. The Italian-language newspaper *Alto Adige,* based in South Tyrol's capital, Bolzano, had been faithfully following Messner's tour of the province. Its correspondent had called Messner every night he stayed in a lodge with a telephone. That evening, when he rang for an update, Messner told him about the discovery in detail and estimated that the corpse was between five hundred and three thousand years old. The correspondent, though excited, thought three thousand was a bit too sensational a figure even for his paper. He argued that it was not until recently that people had ventured high into the mountains.

But Messner disagreed, recalling that Friedrich IV with the Empty Purse, a fifteenth-century duke of Austria and Tyrol, was said to have sought refuge in the Ötztal while fleeing the German King Sigmund of Luxemburg. The correspondent took it from there. The next morning, Sunday, September 22, the story splashed over the front page of *Alto Adige*.

Sensational Find in the High Val Senales [Schnalstal]
An Old Warrior on Messner's Path
A Body on the Glacier: Is It from 5 Centuries Ago?.
The corpse, which is in a good state of preservation,
wore shoes on the feet, had an ax in the hand, and
signs of lashing on the back.

That was just the headline. The text continued:

Val Senales—The Similaun glacier has relinquished the corpse of a man who lived at least five centuries ago. The exceptional find occurred near the Finail Peak, at about 3,200 meters altitude. Reinhold Messner went immediately to the spot to verify in person the importance of the discovery and stood speechless in amazement. The frozen cadaver wore a pair of shoes similar to those used by the Eskimos; in hand the metal handle of what must have been an ax; the head smashed.

"In one hand he is holding a metal ax, at the bottom of which a stone was probably attached," Messner was quoted as saying. Messner had, in fact, not seen the ax, which was now locked in the air-raid shelter in Sölden.

The article continued quoting Messner:

Theoretically, it could reach back even 700 or 800 years ago, although I personally don't believe it myself. I consider it likely that the cadaver may be that of a prisoner of about 500 years ago. Masculine sex. I say prisoner because on the back there are perfectly visible some wounds that look like brands. The legs are still wrapped with some thick leather straps, at the feet, still intact he has some strange shoes that look like those of the Eskimos. In my opinion this is an historic find of exceptional value and importance. It will fall, however, to the experts to examine this corpse with devout attention.

In a separate, short article, the correspondent hypothesized that the man might have been part of the fleeing army of Friedrich IV with the Empty Purse. Messner was quoted as saying he had been told that since the find was in Austria, authorities there were handling the case. " 'They told me'—Messner added—'that tomorrow (today for our readers—ed.) the corpse would be removed by helicopter and transported to a university, probably Austrian, where it would be properly examined.' "2

The next morning, Alois Pirpamer was once again on his way up to the Hauslabjoch, this time with a friend. He knew Messner and Haid believed the corpse might be quite old, but that did not affect his immediate business, which was to dig the corpse completely out of the ice. The night had been cold, and the body was covered from the hips down with an inch of new ice. Using ice picks, the men broke through the crust and then began hacking at the ice that held the hips and legs. The man was naked down to his knees, but Alois observed that the calves were still wrapped in leather. As they worked, the only remaining clothing quickly fell into shreds, which Alois dutifully piled up at the side. He knew the Alpine gendarmes would want every scrap of evidence.

The left foot, which lay under the right one, had been invisible to the Messner group, and now it took all Alois's muscle to wrest it out of the ice. After nearly two hours of strenuous labor, the entire corpse was free except for the pesky right arm, which extended straight down into solid ice. No amount of picking or tugging could free it. Alois almost believed the hand was holding on to something down there.

Having done what they could, the two men covered the corpse again and tossed the leather, wood, fur, and string into a large trash bag. Among the larger pieces they collected was the stick Kammerlander had found to poke around the corpse. But they had to leave the long wooden walking stick behind. It just could not be pulled out, and they could not even determine how deep in the ice it extended.

The two men returned to the lodge with the trash bag of goods just in time to see off Messner and his partner. The Italian cameraman filming the tour was also there recording the men's departure and, at Messner's urging, he and the soundman decided to take a look at the corpse. Once at the site, however, they saw that the plastic was heavily loaded down with blocks of ice and rocks. It did not seem worth digging through all that just to shoot a dead body. They left without even turning on their camera.

Later that afternoon, Alois descended to Vent with the trash bag. He thought some of these items might look nice in a lobby display on early life in the Alps. Calling from his hotel, he informed the gendarmerie station in Sölden that the excavation was complete and that the corpse was ready to be picked up. But the sun set on that day, and the Austrian rescue helicopter still did not return.

By Monday, primed by the South Tyrolean reports of Reinhold Messner's visit to the site, Austrian radio, television, and newspapers were playing up the unlikely idea that the glacier corpse found four days earlier was five hundred years old. At Austria's state-run network, Österreichischer Rundfunk (ORF), reporter Rainer Hölzl was on the story. After speaking by phone with Markus Pirpamer at the Similaun lodge, Hölzl decided to try to get a helicopter to ferry him and his camera team up to the Hauslabjoch to tape the recovery. The weather was poor, and officials were not sure whether the recovery was really going to proceed. There was another problem as well: For environmental reasons, unofficial helicopter landings were not permitted at the altitude of the Hauslabjoch. All morning, Hölzl tried frantically to work something out in case the recovery went ahead.

Up in the Ötztal, meanwhile, Hans Haid was placing an early-morning call to the Ferdinandeum, the Tyrolean provincial museum in Innsbruck. Over the weekend he had done a little research on that ax, and he now felt sure the ax was quite ancient. Concerned about what was happening with this valuable find, Haid urgently wanted to speak with an archaeologist he knew at the museum but

was disappointed to learn she was on vacation. Instead, he was connected to the museum's director, an art historian. In a brief conversation with the man, Haid excitedly described what he and Messner
had seen at the site. He assured the director that this was a very important archaeological find and urged him to do whatever he could
to make sure it was handled properly. The director passed the information on to two junior archaeologists at the Ferdinandeum.[3]

As Haid's appeal trickled along, preparations to retrieve the
corpse from the Hauslabjoch were suddenly, after two days' delay,
moving swiftly through the provincial bureaucracy. From the perspective of the state, the most pressing question was this: Whose
body was it? Since neither the identity nor cause of death had yet
been established, a district attorney in Innsbruck had already issued
the routine order that the body be brought to the office of the medical examiner for examination and a possible autopsy. The order had
been held up over the weekend but was expected to be carried out
first thing Monday morning.

At his university office, Rainer Henn was making plans to accompany the recovery team when he received the call from Konrad
Spindler.[4] Spindler seemed somewhat agitated, and Henn assured
him that the corpse had not yet been recovered from the mountain.

A few young staffers at the Ferdinandeum had also begun trying
to learn more about the corpse. Around midmorning, one employee called the district attorney in charge of the case to say that
the corpse might be of great archaeological importance. The district
attorney listened to the caller's concerns. He was aware of the reports that the corpse was quite old. He would see to it that every
precaution was taken.

Meanwhile, reporter Rainer Hölzl received word that the official
recovery was about to go ahead. Someone at ORF quickly pulled a
few strings, and clearance for their high-altitude landing came
through. At 11:30 A.M., a helicopter carrying Hölzl, his cameraman, a freelance photographer, and a two-man crew took off for the
Hauslabjoch. They wanted to make sure they arrived before the recovery team. A few other photographers who had lesser resources
began driving like wildfire to Vent, where they hoped to catch the
official helicopter on its way back with the corpse.

Shortly after noon, the ORF helicopter flew over the Hauslabjoch, which was now sealed under a fresh covering of powdery snow

that further camouflaged the trash bag over the corpse. In the hope that Markus Pirpamer could help them, the pilot flew to the Similaun lodge. Hölzl stepped out, Markus took his seat, and then the helicopter flew back to the site. Markus pointed out the trench from the air, and the pilot then returned him to the lodge and picked up Hölzl again. Finally, at just about half past noon, the ORF team landed at the site, which the pilot noted was awfully close to the Italian border.

After trampling through the snow for a few minutes, someone stumbled upon the plastic bag covering the corpse. The team made a few preparations to tape and then hunkered down on the frigid pass to wait for the news to happen.

The government helicopter carrying the recovery team lifted off just minutes after the journalists. Onboard were the pilot, Professor Henn, and the Alpine gendarme Roman Lukasser, who happened to be on air-rescue duty that day. To allow for the weight of the corpse, the fourth seat was kept empty. During a brief stopover in Vent, the elder Pirpamer told Lukasser that he had dug the corpse out of the ice the day before, so it was all ready to go. Consequently, Lukasser removed the shovel and ice pick from the helicopter, since they would only contribute dangerous weight when flying at such a high altitude. They also refused to carry a freelance photographer who was on the scene, although the pilot did agree to take pictures with the photographer's camera. The three men then resumed their flight.

The ORF team recorded their landing and the recovery that followed.[5] Henn, hatless and gloveless, picked his way through the slippery snow-covered rocks to get to the corpse. The gendarme, in a bright red snowsuit, straddled the snow-covered mound and pulled up the plastic, dumping the snow off to the sides and revealing the corpse. Still lying facedown, it appeared to have become refrozen into snow and ice.

"*Na ja*," Henn said, using a German exclamation that indicates something unexpected. He could not have been pleased that contrary to what Alois Pirpamer had told them, the corpse was stuck fast in the ice.

"You don't need those," Henn said to Lukasser, who was preparing to put on some plastic gloves before touching the corpse. "He's harmless."

"That's clear to me," Lukasser replied a bit defensively. Normal protocol required people handling corpses to wear such gloves. It was a safety precaution for both the gendarme and the corpse. Why Henn thought it was unnecessary in this case was not clear.

The video camera, in the meantime, was feeding on the sight of the emaciated brown corpse. Occasionally, the cameraman pulled back to get the whole scene. Next to the adult men wearing down jackets, the shrunken corpse looked as small and delicate as a child. "Do we have a pick?" Henn asked, obviously intent on getting the job done. The pass was colder than he had anticipated and windy.

"We probably don't have anything along," Lukasser replied. "I thought he was all ready."

Hölzl interrupted with a question about the age of the deceased. That was, after all, the main reason they were here on this godforsaken pass. If the corpse did not turn out to be a little unusual, he could have trouble justifying the expense of the helicopter.

"I can only say he is surely long dead, has lain here for a while, probably in water, very long in ice. We can say more only when we have the instruments of the Forensic Medicine Institute," Henn responded curtly.

Hölzl had sensed from the beginning that Henn was not happy ORF was here documenting their work, but he had a job to do, and that answer was just not good enough. He was used to experts trying to downplay things that were really interesting. Hölzl refined his question. What about the reports that the corpse might be five hundred years old?

"I can't say anything about that," Henn said wearily. "That's from the rumor exchange. We work with scientific methods, and we'll say something when we have results."

Obviously, the only way to get the man to say anything was to talk about science. Hölzl asked how the corpse's age could be determined.

"With C-fourteen or by measuring the rate of glacier flow, conferring with glaciologists, looking at how much is made of adipocere," Henn replied. "From the type and degree of adipocere, we can draw conclusions."

Now they were getting somewhere.

Henn continued: "It would be nice to [find] an identification card, passport, or an engraved wedding ring." Then, looking at the camera, he added ironically, "For future mountain hikers, remember always to take these things with you to make the work of the forensic doctors easier."

After that morbid bit of advice, Henn got back to work. While he had been talking with the ORF, a passing hiker had offered to lend his ski pole and ice pick to the rescuers. The video showed Lukasser using the pick to hack at the ice around the left hand while Henn tried sweeping water through a gully in the snow with the end of the ski pole.

To test whether he could pop the whole corpse out of the ice in one tug, Lukasser hooked the body on the pick and raised the torso out of the slushy water underneath. The stiff torso bounced up and down on the end of the pick, but the lower end was still stuck in the ice. He let the body slap back into the slush and ice. This was going to be even harder than he imagined. As the two men worked, they occasionally stepped right on the corpse's back.

Hölzl was surprised by the impersonal handling of the corpse. On one hand, the scene was somewhat comical. The body was stiff as a board, and the arms were sticking out at bizarre angles to the right. On the other hand, this had been somebody, a real live, breathing person who perhaps had had a family. Hölzl wondered what had happened to him.

The camera caught the ski pole poking through lumps of hay. The left foot was bare. That was probably the insulation from the shoe Messner and others had mentioned. "Look, it's straw," someone said at one point. "It's woven, look. There are strings."

The camera did not record the moment at which the corpse was finally freed, but it did pick up Henn's voice, announcing, "Now we've got to see that we get a little bit for the archaeologists."

Lukasser and Henn dug in the ice and water with their hands, pulling up pieces of leather. Nearby, the corpse was lying on its back on the ice and, for the first time, the face was visible. The mouth was slightly open, and so were the eyes. Except for what looked like the remains of a shoe, not a shred of clothing was left. The position of the arms looked all the more awkward with the corpse faceup.

Henn straddled the corpse, bent down, and flipped it easily from back to front. It was frozen solid. Hölzl pressed him to say a little more about the person.

"Teeth scraped down, partly mummified," Henn said slowly, thinking carefully before each sentence. "Probably lay awhile in the air before he ended up in the ice."

He paused. "Clothes? Unfortunately none left. Can't say more on the spot."

Henn and Lukasser lifted the corpse from both ends and placed it facedown in a transparent plastic body bag. In the meantime, the ORF helicopter had fetched Markus Pirpamer to the site for an interview.

"You found this body—" Hölzl began.

"No, not I," Pirpamer corrected him. "Two tourists did on Thursday, and they informed us in the lodge, and then I informed the police. My first impression was that he was, like, mummified. From the tools it seemed like he'd been there a long time. The shoes were stuffed with hay, and there was a wooden ax with an iron blade, and there was chamois fur. He could have been a hunter," the young Pirpamer offered.

"How old do you think he could be?" Hölzl asked.

"Hard to say," Markus responded. "In any case older than one hundred years."

Markus told how the first recovery attempt failed and that Reinhold Messner was there and thought the corpse could be two or three hundred years old. This was exactly the kind of footage Hölzl wanted.

In the background, the excavation was still going on. Henn and the gendarme were scraping and poking at the boulder on which the mummy had been lying with the ski pole and pick. Suddenly, they found something. A primitive knife with a wooden handle appeared from the icy pool of water, and someone held it up to the camera, turning it to show all sides. The blade was unusual. It appeared to be made of stone. No one had any idea what that could mean.

Now the man with the ice pick pried at a grass mat lying flat on a boulder. A clump of hair hung from the ice pick, and part of it fell back into the icy water as it was displayed to the camera. The last shot recorded a little mound of leather on the snow. The ORF team, conscious of its deadline, packed up and flew back to Innsbruck.

Lukasser and Henn, too, were ready to quit the site, but they were unable to get the long whittled branch out of the ice. The solution was simple: The hiker who owned the tools stepped up and seized it with both hands. With all the strength he could muster, he pulled back on the branch, and with a mighty crack it yielded, breaking off at the level of the ice. It was then placed into the body bag with the leather pieces and the stone knife. The recovery had taken one hour and ten minutes.

The helicopter flew back to Vent, where, this time, the local undertaker was not disappointed. He had selected a modest pine coffin for this unidentified soul, but when he and Henn tried to place the body inside, a small problem arose. The arms were still frozen straight out to the right, over the sides of the coffin. Normally, the undertaker would try to place the deceased's arms at its sides or cross them on the chest. But these limbs were frozen stiff.

Without hesitation, the men forced the arms down into the coffin and closed the lid. Alois Pirpamer handed the undertaker the trash bag full of material he had collected the day before, and then the undertaker headed down the valley toward Innsbruck, planning one stop in Sölden to pick up the ax that had been stored there since Friday.

Hours after his appeal to the museum in Innsbruck, oblivious to the recovery under way, Hans Haid, the folklorist, still could not get that ax out of his mind. Having learned that it was in the possession of the police in Sölden, he drove to the station to see whether he could get a look at it. An officer brought it up from the air-raid shelter and, a little proudly, showed it to Haid. As soon as he saw it, Haid felt certain that it was a few thousand years old, which put it in the Iron Age, part of which was known in Central Europe as the Hallstatt Period.

Haid was still exclaiming over the tool when the undertaker pulled up at the station with the coffin and the trash bag. The fact that the corpse was being chauffeured to Innsbruck in a hearse made Haid wonder whether any archaeologist had been present at the excavation. The undertaker seemed to be in a hurry. He added the box with the ax to his load and then left on the ninety-minute drive to Innsbruck. Later that afternoon, after hearing a report on the recovery on a local radio program, Haid fired off a peevish fax to the ORF in Innsbruck:

"I was at the site on Sept. 21 with Reinhold Messner. Together we developed some theses," he began. "After double-checking and various researches I conclude that: it is probably a corpse from the Hallstatt Period (or shortly before or after); the 'tools' indicate that."[6] Haid also hypothesized that the man "was searching for minerals" in the mountains. "The hole on the back of the head stems from a trephination (usually for medical purposes) which was entirely common in prehistoric times," he continued. "A rough dating (900–500 B.C.) is therefore permissible."

He concluded with a mild reprimand: "On the afternoon of the 23rd I was at your disposal in the gendarmerie station in Sölden and at home at Heiligkreuz 8. I could have provided some information."

Unfortunately all Haid's endeavors had come a little too late.

It was 4 P.M. on Monday, September 23, and an Innsbruck medical examiner named Hans Unterdorfer was poised, bemused, over the very unusual corpse that had just been delivered to his autopsy table from the ice on the Hauslabjoch. His autopsy apron was tied around his portly girth, and the stainless-steel knives, scissors, saws, and other autopsy tools had been removed from their cabinets and laid at the ready.

But Unterdorfer, a cherubic man much appreciated by his secretaries for his good humor, understood immediately that there was not going to be any autopsy, at least not right away. This was clearly a case for the archaeologists. Still attached to the corpse's right foot were the remains of a primitive shoe. It consisted of a big clump of brownish grass bound around the foot by some shredded string and a few pieces of tattered leather. No one there had ever seen anything like it before. It looked like a bird's nest. "What we have here is the ur-Tyrolean," Unterdorfer joked, and the others in the room agreed.

Together with the district attorney who earlier in the day had taken the call from the museum, Unterdorfer opened up the plastic trash bag and removed several items. The ax was quite impressive. Noticing the gendarme's scratch in the patina, Unterdorfer, too, deduced that the metal beneath must be copper. All these items were assumed to belong to the person who now lay before them, but not a scrap of identification was found among them.

Given the uniqueness of this case, the district attorney declined to issue an autopsy order and instead ordered that the corpse be examined carefully and then turned over to the historians. Unterdorfer immediately began his examination, speaking into a small cassette recorder. The tape was later transcribed.

In his twenty-seven years in this line of work, Unterdorfer had seen all kinds of corpses, including some that emerged from glacial ice, so he recognized immediately that this one was very well preserved. It was extremely desiccated and looked much like an old mummy. Unterdorfer's guess was that it weighed only between forty-four and sixty-six pounds. The skin was reddish in places and almost black in others. The epidermis was gone and with it virtually every strand of body hair. The fingernails, too, had fallen out.

Parts of the body were packed with bits of ice. When Unterdorfer began the exam, a large clump of ice was still wedged in the crotch. As it melted, "leather-like black straps" emerged.[7] He had no idea what they were for.

To get rid of sand and other dirt clinging to the corpse, Unterdorfer rinsed it with cold water. He was particularly alert for wounds, especially those that might explain how the person had died. He carefully examined the neck region for signs of injury but found nothing. Neither was there any visible trauma to the chest or gut, which were so sunken that, Unterdorfer noted, "the skeleton is clearly visible."

He assumed this was a male corpse, but the genital area did not indicate this as clearly as he expected. "The external sexual organs are flat, as far as can be judged, most probably male, desiccated," he dictated.

The most obvious damage to the corpse was in the left hip, leg, and buttock. The flesh there seemed to have been ripped out raggedly and so deeply that the top of the thighbone stuck out. Since the bone showed no signs of exposure, Unterdorfer assumed that this damage was recent. Unaware of the jackhammer and ice pick used to pry the corpse out of the ice, he guessed that the damage stemmed from animal scavengers.

Turning the corpse over, Unterdorfer noticed that the damage extended even into the small of the back. "Ice still present here," he dictated. "As far as can be recognized the skeleton is also affected, displaying something like chipped marginal area."

Unterdorfer also attributed the wound on the head to scavengers. "On the back of the head is an approximately three to four-centimeter wide wound on the skin of the skull, apparently due to animal (bird?) scavenging, which is jagged on the edges, and on the left radiating out, there is scratch-like superficial damage," he noted. "The bony skull shows as far as visible no corresponding break." Unterdorfer was not at this point aware of the trephination hypothesis of Haid, but his observations would have spelled the end of it, since only the skin, not the skull itself, was broken.

Moving down the corpse's back, Unterdorfer next spotted a series of "skin discolorations," the markings that others had identified as brands. There were four groups of vertical stripes, each one above the next. He found that the marks varied in length from 2.8 to 3 centimeters and in breadth from 2 to 3 millimeters. They looked like little grates. "From top to bottom there is first a group of four then in close proximity two groups of three and, lastly, barely visible another group of four," he noted. "The barely visible one is in the region of the left side of the small of the back."

On the right side of the spine, he found a similar group of four stripes. Further down, on the inside of the man's right knee, he spotted another peculiar marking, which he referred to as a tattoo. It was in the shape of a cross, with a vertical axis about an inch high and a slightly longer horizontal axis. Two parallel stripes also ran around the left wrist like a bracelet. Unterdorfer saw tattoos all the time, but these patterns were not typical.

Unterdorfer looked into the man's face. The eyelids had shrunken to reveal two flattened but intact eyeballs. Unterdorfer was struck by the unlikelihood that these two sensitive organs had survived so long in the ice. The man looked alert and seemed as if he was on the verge of saying something. His top lip was shoved up and to the side, revealing a full, if battered, set of yellowing teeth and dark gums. The wild position of his arms enlivened him. The fingers of the right hand were "curved as if in a position for holding a round object." What that object could have been, Unterdorfer had no clue. Neither could he determine, based on this initial examination, what had caused the man to die. That was not unusual. Determining the cause of death is notoriously difficult even in new corpses where all the evidence is fresh.

Around 5 P.M., while the examination was being wrapped up, Rainer Henn, Unterdorfer's boss, finally arrived and told his colleagues that he was going to contact the archaeologists. In the transcription of the examination, Unterdorfer is recorded as saying that "the entire find is being left until the arrival of Professor Spindler of the University's Department of Prehistory and Early History, who has been informed." Unterdorfer and his colleagues expected that the archaeologist would be over as soon as he learned of this strange find, so they stood around in the autopsy room, good-naturedly arguing over the age of the corpse and the bag of odd goods that accompanied it. Nearly everyone in the office came down to ogle the mummy and give an opinion on its age. Outside the sterile tiled walls of the autopsy room, interest had also been growing, since ORF had been broadcasting hourly reports of the recovery. Journalists were frantic to see the corpse, but the district attorney had not yet approved its release to the media.

By 7 P.M., Spindler still had not shown up, and Unterdorfer was growing tired of waiting. He called Henn in his office, who said that he had been unable to reach the archaeologist.* A bit perplexed about why he had been left in a holding pattern, Unterdorfer returned to the corpse. He then allowed two photographers to come in to take photographs of the artifacts. He wanted to be sure this person was not somebody's relative before he let them at the body itself. After they left, he prepared the corpse for overnight storage in a refrigerator set at just a few degrees above freezing. But he was too curious to leave it and too excited to sleep. He spent the night tossing and turning on a cot in the institute.

Shortly after 8 A.M. on Tuesday, September 24, Konrad Spindler arrived at the medical examiner's and was guided to the stainless-steel

---

*Later Henn told Unterdorfer that he had eventually reached Spindler that night, but the archaeologist had not come. Spindler steadfastly maintained that he had not been summoned to see the corpse until the next morning, when Henn reached him in his office.

table bearing the mummified man and the artifacts, arranged neatly next to his head. Years of poring over archaeological artifacts had prepared Spindler well for this moment. He immediately recognized a few items. There was a metal ax and a small dagger with a stone blade. The long carved branch that some had thought was a walking stick looked to him like an archer's longbow. The other artifacts were less familiar but absolutely fascinating. There was a small white disk with a central hole, through which a tassel of twisted leather strips passed, as well as a cylindrical piece of wood, pointed at one end, which looked like a stout pencil. Nearby lay a leather pouch with a small tear, out of which poked a flint blade.

Spindler surveyed the corpse and the array of objects and then focused on the ax. He knew that blade well, but neither he nor any archaeologist had ever before seen one *hafted*. Never had they found an entirely intact tool such as this. It was extraordinary. The leather strip that bound the blade into the shaft looked as if it had been made last week. This was the blade that people across Europe had made during the Bronze Age.

Spindler picked up the ax and examined the cutting edge closely, rubbing his finger along it and turning it from side to side. The blade was narrow, less than two inches across and covered in a light brown patina, which forms on some metals when they are exposed to moisture. Underneath the patina, Spindler expected to find bronze, an alloy of copper and tin.

Except for the click of a photographer's camera, there was barely a murmur in the room as the forensic staff waited for the professor to speak. Nothing in his demeanor had yet betrayed the singularity of what he found himself beholding. After just a few moments of consideration came Spindler's cool and terse pronouncement: "About four thousand years old."

CHAPTER 3

A GREAT MOMENT FOR SCIENCE

THE PRESS CONFERENCE was scheduled for 5 P.M. Rainer Henn, Konrad Spindler, and a few other men filed in silently across the back of the room and turned to face Innsbruck's anxious press corps. Henn, whose forensic work had brought him into frequent contact with journalists, stepped up first. Like a doctor explaining a diagnosis to a patient's family, he began a detailed chronological report on the unusual corpse.

The reporters shifted restlessly. The afternoon deadlines were already gone, and this man was talking formalities. What about this mummy? Smiling composedly, Henn continued his measured account of the corpse's recovery. ORF's exclusive video of the excavation had been broadcast on the national news the evening before, and all Austria had seen how he and the gendarme had hacked the corpse out of the ice with the pick and ski pole. Seemingly unaware of the broadcast, Henn confidently emphasized the propriety of all actions taken by the gendarmerie and his office.

"Please, don't destroy anything, bring along everything, every piece that is lying up there," Henn said, quoting an archaeologist, presumably Spindler, that he had spoken with before the flight. Still smiling kindly, Henn then turned to introduce Spindler, who had been surveying the press intensely through tiny oval glasses and now moved forward self-consciously.

In a low, stiff voice, he praised Henn's work and thanked the office of the medical examiner for its cooperation. Then his voice rose to a new key. The corpse and artifacts, he began, were absolutely unique and highly significant. "When I saw the artifacts, it was immediately clear that we were dealing with a prehistoric find," he said. "The accompanying objects are so typical for the early Bronze Age that an age of 2000 before Christ, four thousand years ago, cannot be doubted in the least." Learning that the rumor that had been flying around all day was true, a few reporters quickly dialed their editors from cell phones.

Spindler scanned the room. The entire Innsbruck press corps seemed to have gathered in this dull university lecture room. Truly, the discovery was a wondrous event, but how could he convey in these few pressured moments how truly extraordinary it was?

By the time this prehistoric individual pulled on his shoes for the last time and began his ascent over the main Alpine ridge, his kind was already long established. Humans evolved over millions of years, and yet the world's histories illuminate just the very end of the story. At the time this man lived, the people in the Alps had yet to develop writing. The start of history, the genesis of the written word, was still at least a millennium in the future. Everything archaeologists knew about prehistoric life came from very ambiguous materials, mainly human and animal bones, tools made of durable stone, metal, or ceramics, and the rare organic remains that survived until the present.

An archaeologist might spend all summer exploring an area and come up with only a few chips from a stone tool. If he found a whole tool, the remains of a campsite, or, better yet, the outline of a dwelling, he could consider himself lucky. When the rare human remains turned up, it was inevitably a grave. One reason burials survived was that they were at least temporarily protected from surface disturbances.

But this person did not appear to have been buried. Henn, who had experience in these matters, guessed that the man had died in some typical Alpine mishap, maybe of hypothermia. That meant the artifacts were probably his own belongings. They were the stuff of everyday life four thousand years ago. Spindler had never seen anything like it. No archaeologist had. These things *belonged* together. Such integrity in an archaeological find was virtually unknown.

Spindler knew he had to establish some scientific context for the journalists. Briefly he mentioned the few comparable finds that came to mind. There were, of course, the bodies found in British and northern European bogs, such as Lindow Man. But the only frozen bodies he could think of were from the fifth-century B.C.E. tombs of a southern Siberian culture. Known as the Pazyryk burials, the tombs were constructed in a way that had, by chance, created a permafrost microclimate within, freezing and perfectly preserving the contents.

But all those corpses were much younger than this one. There was nothing quite like this. Guilelessly, he uttered the words the tabloids had been hoping to hear. "You know," he concluded, "the scientist does not like to take words like 'great moment,' 'hundred-year find,' or other superlatives in his mouth, but in this case it appears really justified that even the dry scientist gets a little excited and lets himself reach for words that do not belong to his usual vocabulary."

That was the only moment in the press conference in which Spindler ever let on that, beneath his placid veneer, he, too, was thrilled. To the journalists, Spindler's endorsement of the discovery was as good as gold. The reemergence of a person after thousands of years frozen in ice certainly sounded impressive, but journalists relied on scientists to verify the sensation. Most had no idea what was going on in the Bronze Age, or even when it was. Now they had a scientist's confirmation that the frozen corpse was a bona fide archaeological sensation.

The press conference was not over. Everyone wanted to see this corpse, and the scientists' impulse was to share him with the world. To the journalists' delight, they were ushered into the autopsy room. Photographers and journalists swarmed around the body and the artifacts. Aware that the cameras' heat and lights could damage the find, Spindler warned the teams not to leave their lights on for more than two minutes. Rainer Hölzl approached Spindler for another interview on video as he stood beside the autopsy table.

"Without a doubt it's an early Bronze Age ax," Spindler said in a funereal whisper. "The other things fit into it. The combination of metal and stone shows we're in a transition period from stone to metal."

Hölzl asked, "That means a mistake is therefore out of the question?"

Spindler replied, "From the archaeological point of view, yes."

Spindler even conjectured that the person might have been a hunter, evidenced by the longbow, or a prospector, since prehistoric people were exploring the mountains for ore deposits at this period. Or maybe, Spindler added, his serious mien admitting a tiny grin, he wanted to visit his girlfriend in the neighboring valley. Even a "dry" scientist could see the man as an individual with a story rather than just a pat scientific discovery. Already, Spindler had granted the corpse a personality.

Several minutes later, the ORF video picked up another discussion between Hölzl and Spindler. Hölzl was apparently trying to entice the prehistorian into the ORF television studios for a live interview. He told him to take a taxi to the studio. Of course, he added quickly, ORF would pay all expenses. Spindler made a few agreeable noises but said nothing right away. Until now, he had been unknown, his work routine varied rarely, and he never took a vacation. Yet before the end of that day he was to be offered flights to television studios in London, Hamburg, and Mainz.[1] The power and wealth of the media were quickly becoming apparent to him.

Given the enormous responsibility that had descended upon Spindler just nine hours earlier, he carried off the press conference with remarkable panache. In fact, he, Henn, and Unterdorfer had spent the entire day trying to make sense of what this thing was and what should be done with it. Initially, the forensic staff had not believed Spindler when he said the corpse was four thousand years old. Neither Henn nor Unterdorfer had ever heard of a glacier corpse more than a century old. How had this one managed to stay preserved? The only ready answer was that the ice had somehow preserved the man, just as a freezer kept meat from spoiling. Yet how did he get in the ice? Had he fallen into a crevasse? Unterdorfer had found no apparent fatal wounds, so how did he die? His flesh did not appear to have been transformed into adipocere. Henn thought wind might have quickly desiccated the corpse, which had then continued to dry out under loose snow.

Everyone was glad that Spindler seemed willing to take charge. There were no protocols to follow for a case like this. They were going to have to improvise. But first, were they sure this was not a fake? Reinhold Messner's presence at the site was noted with a bit of discomfort. Could this be another Matterhorn joke? Or another of Messner's Yeti stories? In 1986, while in Tibet, Messner had reported observing a strange animal that he said looked exactly like the mythical creature known as Yeti, the Tibetan abominable snowman. Skeptics suggested the sighting had to do with Messner climbing mountains without supplemental oxygen. But Messner, who said his brush with the animal occurred at an altitude where oxygen was no problem, had stuck to his story. He said the animal was about two meters and twenty centimeters tall, black, and had big feet.[2] That claim hung like a cloud around all he said and did. Could someone have planted this find in order to embarrass Messner or even the scientists themselves?

Spindler, who said he was familiar with archaeological fakes, doubted it. Among the kinds of artifacts present were a few he had never seen before. It seemed unlikely that a forger would invent prehistoric tools. The ax appeared genuine. In the two million years that humans have made and used tools, their shape and the material used to make them have changed considerably. The ax had all the characteristics of one from the Bronze Age. The most obvious feature of the blade was that it was made of metal rather than stone. That was significant because it meant that the tool had to have been made sometime after humans began to use metals, which, based on what archaeologists already knew of the Alpine region where the corpse was found, could not have been earlier than about 3000 B.C.E.

Unterdorfer and others had deduced from the scratch made by the gendarmerie commander in the Ötztal that it was copper. But for Spindler, the important feature was the *shape* of the blade. The shape was nearly identical to those of bronze blades he knew from the early Bronze Age, which began in the Alps as early as 2000 B.C.E. and lasted for over a millennium until bronze was eventually replaced by iron. His guess was that this blade, too, was made of bronze. Other facts supported that. The wooden handle in which the blade was fixed looked similar to Bronze Age shafts. It had been cut from the nook of a tree branch and trunk and was known as a knee-joint shaft. The small stone-bladed dagger, obviously flint, could also have been used in the Bronze Age, even though it was of a style that had been in use long before.

Spindler was comfortable placing the find in the Bronze Age, but he knew radiocarbon dating could provide a more precise age. Samples would have to be sent to laboratories as quickly as possible. He also wanted to get up to the location where the discovery was made. Henn said he had brought everything down, but Spindler said an archaeologist still needed to evaluate the site immediately. More artifacts, or even more corpses, might still be up there, and they should be salvaged before souvenir hunters got there. But first, they urgently needed to decide what should be done with the corpse.

Unterdorfer had kept it cooled on Monday night, but by the time Spindler first saw it, nearly a day had passed since its recovery, and it had completely thawed. The situation was critical. The body would turn foul quickly if nothing was done to stabilize the decay. Most human remains unearthed by archaeologists consisted of skeletal material, which needed little attention once out of the ground. But with intact flesh, hair, and clothing, extraordinary preservation efforts were required to keep them from rotting away.

Spindler was concerned about the condition of the organic materials as well. Already, the unique leather pouch, which was attached to a long leather belt, was in a delicate state. A small flint blade had poked through the soggy leather, and everyone wondered what else was in there. But Spindler was not rash. He knew that before taking any irreversible steps, such as emptying the pouch, everything was going to have to be carefully and completely documented. The first priority was to get them preserved.

Spindler was convinced that his own small department had neither the facilities nor the expertise to handle the artifacts, much less a human corpse. After discussing the situation briefly with Henn and Unterdorfer, who said they, too, would nose around for some advice, Spindler hurried across campus to his office to see what kind of preservation he could line up. Several museums in Austria had conservation departments, and any one of them would have been thrilled to assist. But Spindler called the Roman-Germanic Central Museum in Mainz, Germany, one of Europe's premier conservation workshops. He had worked previously with conservators there and knew them to be excellent. Spindler easily convinced the museum director to accept the artifacts for restoration and conservation. But the director declined to take the corpse. The museum had no doctors on its staff and had never worked with human remains. Neither could he offer any advice on what immediate steps the Innsbruckers should take. Spindler made other calls as well; to Austria's Federal Office of Monuments, to plead for immediate funds to fly back to the Hauslabjoch; and, unsuccessfully, to the Hermitage in Saint Petersburg to ask curators there how they had preserved the frozen Pazyryk finds.[3]

By the middle of the afternoon, the corpse was still lying in the autopsy room. In the meantime, the phones had begun to ring ceaselessly with inquiries from the media. A few reporters had infiltrated Henn's and Spindler's offices and were trying to set up interviews. With accommodations for the corpse still in the air, the men decided to call the news conference.

During the media's viewing of the corpse, someone noticed what appeared to be a fungus growing on the desiccated skin. None of the doctors present knew what the splotchy dark stuff was, but it did not look good. Was the corpse disintegrating before their very eyes?

Pinning down the genesis of a decision is tricky. Ideas often have many authors, and in a high-pressured, hierarchical environment not everyone may end up getting the proper credit. Precisely who first thought to refreeze the corpse is not clear. Probably it had crossed the minds of several of the scientists present. After all, it was the commonsense solution. Even more decisive was the fact that Dr. Werner Platzer, head of the university's anatomy department, had recommended it. By most accounts, Platzer was one of the university's most powerful professors. Sixty-two years old, he had firmly directed the Institute of Anatomy since 1968 and was now approaching retirement. His impact on Austrian medicine had been deep and wide. One of his books, a pocket atlas of anatomy first published in 1975, was in its sixth German edition and had been translated into more than a dozen languages. Many of the country's doctors had once been his students.

A proud, hunched man with bushy black eyebrows, Platzer had never been content to harness his energies solely to the rather conservative study of anatomy. For decades he had also served on important budget committees on the medical faculty, where he had proved himself to be highly adept at choreographing relations between the university and the federal government in Vienna, which exercised great control over the country's universities.

Platzer's qualifications as a consultant on saving the thawed prehistoric corpse lay not only in the fact that he had experience in the preservation of human tissue but in that he had two walk-in freezers that were not contaminated, like those in the morgue, where it no longer mattered much if some virus or bacteria was lurking about. Platzer was out of town at the time and had to be reached by phone. He immediately grasped the urgency of the situation and backed the idea to refreeze, overriding the concerns of those who feared that this could damage the tissues. This, Platzer said, was how his department preserved its own specimens. In fact, at the moment, his freezers were filled with every possible body part—all specimens that he and his colleagues had carefully prepared for study. Yet he readily offered to make room for the mummy.

After learning from Henn about the conditions in which he had found the corpse, Platzer had one of his freezers cleared out and washed down. The temperature was set to twenty-one degrees Fahrenheit. In another conversation after the press conference, Platzer also said he knew what to do about the fungus. He advised the forensic doctors to swathe the body in wraps soaked in carbolic acid, a common disinfectant. The procedure accomplished, the mummy was rolled in, and the door was locked.

Platzer now had possession of the world's oldest mummified human remains. Spindler had first recognized the significance of this find, but from now on Platzer had authority over the corpse, since it was in his freezer. The scientists had made a timely decision, but on that night they could not know whether their solution would salvage or destroy a once-in-a-century treasure.

At nearly noon on Wednesday, dark clouds were billowing over the ridge from South Tyrol. As Gernot Patzelt hurried up to the Hauslabjoch, he suddenly heard his three good friends and university colleagues—Heralt Schneider, Ekkehard Dreiseitl, and Gerhard Markl—laughing, whooping, and excitedly summoning him up the last hundred yards. They had started off from Innsbruck that morning a few hours ahead of him and now, obviously, they had located the spot where the corpse had been found, thought Patzelt as he stepped rapidly over snow and rock.

Yet as he drew closer, before he could even utter a greeting, the men blurted out another discovery and steered him to one side of the trench. Patzelt crouched down and stared in amazement. There, half buried among crystals of ice and dirty snow, lay a bunch of wooden arrow shafts, sticking out from a long, narrow leather bag. Amazingly, a few feathers, battered and wet but more or less intact, were still attached to the shafts. It must have belonged to the four-thousand-year-old man.

As Patzelt exclaimed in excitement, his friends recounted how Schneider had noticed it almost as soon as they had arrived. It lay just a few yards away from the spot where the mummy had apparently been found and must have emerged in just the last forty-eight hours. Otherwise, it was incomprehensible that no one had noticed it during the recovery of the corpse two days earlier.

A glacier expert at the University of Innsbruck, Patzelt had come up here as quickly as he could, having abandoned a geographers' conference in Switzerland as soon as he learned of the corpse. Schneider, a math professor, and Dreiseitl and Markl, both meteorologists, were all volunteer glacier monitors for the Austrian Alpine Club, and they were just as curious as Patzelt. They had left Innsbruck at the crack of dawn while Patzelt lingered in Innsbruck to speak with Spindler, whom he knew vaguely.

Patzelt now reported that Spindler was planning to fly up in a helicopter that same afternoon with a group of students. Certainly they would have excavation tools that could dig the quiver out. Until then, they would wait, resist touching the quiver and arrows, and guard the site.

In the meantime, Patzelt turned to explore the land. A generous, good-natured man with a ruddy, boyish face, he had an insatiable love for the mountains. He had grown up in a small Alpine village in central Austria and had hiked all through the country's Alps. The Ötztal mountains were among those he knew best. For years, he had taught a course each summer in the Gurglertal, the nearest valley to the east, and in the last several years he had observed and measured the retreating glaciers of that region. How, he wondered, had the corpse remained in glacial ice for so many years?

The trench in which the four men were standing was just above a relatively flat and wide pass that cut right across the main Alpine ridge dividing Austria from Italy. Patzelt knew that just a few decades earlier the rocky landscape on which they were now assembled had been completely obscured by the massive Niederjochferner glacier. Formed over thousands of years as layers of snow became compressed under the weight of additional precipitation, the glacier was constantly in a state of flux, either growing or shrinking, depending on accumulation and temperature. Like a slow-moving stream, it was flowing down into Austria. Because their slow downward movements, the rate of which is determined by the angle of the slope and the thickness of the ice, cannot be discerned with the eye, glaciers can appear to be rather placid geological entities. But they pack immense force. A glacier picks up boulders and earth and other things in its path and, like a conveyor belt, transports them to its end. At a glacier's terminus, where it is melting, this till is deposited in a heap called the end moraine. The movement of ice within the glacier itself varies. Generally, the ice near the surface moves most quickly, sliding and slipping over layers of ice beneath it. The ice on the bottom moves most slowly, since it often freezes onto the ground below. If the land is level, the ice might not move much at all.

Other Ötztal glaciers visible from the pass were also melting, and scientists debated whether the melting is due to a man-made global-warming effect or a natural fluctuation in the earth's temperature. Every fall, Patzelt and his friends trudged out to the tongues of the glaciers and, consulting markers they had planted the previous year, measured the ice's advance or retreat. In some cases, the ice was disappearing so quickly that Patzelt could see the difference with the naked eye from one year to the next, and he was far from indifferent to the trend. He sympathized with the languishing glaciers, preferring to see them grow robustly down a slope.

In recent years, he had noticed that more and more of the rocky outcroppings on this pass were emerging from the melting glacial ice. Over the years, one of these outcroppings—the low ridge opposite the one the Simons had stood atop when they first discovered the corpse—had become a favorite resting point for tourists. A century's worth of tourist trash lay about the site, such as the blue ski clip, soda cans, and broken glass.

The Niederjochferner glacier had completely retreated from the pass now, but he could see the glacier's new head not far below on the Austria side. As it melted, it had left ice behind in a number of low-lying areas, like pools on a beach after the tide retreats. In one of these icy pools, formed by the walls of the trench, the corpse had been found.

Patzelt's friends had easily established the exact location of the discovery from the concentrated footprints around it. Water covered the spot, but they could see ragged bits of leather clinging to the rock below, which suggested that the man had died right on the rock. If so, Patzelt thought, then the ground here must have been free of glacial ice or water at the time. Snow must have covered the corpse and then changed into ice during successive thaws and freezes, eventually forming a glacier that packed the man into the trench and grew above it. The corpse itself would have been frozen onto the boulder on which it lay, just as the ice at the bottom of glaciers freezes onto the rock below.

If his assumptions were correct, Patzelt thought he understood why the corpse had not been destroyed. The ice in the trench must have been trapped and did not budge even when the glacier above it moved. The corpse lay frozen in an immobile mass of ice about nine feet, Patzelt estimated, beneath the stream of the glacier. This little pocket kept the corpse from being transported down the mountain in the main body of the glacier. Even when the glacier had covered the pass, it would not have moved much across this relatively flat terrain.

To be certain that the trench had indeed been under the glacier, Patzelt compared the rock around its edge with the same type of rock many yards away, at the edge of the mountain ridge that would have been covered by glacial ice for a much shorter period. As he expected, the rock along the trench edge was far less eroded than that along the main ridge, which had been battered for centuries by wind, rain, and snow.

Patzelt was quickly forming an informal hypothesis about what had happened. The man was probably on his way from one side of the mountain to the other when a terrible storm suddenly kicked up, blinding him with snow or sleet and obscuring the landscape. Unable to orient himself on the treacherous terrain in the storm, he wandered off the path and crouched down beside the trench wall.

Perhaps he had also been cold, wet, or ill. People who are not acclimatized to this altitude can suffer severe headaches, nausea, and exhaustion. Yet a man who had grown up in the mountains, as he presumably had, probably would not have succumbed to altitude sickness. The trough probably offered only minimal protection, and Patzelt doubted that the man would have wanted to remain here long. Camping overnight at this altitude without shelter or even wood for fire was almost out of the question. Yet for some reason the man had not been able to go on, and he had died here. His body then must have been quickly covered with snow. Patzelt believed that if the corpse had ever been exposed for more than a day or two it would have decomposed rapidly, or been devoured, or at least molested, by scavengers. Yet the corpse apparently showed few, if any, signs of damage by animals. As unlikely as it seemed, Patzelt concluded that the corpse must have been sealed in snow or ice since shortly after the man's death. Altogether, Patzelt thought, this was a highly extraordinary string of circumstances.

As the four men discussed their findings, they suddenly caught the sound of an approaching helicopter. That must be Spindler. Unfortunately, however, the fog had grown thicker, and visibility had been reduced to just a dozen yards. They knew the pilot would not be able to see, much less land on, the pass.

As fast as he could, Gerhard Markl ran straight down the slope, intending to signal to the helicopter from an opening in the fog just below the ridge on the Austrian side. But before he got a glimpse of the sky, the sound of the machine faded and then died. Frustrated, he walked back up to the others, where they discussed what to do.

An hour passed, and then they heard the helicopter again. This time Patzelt set off on the same course Markl had taken. He, too, failed to signal the helicopter before it retreated. Now the men were deeply frustrated, and they wondered why the helicopter had not just landed where it could see the ground. Almost anyone could have made the walk from the site.

It seemed too late for another landing attempt by the helicopter, and they knew they had to make a decision about the quiver. Fearing that publicity would encourage others to seek out the site, the men decided to recover the quiver themselves. Before they started anything, Patzelt took a few photographs of the situation. Then, using the spoon of a pocket knife, they began gently picking away the snow and ice that surrounded the quiver. Gradually, its edges came into view. Using a plastic lunch bag as a bucket, they collected water from the icy pools around them and poured it over the quiver to slowly melt the ice off. As they worked, they took more pictures.

Meanwhile, an Italian customs official named Silvano Dal Ben was on his way up the mountain from the Italian side. His post in the Schnalstal was responsible not only for customs but also accidents involving hikers. Technically, Dal Ben was on vacation this week. But when he had learned of the discovery of the corpse, he had grown a little suspicious. The location of the find sounded like Italian territory to him. Among his colleagues, Dal Ben, a burly ethnic Italian, was something of a legend. He was known not only as the post's most vigilant officer, with a bloodhound's sense of the border, but as an amazing athlete. Dal Ben was actually jogging up the mountain, dressed in a fashionable running suit and all-terrain shoes.

Just ahead, on the Hauslabjoch, Patzelt had begun collecting everything else on the ground that might have been part of the find. Near the ledge where the bow and ax had been found, Patzelt saw string, leather, and hair. He also spotted a clump of leaves, and he bent to pick them up. They seemed to be packed in a kind of parcel, as if someone had intentionally folded them up together.

Carefully, he pulled back a corner. To his astonishment, they were maple leaves. There wasn't a maple tree within two or three hours' walk, he thought, as he put the packet in a safe place for transport back to the valley. Did these belong to the corpse, too?

Lots of leather was still stuck to the rock on which the body had been found. Most of it was covered in more than a foot of water, though, and since it would probably freeze that night, they decided to leave it for the archaeologists.

After two tedious hours of work, the quiver was free, and the scientists gently began to lift it away. Just a few hundred yards to the south, Dal Ben, breathing hard, was scrambling up the scree on the Italian side of the ridge. He knew he was close because he could see the slope flattening out at the pass just above his head. The discovery spot was supposed to be right around there.

Ignorant of his approach, the Austrians were discovering just how delicate soaked leather can be. It ripped as easily as wet paper. Fortunately, ice seemed to be packed inside the quiver, securing the arrows in place. They placed the quiver inside a plastic bag one of them happened to have along and then wrapped it securely in Patzelt's down jacket. They had just inserted the quiver upright into Schneider's backpack and splinted it with two ski poles when they were startled to hear an unfamiliar voice coming out of the fog. Dreiseitl had stepped away for a moment and bumped into Dal Ben, who flashed his customs badge. They were surprised by how he was dressed. "What should I do?" Dreiseitl asked, turning quickly back to his colleagues, as the man stood several yards away.

"Does he speak German?" one asked in heavy dialect, to make it more likely that the man would not understand if he did. "Just keep him busy." In the next moment, Schneider disappeared into the fog with the quiver in the backpack, and the three Austrians turned to the Italian. In a mixture of English, Italian, and German, he asked where the corpse had been found. The Austrians pointed to the pool around the rock, and the Italian took a long look through the clear water to the scraps of leather, which swayed back and forth like reeds at the bottom of a pond.

"This is Italy," he announced in Italian. That was the last thing the Austrians wanted to hear. Whether he was right they could not say, but the possibility had occurred to them. Patzelt knew where the border markers were, but because of the fog he had not been able to see both of them clearly at the same time. If the Italian was right, then the scientists had just successfully smuggled out one of the greatest treasures ever found on Italian territory. In any case, they did not even consider telling the customs agent about the quiver. Before he could ask any further questions, the Austrians politely excused themselves and rapidly caught up with Schneider, who had been waiting out of view not far away. With great reluctance, they decided to forgo the glass of wine they had been anticipating in the Similaun lodge, since they feared they could meet the Italian there again and on Italian territory at that. Instead, they started down the mountain for the long and dark hike to Vent.

As Dal Ben watched them go, he had the feeling that they were up to something. Part of his job was to detect funny business—

smugglers, illegal immigrants, and the like—and this little group had obviously been up to something. He wondered why the fourth one had disappeared so quickly. He hoped he hadn't missed anything. Straddling the hole where the body had been found, he sighted first one border marker and then the other. Exactly as he thought. His colleagues in the carabinieri had erred and erred badly. They must have consulted the Alpine Club map to determine the border, not realizing that it contained a little error in the representation of the border. According to that map, a tiny triangle of territory that actually belonged to Italy appeared as part of Austria. The corpse lay in that little triangle. It belonged to Italy. Dal Ben was going to have to do something about this.

On Saturday, fully three days after their first attempt, Spindler and his crew of archaeologists and students finally arrived at the Hauslabjoch. Over the last several days, bad weather and low clouds had repeatedly obstructed their efforts to get to the site by helicopter. Though no other archaeologist in Tyrol had openly challenged Spindler's right to handle the amazing discovery, the delay had occasioned a little grumbling in Innsbruck's tiny archaeological community.

On Thursday, Spindler had conceded to a request from the Ferdinandeum to send two of their young staffers up to the site on foot. The two young men, the same ones who had learned of the discovery on Monday from Haid's call to the museum, planned to arrive there on Friday, search for more artifacts, and stay, sleeping in the Similaun lodge, until Spindler arrived. On Friday evening, Spindler learned that the two had reached the site and recovered a single, bluish, berry-sized fruit, the skin of which was slightly wrinkled, and a few pieces of leather and grass before being forced by a bad storm to retreat to the lodge for the night. Everyone in Innsbruck breathed a little easier knowing that archaeologists had at last arrived on the scene.

As Spindler and the others climbed out of the helicopter, they were blasted by a fiercely cold wind that scoured the pass and sent streamers of powdery snow flying into the air. Though Henn had described how remote the spot was, Spindler was taken aback by the bleakness of the terrain. In the chaos leading up to the flight, Spindler had not had time to outfit himself properly, and he arrived wearing jeans, which the wind quickly turned stiff.

As the group stood shivering on the pass, Spindler noticed several people in the distance, walking single file in their direction. The police had closed off the trails to tourists, so these could not be hikers. Nevertheless, they were clearly headed toward the Hauslabjoch. Slowly, the party drew nearer, and Spindler recognized the silhouette of the man in the lead. Though just a few years younger than Spindler, the man moved nimbly over the rock and snow. He was outfitted appropriately in colorful Alpinist gear and seemed not to notice the chilly gales as he bounded toward the professor with a crescent grin on his face and a healthy rouge in his cheeks.

It was Andreas Lippert and an eager, seasoned crew of student excavators.

Andreas Lippert was Spindler's departmental rival, a colleague who stood just beneath him in the hierarchy. Three years earlier, Lippert had been beaten out narrowly by Spindler in the search for the department head. Ever since, relations between the two men had been at best frosty. The son of a well-known Viennese architect with a notable genealogy, Lippert had the bearings and manners of the old Austrian nobility. He was tall, elegant, and unfailingly polite. In his youth, he had been among the dancers who opened Vienna's famed Opera Ball, the most important society engagement of the season.

Since Tuesday, he and his students had been following the news from the site of their own excavation of a Roman street in the Austrian province of Salzburg. At first they had all agreed that they should finish up their dig as planned and refrain from butting in on Spindler's big find. But by Thursday afternoon, Lippert had changed his mind. He had learned on the midday news that lay people rather than archaeologists had excavated a quiver from the site. It was a spectacular find. The discovery of just one wooden arrow was unusual, but a whole cache was nothing short of miraculous. Lippert wondered where Spindler had been when that was going on. Such sensitive work ought to be done by specialists. Technically, Lippert was supposed to have been informed of a find like this, but he had heard nothing from Spindler. That afternoon, he had finally reached Spindler in his office. In a brief discussion, Lippert told his colleague that he and his students would cut off their work and head to the site.

Spindler had not protested, and this was now the result: one site and two ambitious archaeologists, one of whom was keen to get started. After greetings were exchanged, Lippert began pushing for a preliminary excavation to be mounted as quickly as possible, before snow sealed off the site for the winter. Spindler wanted to wait until the next summer, when they would have enough time to clear the entire trench of snow and ice. Lippert insisted that the snow now protecting the site could melt off again that month, revealing whatever still lay there to the elements and whomever happened to be passing by. There was a good chance that more artifacts were still here, and he did not want to abandon them to the luck of the weather. Already they had cause for concern. Patzelt's group had observed but not touched many pieces of leather on the rocks where the corpse had been. Yet the two archaeologists who had visited the site the day before had found only tiny scraps of leather. Much more seemed to be missing.

Ultimately, Spindler seemed to agree. The dig would proceed this year. As soon as Lippert got down the mountain to Innsbruck, he at once set to planning the excavation for the middle of the following week.

Nine days had now passed since the Simons had stumbled on the corpse and four since Spindler had identified it in the autopsy room. At last the scientists and their overworked staffs in Innsbruck had a moment to assess what had hit them. Two conservators from the Roman-Germanic Central Museum in Mainz had sped to Innsbruck to take charge of the artifacts. The quiver with arrows, the tiny fruit, and the grass and leather were handed over to them. The corpse was still in Platzer's freezer, and the application of carbolic acid seemed to have at least arrested, and perhaps destroyed, the suspected fungus.

For the archaeologists and scientists, the sudden pressure of the world's media was relentless and thrilling. The unlikely discovery had propelled the provincial university onto the world stage. There was no public-relations department at the university, so the professors were left on their own to deal with the crush of journalists. The attention was flattering but also deeply distracting.

Media tyros all, the complaisant scientists consented to one interview after another, and even took turns appearing in live broadcasts during Austria's evening news programs. Next to their neat and composed interviewers, they looked a little sweaty and disheveled. They spoke excitedly but inevitably they never got enough time to say everything they knew. Interrupted by interviewers in midsentence, the scientists looked a bit startled, but they just swallowed their next words and smiled. This thing was already bigger than they were. Overnight they had become experts in an entirely new field. There was talk of book contracts and exclusive articles and movies and agents. There were offers of money everywhere.

Sharing the spotlight with the Innsbruck researchers were the people who had played a role in the corpse's discovery and recovery. Anton Koler had been tracked down at his station in Imst and interviewed a dozen times about the initial recovery attempt. Reinhold Messner had made several comments and appeared on television with Spindler. Even the voice of the folklorist Hans Haid was heard on radio throughout the land.

Helmut and Erika Simon had returned to Nuremberg to discover that they were celebrities. Their phone rang incessantly with requests for interviews. As soon as they got their photographs from their vacation developed, they found their one shot of the corpse and showed it to the journalists who were flocking to their cozy home. The slightly blurry image showed the corpse's head and upper back, face down over a dark pool of water. Naturally, everyone, including the archaeologists in Innsbruck, wanted to see the picture, and at first the Simons just passed copies out for free. But soon enough they realized that there was a bit of money to be made in those shots and, rather self-consciously, they began to sell them. They had been home less than a week when an Innsbruck lawyer called to inform them that he believed they might have some claim to the corpse. At first, the idea struck them as absurd. It was a treasure that belonged to all humanity, and they felt honored to have discovered him. Then again, they thought they should at least inquire. But first they hired another lawyer to deal with the Innsbruck lawyer.

Meanwhile, the discovery had already acquired a catchy name. In English, the press called him the Iceman. The Italian press had dubbed him L'Uomo del Ghiàccio, the man from the ice. In German he was Eismann, the Iceman, or Der Mann im Eis, the man in the ice. But the name that stuck in the German-speaking world was Ötzi, dubbed by a Viennese headline writer, after the Ötztal. It was an endearing name and sounded somewhat like the English word *tootsie*.

But no sooner had he been baptized for the Austrian valley in which he had died than the rumor arose that he was not, after all, Austrian. Silvano Dal Ben's insistence that the corpse was found on Italian territory had finally penetrated the upper levels of the South Tyrolean bureaucracy. All of a sudden, Reinhold Messner, too, was quoted as saying he believed the corpse was found on Italian or, more precisely, South Tyrolean territory. In a flash, South Tyroleans and Italians were saying the frozen mummy belonged to them.

To some of those involved in the corpse's recovery, Italy's claim rang true. Markus Pirpamer had been unsure about which side of the border the body had lain. Gernot Patzelt had also suspected the site might be in Italy. Over the next few days, gendarmes, carabinieri, and customs officers began making unofficial measurements at the site. At first, the Austrians said it was in Italy, and the Italians said it was in Austria. Then the Italians issued a news release expressing doubt about their own result. On the day Lippert and Spindler met at the site, a group of carabinieri and customs officials together with a few Austrian police had again tried to measure the position of the site. Again, the verdict was for Italy. But until a team of government surveyors was on hand, no one could say with authority on which side of the border the mummy's resting place lay. But as the debate heated up, so, too, did the import and value of the Iceman.

Across the border, in the South Tyrolean capital of Bolzano, Hans Nothdurfter, a graying, soft-spoken archaeologist in the province's Office of Cultural Treasures, had been monitoring the discussion over the corpse and the border with consternation. As a young boy growing up in a tiny Tyrolean mountain village during World War II, he knew well how seriously people took borders. On several occasions as a child, he had been dispatched with messages to some neighboring village. When he arrived there, he hid behind an out-lying house until he saw a familiar adult face. Then, checking around quickly, he sprinted over to the person as quickly as possible, delivered the message, and then got out. If he was spotted by one of the older boys in the village, he faced a certain beating. All were Tyroleans, and all spoke a very similar dialect of German, but Nothdurfter was different just because he was not from there.

In some ways, the battles of his childhood were analogous to those in the region's—perhaps any region's—history. Over at least the last two thousand years, the mountains and valleys had been occupied and inhabited, trespassed on, fought over, and abandoned by many different peoples, from the natives and the Celts in the fifth century B.C.E., to the Romans in the first century B.C.E., to the Germans, Austrians, and Italians in the twentieth century. Nothdurfter saw the traces of these populations and their languages in his work almost every day. In recent years, he had devoted himself to the excavation and restoration of the numerous little medieval churches of South Tyrol. The language in the beautiful frescoes that covered the walls of these churches was Latin, but the language in the pews had been German, probably brought here in the sixth century by immigrants from Bavaria. As soon as a church was restored, it became a destination for tourists from Italy, Germany, and other places. In some ways, all could consider it part of their heritage.

For all but a few years since 1363, Tyrol had formed part of the western flank of the Austrian-Habsburg Empire.* But upon the empire's defeat in World War I, Austria was forced to cede the portion of Tyrol south of the main Alpine ridge to Italy, and the 1919 Treaty of Saint-Germain established the new border between Austria and Italy along the watershed of the Austrian river Inn and the Italian river Adige.[4] Suddenly, the German-speaking Tyroleans who made up an overwhelming majority in the ceded region became Italians, divided from their ethnic brethren in Austria by the new border. Mainly poor farmers who lived in isolated villages, they scarcely had the political might to protest their fate. After Benito Mussolini came to power in Italy in 1922, he began a massive Italianization drive in the region. The German language was forbidden

*From 1810 to 1813 much of South Tyrol was ruled by Italy.

in schools, German place-names were changed to Italian, and official business could be conducted only in Italian. Even the name *Tyrol* was banned. Beginning in 1935, Mussolini sponsored the settlement of tens of thousands of ethnic Italians in the province, mainly in the cities of Bolzano and Merano. The rural German-speaking population was almost entirely disenfranchised.

On the eve of World War II, the status of native German speakers in the Italian province grew more confusing still. Even Hitler compromised his pan-Germanic expansionist policies when it came to the German South Tyroleans, many of whom supported him. Respecting Mussolini's desire to hold on to the region, which included half of the strategically important Brenner Pass, Hitler consented to a regional plebiscite in 1939 in which the population either had to accept German citizenship and emigrate to Germany or keep Italian citizenship. Under immense pressure from Italy and the local Nazi-backed party to choose emigration, at least 70 percent of the population of the province of Bolzano voted to leave their native land. Almost 75,000 people left before the war made civilian transportation too difficult.[5]

After the war, Austria, which still viewed itself as the German Tyroleans' protector, pushed for another plebiscite in South Tyrol on whether the region should remain part of Italy or be annexed to Austria. But the Allied powers were in no mood for Austrian expansion, and they never seriously entertained the idea. Though Italy officially agreed to protect the rights of the province's German speakers, the discrimination continued.

Then, in 1960, Austria went to the United Nations, charging that Italy was not abiding by its agreement. As various commissions debated how much autonomy the region should be granted, a pro-Austrian terrorist group initiated a bombing campaign against public works in the province. Their rallying cry was "One Tyrol." No one was hurt in the explosions, but the terror sent a chill through the population.

Finally, in 1969, Austria and Italy agreed on a set of terms for a largely autonomous province called Südtirol (South Tyrol) in German and Alto Adige (High Adige) in Italian. By 1991, the 440,000 people of the province—65 percent German, 26 percent Italian, and 4 percent Ladin[6]—were largely independent of the federal government in Rome; German and Ladin, a Rhaeto-Romanic language, were placed on equal footing with Italian in schools and offices, and public offices were divided proportionately among the ethnic groups.

But despite the overall success and cooperation among South Tyrolean, Italian, and Austrian officials, hard feelings, suspicions, and stereotypes persisted all around. Some South Tyroleans and Austrians still yearned for "one Tyrol." Some Viennese had a soft spot for this idea, but this nostalgic fondness was also tinged with the same mild arrogance they adopted toward all provincials. Tyroleans in Austria felt protective of their unharbored brothers and sisters in South Tyrol, yet they were also slightly patronizing toward them.

Italians outside South Tyrol viewed the province as spoiled by government funds, while German speakers in South Tyrol believed the federal government in Rome might swipe away their hard-earned minority rights if they were not vigilant. Though Messner's exhortations to build a unique South Tyrolean identity had found support among large segments of the province's German-speaking youth, the ruling conservative party's line was that there was only one Tyrol, one culture, one history, which now, alas, was divided between Austria and Italy. The historical capital of Tyrol was Innsbruck, and the University of Innsbruck was Tyrol's university. If the letter of that policy were followed, then Austrian Tyrol's possession of the corpse should not matter much to the South Tyroleans, since the university served Tyroleans everywhere.

But authorities on both sides of the border had quickly realized that more was at stake here than science. The Iceman was already drawing international media attention, and he was bound to draw tourists as well. Ideology and war had defined the region's ethnic struggles in the first half of the century, but the current form of ethnic struggle was economic. Tourists came to places with traditions, museums, and a sense of identity, and the money they left behind helped a place further shape its profile.

Nothdurfter was thus hardly surprised to see a debate emerge over the jurisdiction of the prehistoric mummy. The first salvo came just a week after the corpse's arrival in Innsbruck, from the governor of Austrian Tyrol. Calling the ownership controversy "unworthy," he stressed that any way one looked at it, the find had been made in Tyrol.[7]

The comment was a thinly veiled caution to both the Austrian and Italian federal governments that they should butt out. If the official survey determined that the Iceman had died within Italy, then autonomous South Tyrol would be responsible for it. Of course, Ötzi had lived long before the concept of nation, but the governor's comments demonstrated that the Iceman had become not only a worldwide archaeological sensation but also a national icon for a nation that did not exist.

Tyroleans, wherever they might be, were not the only ones interested in holding on to the mummy. Just as the issue of the jurisdiction was heating up, Helmut and Erika Simon's lawyer filed a claim on their behalf with Austria's Federal Forestry Office, which apparently owned the land on which the corpse was found, and the University of Innsbruck. The basis for the claim was an Austrian law that entitled those who find something to half its value. The lawyer was not yet willing to guess how much the corpse was worth, but he believed the value might be considerable.

On September 30, Spindler, Platzer, and Henn were summoned to meet government officials in Vienna. Here, too, the discovery was being viewed in national terms. Spindler's request that export licenses immediately be issued so that the artifacts could be transported speedily to the Roman-Germanic Central Museum had met with a bureaucratic pause. This was a standard request, and other Austrian finds had occasionally been restored in Mainz. But the minister in charge of science and research must have liked the publicity this discovery was bringing the country. The minister wanted to know why Austrian conservators and archaeologists could not handle the artifacts.

No one disputed that such an arrangement would be politically gratifying. But was it scientifically responsible? Already the University of Innsbruck was being accused of bungling the recovery, and they did not want to see amateurism added to the charges. Though Austria had produced more than its share of Nobel winners and artists in the first half of the century, not to mention people like Sigmund Freud, it was no longer considered a European science powerhouse. That reputation belonged instead to Germany.

At last the scientists, conservation experts, and government officials reached a compromise. With a discovery of world import like this one, the safest bet was to send it to the best. The official survey of the border would take place in a few days. Until then, the corpse would remain in Austria, but the artifacts could go to Mainz. Austrian conservators were to be permitted to follow the work there until its completion. At that point, everything would come back to Austria.

Klaus Oeggl grabbed his research proposal, rushed down the stairs and out the glass doors of the Institute of Botany. His jaw clenched in determination, the young assistant professor began marching through the botanical garden, toward the tiled roofs of Innsbruck below. Down there was the Institute of Forensic Medicine, where the artifacts were still being kept. Oeggl had only just returned from vacation in Italy with his wife, also a botanist, and their small children. But upon hearing the basics of the corpse and his equipment, he had immediately realized that this was a terribly interesting find for paleobotany.

Many summers ago, as an ambitious doctoral student, Oeggl had spent endless days in knee-high boots, drilling thirty-foot-deep samples out of a mucky Tyrolean bog. Because of the bog's special preservative powers, some things that fell in it—such as pollen and human bodies—were preserved indefinitely, creating an archive of organic life centuries or even millennia old. The botanists could then study the organic material for information on past environments and the crops, plants, and trees that grew nearby.

Like anyone who probed into bogs, he was aware that corpses had occasionally turned up in their murky depths. As he labored away, carefully packing the cores he brought up, he once mused idly about what a rich find a corpse would be, but he knew it was an unlikely scenario. No bog bodies had ever turned up in Austria.

Now, many years later, that unlikely fantasy seemed to have materialized. Though the Iceman had emerged from glacial ice rather than a bog, the possibilities were the same. The opportunity to reconstruct a prehistoric environment came around exceedingly rarely. Indeed, Oeggl believed it might never come again.

Arriving at Henn's office, Oeggl was welcomed warmly by the forensic doctor, who seemed to have the authority to decide who was going to work on the project. Oeggl immediately handed over his detailed proposal for a complete paleobotanical research project on the organic material found with the corpse, and the two men briefly discussed the corpse's state of preservation and Oeggl's previous botanical work. Henn was impressed with the young botanist's knowledge of bog bodies, and he could not mistake Oeggl's eagerness. As Oeggl left, Henn told him that since he worked in the Alps and knew the native flora well, he would likely be invited to participate in the research.

Hours later, Oeggl's boss, the head of the botany department, Sigmar Bortenschlager, showed up in the autopsy rooms to take a few samples of the organic material. But when Markus Egg, a conservator from the Roman-Germanic Central Museum, saw what Bortenschlager was about to do, he insisted that nothing, not even a blade of grass, be removed without first being inventoried in Mainz.

Egg respected the Innsbruck botanists, but not everyone who wanted a material sample of an artifact could get it. Even minute scrapings such as the ones the botanists wanted to take would not be sustainable over the long run. Egg believed that, as far as possible, every step taken in the conservation and restoration of artifacts should be reversible. The basic goal was to keep the materials in a condition as near as possible to that in which they had been found. The conservators and researchers always had to keep in mind that new technologies were continually becoming available that would suggest questions scientists did not even pose now. Therefore, the wise conservator tried to be as noninvasive as possible while still allowing samples and access.

Bortenschlager, a feisty strawberry blond with a reputation for judiciousness, saw no sense in waiting. Once the finds were in Mainz, the Innsbruckers might not have the opportunity to get samples. After a few tense moments, Egg backed down and fetched a sterile razor for the botanist. With Oeggl, whom he had summoned, Bortenschlager took tiny bits of grass from the shoe and the string, as well as a tiny splinter of wood from the ragged broken end of the longbow. Oeggl could hardly believe the variety of organic material, which Egg and another conservator arrayed carefully on pieces of Styrofoam. The prehistoric organic finds he had examined up to this point in his career had been won only after tremendous effort, and even then the information they yielded was measly. But now he was overwhelmed by the possibilities for interesting research.

The woods and grasses the man had used in his tools would provide a snapshot of the prehistoric environment in which he lived. Oeggl thought they might learn what types of trees and plants were available to the man for his equipment and what he knew about woods and their different properties. Plenty of other botanical evidence invisible to the naked eye was also contained in this find. Microscopic pollen might still be clinging to the corpse's clothes or be present inside the corpse itself. They might reveal the season in which he died or the particulars of his diet, including information on the kinds of crops, if any, being cultivated in the area.

Already the media reports were full of speculation by the archaeologists in Innsbruck about what this fellow had been doing up there in the mountains. There was talk that he might have been a hunter. He might have been in the mountains looking for metal ore. His possession of a metal ax indicated that he was familiar with metal, though most of his other tools were made of stone. Lippert had suggested that the man might be a shaman who had hiked up to carry out some mysterious ritual. That might explain why he had stopped on the lonely pass.

Oeggl bristled at such speculation. When he heard something he did not like, he often paused and almost seemed to stop breathing as he considered how to respond. Sometimes he decided not to say anything. Often, people were unnerved by his silences and took his mysterious caution as arrogance. His temper could be quick, but with his students and his own children his generosity and patience were bottomless.

As any scientist would be, Oeggl was astonished that this prehistoric human corpse had survived to the twentieth century. Yet he believed that scientists should resist animating the corpse and speculating about his story or his motive for going into the mountains, and instead try to view the corpse and the artifacts as an archive. Oeggl did not want to hear a single word that would prejudice his analysis. He wanted to begin with clean facts, unblemished by assumption or speculation. Already he had been disappointed to hear speculation that the good preservation indicated that the man had been embedded in snow and ice since shortly after his death. Since the corpse was found lying partially in meltwater, Oeggl wondered how the archaeological site could be pristine.

Later that day Spindler gave the botanists the tiny oval-shaped fruit recovered days earlier by the two archaeologists from the Ferdinandeum. Spindler guessed that it was part of the man's provisions and had perhaps slipped out of his hand or some other container. He was eager to know what it was and especially whether it was edible. He was also curious to learn what kind of wood was in the bow.

Oeggl went back to his lab and immediately got to work. Despite his welcome from Henn, he knew he had competition for this job. The Roman-Germanic Central Museum was the home of Maria Hopf, Europe's pioneering paleobotanist. Oeggl feared that his own slim résumé could be easily dismissed and that he would be locked out of the research.

Bortenschlager, meanwhile, was taking nothing for granted. The first step was to get the organic material properly carbon-dated. He removed a few bits of the grass samples and sent them off to labs in Paris and Uppsala, Sweden, for testing. He made a mental note that the results were due back about the first week of December.

The official survey of the border was set for October 2, just a day shy of the two-week anniversary of the discovery. Confusion over the course of the border had grown so large that only a grand gesture, captured on live video for all to see, would suffice to settle it. Accordingly, an ORF camera crew was there as Austrian surveyors, the first to arrive at the windy Hauslabjoch, quickly staked out the three granite border stones at issue: b-34, b-35, and b-36. Soon afterward, Italian officials on the site reported that bad weather in the Schnalstal was delaying the helicopter carrying the surveyors from Italy's Military Geographic Institute. But since the measurement was deemed of such political import, the Austrians agreed to wait for the Italians before proceeding.

The 1919 Treaty of Saint-Germain had defined the border between Austria and Italy in language, but it had been up to the surveyors of the time to figure out where it actually ran. Between 1921 and 1923, an international team had mapped out the watershed between the Inn and the Adige and set the border stones. Finding the watershed had not always been easy, since the mountains were partly covered by glacier and the lay of the land beneath could not be determined. The commission appointed to carry out the measurement directed that where the ground was concealed by ice, a straight line should be drawn between the two closest identifiable border points. The glaciers around the Hauslabjoch had been one such problematic area. The commissioners drew the border in a straight line between the Hauslabjoch, where border marker b-35 was placed, and a nearby ice-free point at an altitude of 10,525 feet that was labeled b-36.

After two hours, the Italian helicopter still had not shown up. Conditions at the pass were frigid, so the head of the Austrian team decided to go ahead. Everyone present had already seen with the naked eye what the surveyors subsequently measured: The site lay in Italy, just 101 yards from the border.[8]

The result had been predictable. The surveyors had seen just by looking at the map that the body had been on Italian soil.

But the exercise did uncover a small surprise for the geographers. In the seven decades since the original survey, the glacier had melted so much that the surveyors could now see the true watershed. It swung out more than one hundred meters to the west of the actual border and around the site of the find. The corpse, then, had lain inside the Austrian river Inn's watershed! If the true watershed had been discerned in the 1920s, the mummy would have been Austria's; only the ice cover of the time had prevented a true reading of the terrain. For the surveyors, this was nothing more than an ironic footnote. No matter how the true watershed ran, international law as well as the current border markers now said the corpse had been in Italy.

As the Austrian surveyors wrapped up their work, their Italian colleagues radioed up that fog was still preventing them from getting off the ground in the Schnalstal. They offered to drive around the Brenner Pass to Vent to meet the Austrians to discuss the results. Their job might be about fine-tuning border questions, but as Europeans in good standing, they were free to cross into Austria

with just a passport. A few hours later, in the tavern of Alois Pirpamer's Hotel Post, the two teams went over the maps. There was
no doubt that the site lay on Italian territory.

On the Austrian side, the politicians and local officials who had
been ready to welcome the remains of the prehistoric body into
their little villages were quietly disappointed. Among the scientists
at the University of Innsbruck, the reaction to the finding was even
more muted. Professing indifference over precisely where the
corpse was discovered, they insisted that the important thing was
that science proceed. The unspoken but clear message was that science should never bow to the narrow parochial concerns of an individual, a city, or a nation. As one Innsbruck headline writer put it,
"Science is international."9

The day after the official measurement, Hans Nothdurfter and a
few of his colleagues were hastily summoned to meet with Luis
Durnwalder, the province's ethnic German governor. For years,
Durnwalder's conservative party had insisted that the border was irrelevant to the cultural life of the province. Yet if they followed that
line now and said nothing, what would the consequences be?

Nothdurfter and the others were concerned that the powerful
federal government in Rome might try to get possession of the
mummy if South Tyrol failed to act first. Normally, finds of archaeological interest belonged to the state, but South Tyrol's unique autonomous status gave it special powers, including ownership of
archaeological finds. As long as South Tyrol made its claim, the
mummy and artifacts belonged to them.

But could South Tyrol take care of the corpse and the artifacts
once it possessed them? The province had no university of its own,
and its archaeologists were not prepared to handle the restoration
of the artifacts or preserve the corpse in a freezer like Innsbruck's.
The lack of appropriate facilities had been demonstrated the week
before when Italian customs officials had arrived with a bag of
leather pieces said to have been retrieved from the Hauslabjoch.
These were the shreds of leather Patzelt and his friends had decided
not to pull out of the water for fear of damaging them. Silvano Dal
Ben, the Italian customs officer who had surprised them at the site,
had later ordered his men to remove the pieces. The archaeologists
in Bolzano had no idea exactly where the pieces came from or what

to do with them. So one of Nothdurfter's Italian colleagues just took them home and put them in his freezer. Clearly this was not a long-term solution.

Despite their evident lack of preparation, Nothdurfter and the others believed that South Tyrol should exercise its hard-earned right to the corpse and artifacts. Durnwalder agreed. The find was bound to bring favorable publicity to the province, whose livelihood was heavily dependent on tourism. The very future of South Tyrol's heritage hinged on the province's economy.

After some discussion, the men came up with a compromise: South Tyrol would claim ownership of the corpse but would allow the University of Innsbruck to carry out the research. The idea seemed particularly palatable since many German South Tyroleans studied and taught at the university. To demonstrate the province's good intentions toward the university, the governor also decided that Andreas Lippert's excavation at the Hauslabjoch could go ahead.

Twenty-four hours after permission came, work at the site began. The early autumn weather had already added two feet of fresh snow, and Lippert knew he had to work fast. Normally, Markus Pirpamer closed up the Similaun lodge for the winter on October 1, but he offered to hold it open for the team. Lippert and Spindler had decided that a thorough excavation of the entire trench would have to wait until the following summer. The goals of this emergency excavation were to plot out the site, lay bare the large boulder on which the man had apparently died, and explore superficially the snow- or ice-covered spots where other artifacts had been found.

Lippert soon realized that few, if any, of the bits of leather, string, tiny lumps of charcoal, and leaves they gathered near the top surface of the ice lay in their original positions. The rescuers' actions, as well as the casual movement of the other visitors around the site, had disturbed almost everything. If the archaeologists had been called in at the moment of the discovery, they would have gently melted the ice from the corpse and documented its position fully before attempting to lift it. Clothes, shoes, and all the equipment would have been photographed and drawn in order to exactly represent the context. But now almost all of that was lost. The clothes were in shreds, the shoes badly damaged, and it seemed impossible to figure out where the tools had been in relation to the man and each other. What remained, Lippert concluded sadly, were the fragments of that violent excision from the ice.

The modest finds included a portion of a grass net, a fragment of a woven grass mat still frozen to the vertical side of the boulder on which the Iceman had died, bits of fur and leather, two pieces of animal bone, and a maple leaf. On day three of the excavation, the weather turned nasty. They could not continue when the falling snow covered up areas as fast as they were excavated. Work was stopped. The rest would have to wait until the following summer. A bit disappointed that nothing spectacular had turned up, Lippert and his students packed up the equipment and returned to Austria.

A few days after the excavation ended, Luis Durnwalder, accompanied by Hans Nothdurfter and a few colleagues, drove to Innsbruck for a meeting with the Austrian Tyrolean governor, Alois Partl, Platzer, Spindler, and several other researchers. In the library of Platzer's Institute of Anatomy, politicians and scientists sat down together while the media waited outside. Since the two governors knew each other well, the three-hour meeting was friendly but frank.

One of the first items on the agenda was the name. Spindler noted that the press was using a variety of names for the body. Traditionally, an archaeological find was named after the field in which it was found. Since a field was lacking in this case, the find should be named after the nearest named geographical site—namely, the Hauslabjoch. *Joch*, he said, meant a connecting point, a pass, and would symbolize the cooperation between North and South Tyrol.

Nothdurfter, who had a knack for representing the minority view, objected. *Hauslabjoch* was difficult to say in Italian, he argued. *H*'s at the beginning of words did not occur in Italian. To deflect any more ethnic or national claims on the corpse, the scientists should agree on a neutral name that all factions along the main Alpine ridge could understand and pronounce. A few others agreed, and they now turned to the one ethnic Italian in the room, Lorenzo Dal Ri, who studied Roman archaeology in South Tyrol. What did he think of *Hauslabjoch*? A moment of silence ensued, and then the normally shy Italian gave his response. "It's fine," he said, shrugging just a little. Science might just win out over politics after all. Hauslabjoch Man it was.

Now Durnwalder outlined South Tyrol's position on the body itself. The province of South Tyrol owned the corpse and the artifacts, but it would draw up a treaty under which the University of Innsbruck would be charged with the research and preservation of the finds. South Tyrol would name the members of a commission that would oversee research, but Durnwalder agreed that the University of Innsbruck could select the scientists who would work on the project.

Apart from the treaty, there was just one more small bureaucratic hurdle. Despite the fact that the body and artifacts were the property of South Tyrol, the federal government in Rome still had control over the export of archaeological finds. In order for the artifacts and the man to remain legally in Austria and Germany, Rome would have to issue an export license. If, for some reason, Rome decided against the license, then the finds would have to come back to Italy immediately. The chances of that happening were considered slim. So far Rome had kept itself out of the debate.

Despite the involvement by the states in what was basically just a matter for science and archaeology, the Innsbruck researchers, including Spindler, were satisfied with the agreement. Led by Platzer, who in the last several days had emerged as the Innsbruck researchers' dominant spokesperson, the university accepted South Tyrol's proposal. The meeting ended with handshakes all around. Under the scrutiny of the cosmopolitan world press, no one in this corner of Europe wanted to be accused of letting local concerns taint a world treasure. The participants congratulated themselves. So far, the cool, rational head of science seemed to be prevailing over the sloppy beast of politics and history. But the battle for the Iceman was not over.

CHAPTER 4

ITALY IS WATCHING

MARKUS EGG slipped into the basement workshop and shut the door behind him. At last, he was back to the artifacts. It was late October, two weeks since he and Spindler had ferried the artifacts here to the Roman-Germanic Central Museum in Mainz, and the media interest in the find had barely abated. Only one phone number connected the museum to the outside world, and it was jammed with calls for Egg, who had taken charge of the conservation of the Iceman's belongings.

The lively young Austrian with enormous eyes, magnified by glasses, had quickly become journalists' favorite interview. Egg could act silly, but he spoke authoritatively, even a bit loudly, in sentences that were so long that he often ran out of breath before he could complete them. Then, from nowhere, he would issue a boom of a laugh and toss his head, sending his auburn hair shuttling across his forehead. Through it all, he managed to come across as earnest and amiable. This was especially effective on television. Egg complied graciously with almost every journalist's request, but he also knew where to draw the line. An immense amount of work needed to be accomplished.

In continental Europe, archaeologists usually approached prehistory through the idea that much of prehistoric Europe had been populated by distinct and bounded populations that could be distinguished by the materials they left behind. When the same artifacts, the same types of dwellings, and the same types of burials showed up together repeatedly, they were then said to define a culture. Pottery styles were frequently one key to identifying a culture. All the people who made their pots according to one style were said to be part of the same culture, and sites where that style recurred in association with certain other cultural indicators were said to belong to that culture. Archaeologists named the cultures after the sites. The maps they drew of prehistoric Central Europe showed the land carved up into discrete cultures, almost like modern nation-states. The region of northern Italy to the south of the Hauslabjoch was similarly divided, though there was less information available.

Recently, this culture-based approach had been criticized as archaeologists have come to realize that archaeological cultures have often been equated with ethnic groups. Some have questioned the assumption that an easy correlation exists between material culture and ethnicity and challenged the very idea of bounded, internally homogeneous, and fixed cultures with deep roots in history. Shared habits and traditions—such as dwelling construction, language, or religion—are not necessarily indicators of communal identity. One need only look at the people of the former Yugoslavia to see that ethnic identities shear across common traits such as economy, language, dress, class, tradition, history, and physical appearance.

And even when clear geographical breaks between groups can be demonstrated, rarely do archaeologists know why a method was preferred. Why did some people make pots with fat lips and others make pots with square mouths? Sometimes there are economic reasons, or reasons having to do with available materials, the landscape, environment, or one of any other number of factors.

Despite its theoretical problems, most European archaeologists have adhered to the culture approach. Ironically, however, the region in which the Iceman was discovered had not been assigned to *any* culture. Virtually nothing was known of the people who lived in the mountains around the Hauslabjoch, which made it all the more incredible that one of them had apparently ended up preserved in a glacier for millennia. Indeed, the Iceman and his things were the only prehistoric artifacts ever found in the Ötztal, which had led to some speculation that the man had been an outcast or hermit who lived off his wits in the mountains far from any contemporary villages, and carried everything he owned on his back. Over the last centuries Tyrolean farmers and archaeologists had occasionally stumbled upon an isolated artifact, mainly flint blades. To the south of the Hauslabjoch, the closest contemporary finds were a few potsherds from Schloss Juval, the medieval hilltop castle owned, coincidentally, by Reinhold Messner.

The lack of a clear cultural context made the Iceman's possessions more difficult to understand. His metal ax could have been a rarity, but it was possible everybody had one. Unless archaeologists found more such artifacts, they could not say much. Egg was not pessimistic. They were just getting started, and in his years as the chief conservator he had seen a lot of interesting information sifted out of what looked like very little.

Egg happened to know a lot about Tyrolean prehistory. Egg's father had served as director of the Ferdinandeum, and the young Egg had grown up steeped in the history and culture of his native land. In a country the size of Austria, however, it was not easy for a son to avoid the wake of a famous father. So, upon the completion of his doctorate at the University of Innsbruck at the tender age of twenty-four, he had eagerly accepted a position in Mainz. Now, thirteen years later, he had risen to the position of chief conservator. Andreas Lippert often said that Egg had now far surpassed his teachers, but Egg just shrugged off such comments.

His immediate task was to make sure that these unique artifacts were properly conserved in a timely fashion so that they could be made available to other scholars, and eventually also to the public. But though his title was conservator, he was also a prehistorian, and already he was toying with a surprising hypothesis about the bow.

Egg had laid eyes on precious few of these prehistoric bows. Only a few dozen or so were known to exist. This one was a classic longbow, the product of millennia of refinements in the bowyers' craft. When Egg first saw it, the cross-section had tipped him off to its function. At its center it was D-shaped, like most prehistoric bows, and the one intact end tapered to a blunted point. He examined the broken end. The break was ragged, like a branch that had snapped off in a violent storm, and Egg wondered how and when it had happened. The bit that had broken off was nowhere to be found. Even with one tip missing, the bow was nearly as tall as the man who had presumably carried it. Yet something about this bow was not quite right.

The surface of the dark, purplish wood was rippled with fine, shallow whittle marks, half an inch to an inch long. Their regularity was remarkable. Why were those whittling marks visible at all? Egg rubbed his gloved thumb in the slight indentation left by the bowyer's tool. Other surviving prehistoric bows had smooth finishes or high polishes, and they were slenderer. No bowstring had been found. That was why the first people to see it in the ice had taken it for a walking stick or a pole.

No bowstring, indeed. That was the tip-off. There was not even a notch on the end of the bow where the string could have been attached. This bow was unfinished. The man had died without a working bow in a region that was probably swarming with wolves and bears, not to mention animals the man might have hunted. Egg was puzzled. It just did not fit. The outcast idea might explain why he was in such a desolate, apparently remote, location but it did not explain the unfinished bow, which, Egg thought, might even have something to do with the man's death.

Egg lay the bow back in the water bath that was the first step in the conservation process and moved over to the ax blade, which had fallen out of the haft. He plucked it off the mat and examined the dull edge. Had the Iceman used this very blade to fashion the longbow?

This ax was the epitome of the technology of the day, but Egg's colleagues in archaeology could not agree on whether such axes were really put to use. Lippert, for one, was convinced that they were symbolic rather than functional, since their blades were small and made of relatively soft metal. Egg noticed a few nicks in the cutting edge, but he could not say whether they were of recent or prehistoric origin. He wondered why the man would have carried the relatively heavy ax with him up into the mountains if it was not useful. Maybe he needed it to show off or to demonstrate his position in society. Perhaps he was going to trade it.

The ax handle was a wonderful example of how people had taken advantage of nature's forms. Egg could see that the entire wooden haft had been cut from the strong and durable joint of a trunk and branch. The blade had been inserted into a notch carved into the branch end and then secured with a black material Egg guessed was pitch. This had then been wound up by a strip of leather or skin, which had subsequently come loose.

The entire history of axes revolved around the haft. The basic construction problem involved preventing the blade from slipping out of or bursting through its handle. Part of the solution in this ax was a flange, a concave indent on the facets of the blade that fit into the corresponding convex bulges in the wooden haft. That grip helped to keep the blade from being knocked to the side as it struck an object.

Egg was not the only archaeologist in Europe pondering the Iceman's ax. From her office in Trento, Italy, about sixty miles south of the Hauslabjoch, Annaluisa Pedrotti had been learning all she could about the remarkable find from press reports and discussions with friends in South Tyrol. Pedrotti, a newly minted Ph.D. who worked at the Province of Trentino's Office of Cultural Treasures, studied the populations who lived in the northern Italian Alps between about 5000 and 2000 B.C.E., the period to which the Iceman had been assigned.

Though just in her early thirties, she had already devoted more than half her life to archaeology. As a teenager, Pedrotti had toiled away each summer at excavations under Bernardino Bagolini, a pioneer in the study of northern Italian prehistory. She began with the lowly task of washing and sorting ceramic pieces, and gradually moved up to cataloguing artifacts. She thus knew the business of archaeology from the ground up and had been present when a lot of what was known about the northern Italian Stone Age was unearthed.

In one moment, Pedrotti could be giggling compulsively over some devilish comment and in the next delivering a brief monologue on the development of the tanged flint dagger. Stopped by a crowd of her mother's talkative friends while walking down a Trento street, she could carry on about the weather and everyone's family's health for a good ten minutes. But as soon as they parted, her attention would snap back to some problem she had been contemplating. She had studied first at the University of Bologna, and then at Vienna, writing her doctoral dissertation on the connections between southern Austria and northern Italy in the fourth millennium B.C.E. The Iceman seemed like a test case for a lot of what she had learned, and she was eager to get involved in the project, though she did not yet know Spindler, who was now firmly in charge of the archaeological side of the investigation. In her view, the find had to be understood in the very broad context of the settlement and development of the Alps, a story that began one hundred thousand years earlier.

Traditionally, archaeologists divided Western prehistory into several periods, based loosely on the development of technologies. The Paleolithic period, or Old Stone Age, marks the time from the use of the first stone tools, some 2.5 million B.P., to about 10,000 B.P. There follows the Mesolithic period, or Middle Stone Age, which lasts until the emergence of agriculture and refinements in toolmaking, such as the production of very fine flint blades. The Neolithic period, or New Stone Age, is marked by the introduction of agriculture, and its final stage is often called the Eneolithic period or Copper Age, in order to designate the beginning of metallurgy. The latter was the period in which Pedrotti specialized. Around 2000 B.C.E. in Central Europe began the Bronze Age, the period in which Spindler said the Iceman belonged.

Pedrotti was not convinced of that dating. While the dating system was fixed according to the appearance of new technologies, archaeologists were increasingly coming to realize that change occurs constantly and not always along a linear path. The point at which the archaeologist chooses to end one period and begin another is arbitrary, fixed largely to the changes he or she believes are important.

Nevertheless, there were a few important guideposts. Humans first set foot in the interior of the Alps during a warm period as long as one hundred thousand years ago, toward the end of the Paleolithic period. Their stay was apparently short-lived. The glaciers soon began to advance again, and people retreated to more hospitable regions outside the mountains for tens of thousands of years.

About ten thousand years ago, at the end of the last Ice Age, humans returned to the Alps. As temperatures rose, the rocky, barren land that had been covered by glacier was slowly reclaimed by vegetation. Generations of plants lived and died and the humus built up, creating soil in which bushes and later trees like fir and pine grew gradually up the mountains. The animals that fed on grasses and small bushes followed plants in their colonization of ever higher altitudes and, in turn, were followed by those creatures that preyed on them.

From the Po River plain in north-central Italy, Mesolithic hunter-gatherer populations moved up the broad Adige Valley, past the sites of the modern-day towns of Verona and Trento, Bolzano and Merano, and into the Alps. Similar populations from what is today southern Germany migrated into the northern Swiss Alps. These people did not live in permanent settlements but followed the herds of deer, ibex, and other animals during their seasonal migrations. With the arrival of the first heavy snows, they probably returned to sheltered camps at lower altitudes.

Pedrotti believed these people did not confine themselves to the valleys but also crossed the high mountain passes, just as the Iceman did thousands of years later. She and her colleagues sometimes found stone tools—blades and scrapers, some just a few millimeters long—in passes that were clear of snow only in the summer months. On both sides of the main Alpine ridge, archaeologists also found harpoons that were virtually the same style, which convinced them that at least in this period the mountains were no barrier to trade or communication.[1]

Upon reaching a pass, a Mesolithic hunting party might have stopped for a few moments. Sometimes they made a fire and sharpened a flint blade, a process called retouching, leaving tiny chips of flint that archaeologists unearthed millennia later. At some sites, Pedrotti found several pieces from one tool. Back in her office, she would try to fit the tiny flakes back together in order to determine the order in which they were removed. This is known as refitting, and it might seem incredibly tedious. But when it worked, an archaeologist could re-create the shape of the material with which the toolmaker had begun and come to understand what the desirable qualities of such tools were.

In the 1980s, an Italian archaeologist excavating one high-altitude site had uncovered the skeleton of a man next to a solitary large boulder. Most likely he had died during a hunting outing and had been buried on the spot with his belongings, which included tools made of stone, bone, and antler. Though this man died a few millennia before the Iceman, Pedrotti and Bagolini noticed that the tools he was buried with were very similar to those found with the Iceman. No matter how much the Hauslabjoch find looked like an accident, Bagolini said, archaeologists must consider the possibility that he, too, had been buried.

Pedrotti's own work was mainly on the Neolithic, the period generally characterized by the domestication of plants and animals. Agriculture appeared in the Alps around the beginning of the fifth millennium B.C.E., well before Ötzi's lifetime, but many millennia after it began in the Fertile Crescent of the Near East, around 8000 B.C.E.

Archaeologists have come up with many theories to explain why and how people became farmers and how the domesticated varieties of plants native to the Near East came to grow in Europe. The abandonment of the hunter-gatherer lifestyle for the rigors of farming must have involved far more than the realization that seeds stuck in the ground will grow into useful plants. Modern hunter-gatherer populations know full well how things grow, and yet they do not support themselves in this way. A perennial question for anthropologists is why some populations turned to farming while others did not.

One possible answer is that rising population, combined with climate changes, led people in the Near East to try more efficient ways to feed themselves.[2] People began to eat more wild grasses and manage herds of animals because their traditional sources of food were harder to find. Hunter-gatherer populations might have been attracted to stands of wild grasses and settled near them, knowing that they were a constant supply of food. Over time, human interaction with these grasses and other animals altered their genetic makeup to the point where it became virtually impossible for them to survive without continued human intervention. Cereals, as the cultivated grasses are known, had to be planted and tended because they could no longer effectively propagate themselves. Likewise, without human attention, domesticated animals were no longer capable of successful competition with their wild cousins or other animals. This was the dawn of farming and also the start of the human genetic engineering of plants. Over the next several millennia, the farming villages of the Near East grew into small towns and cities, and the societies they housed grew more complex. New technologies such as the wheel, baked clay pottery, and copper metallurgy arose and spread. Societies grew more complex, and writing was developed.

In the meantime, the practice of agriculture was moving across Europe. Importantly, the wild progenitors of the cereals were not native to Europe. Domesticated cereals such as wheat were introduced to the region by farmers who either acquired the seeds from others or who migrated into the area, possibly pushing out the people who were already living there. In some parts of Europe, archaeologists have found indications that hunter-gatherer groups persisted for several millennia after the first signs of agriculture, raising the question of how the two groups coexisted. Ultimately, however, the Neolithic population growth probably put pressure on resources—abundant herds on large tracts of land—that were vital to the hunter-gatherer way of life, eventually forcing them into settled lifestyles.[3]

At the start of the Neolithic period, just three domesticated grasses were grown in and around the Alps. They were einkorn, barley, and emmer. The most important of these was einkorn, a durable species that grows well in poor soils such as those in the high mountains. For the farmer, the crucial difference between the wild and the cultivated version of einkorn lies in its development. In the wild version of einkorn, which grows only in the Near East, the rachis, the segments of the stalk to which the spikelets of wheat are attached, becomes brittle gradually, starting from the top of the head and working down, as the seeds ripen. A gentle wind, the brush of an animal, or eventually even its own weight is enough to snap the rachis, which then spills the seeds to the ground where they reseed themselves. Since the entire head does not break off at the same time, the seeds do not normally fall in exactly the same place and thus do not compete directly with each other.

The domesticated version of einkorn ripens differently. A farmer does not want a plant whose seeds fall at the slightest touch or ripen over the course of several weeks. He wants them all ripe at the same time and still on the stalk, so the harvest can take place efficiently when he comes by with a sickle. That is precisely what these grains do. The individual grains ripen at more or less the same time, and come off only when threshed, so little goes to waste.

The arrival of agriculture in the Alps marked the start of a new relationship of people to their land, to their gods, and to each other. At the time the Iceman lived, Europe was dotted with small agricultural settlements that hugged the shores of lakes or sat atop grassy hills or other areas where the forest was not so thick. A few remnant bands of hunter-gatherer populations moved around its fringes. There were no cities, no writing, and, in the Alps, probably no wheel. The complexities of civilization, as archaeologists term the societies that evolve around cities, were still millennia in the future. But cultural influences of populations who lived nearby might well have been at work on the people who lived in the Alpine valleys around the Hauslabjoch.

The most impressive and significant remnants of those people were the huge, anthropomorphic figures sculpted out of stone slabs, which archaeologists call statue-stelae or, more generally, statue-menhirs. Pedrotti had just begun studying a group of six statue-menhirs recently unearthed during a construction project in the town of Arco, near Lake Garda, about seventy miles south of the Hauslabjoch. The striking similarity among widely separated statue-menhirs in northern Italy suggests that the people of the region were in contact with each other.

Pedrotti believed that the statue-menhirs had to do with the spiritual life of the communities they came from. Were they art or religion? Ancestors or gods? Did the statue-menhirs represent particular individuals who had really lived? Were they spirits or idealized figures?

The largest of the six was a pentagon-shaped slab of rock more than six feet tall, nearly three feet across, and just under a foot thick. With one carved line, the creator had given it a pointy nose and two eyes, very much like those one might expect in a cartoon character or a Picasso sketch. Below the face was a beaded necklace, and below that, on the figure's chest, was an impressive display of weapons. Long-handled axes and pointed daggers with prominent ribs were arrayed across the front like a military man's war medals. Pedrotti wondered whether the representations indicated that these people possessed the daggers, desired them, or despised them. Below the armaments, encircling the statue-menhir's midline was a band of wavy lines, usually interpreted as a belt, possibly made of cylindrical copper beads strung together. Patchwork-like rectangular designs were common on the backs of the statue-menhirs, and probably represented clothing.

Below the belt, the stone was rarely carved. Legs were never depicted, and, as far as the archaeologists could tell, neither were the genitals. But some had prominent breasts and were assumed to be female; additionally, no statue-menhir with breasts was also carved with weapons or a belt. Two Arco statue-menhirs were male, three were women, and one was so small that Pedrotti thought it probably represented a child or possibly an adolescent who had not yet gone through some rite of passage.

Pedrotti's study of the Arco statue-menhirs had convinced her that the society in which they were constructed was hierarchic. She assumed that the statue-menhirs belonged together and that their relative characteristics were therefore meaningful. Whether this society mirrored the one in which the Iceman lived, Pedrotti could not yet say. But given the ax's prominence in the statue-menhirs, she did believe it was highly significant that the Iceman carried his ax with him, whether or not he used it.

The statue-menhirs and the Iceman also had one material connection. Five of the six statue-menhirs were cut from a gleaming white marble that was quarried from a site in the Vinschgau, the wide valley to the south of the Hauslabjoch. Somehow those people had transported the enormous slabs to Arco, probably down the river Adige. The Iceman, too, had a piece of white marble, the little disc to which was attached the tassel of leather strips, and Pedrotti suspected that it also had come from the Vinschgau. The purpose of the object was not yet clear, and Pedrotti wondered whether the marble itself was considered sacred and whether the disk was a religious talisman.

Apart from the statue-menhirs, Pedrotti knew of one other site that immediately struck her as relevant, and possibly crucial, for understanding the Iceman. In the late nineteenth century, Italian archaeologists had uncovered a large Copper Age graveyard near Remedello Sotto, a modern town on Italy's Po plain, just south of the Trentino. The archaeologists had no idea what kind of dwellings these people lived in, or exactly how they made their living, because the only finds came from the settlement's graveyard. The people who buried their dead there, beginning around 2800 B.C.E., were believed to be the first metallurgists in northern Italy, the first to add copper to their list of raw materials. So many copper objects were found in the graves, and they were so distinctive, that the archaeologists inferred that the Remedello people themselves knew how to smelt copper and had developed their own style of tools and ornaments. At the same time, however, they had not abandoned their reliance on stone. The artifacts excavated at the site, such as daggers and axes, testified to the technologically diverse nature of the period. They made their daggers out of copper, but also of stone; they made axes of copper, but also of stone. Their arrowheads were knapped out of flint. These people may have known how to use copper, but they still had one foot in the Stone Age.

Pedrotti knew Remedello well and had noticed right away that the materials in the Iceman's tool kit were similarly diverse. He had two flint arrowheads, a flint dagger, and several smaller flint tools, yet his ax was made of metal. This combination of materials as well as the particular shapes and kinds of his stone tools hinted to Pedrotti that the ax might be from an early stage in the development of metallurgy. In this phase, people made their tools out of more or less pure copper. They had not yet developed the technology to make bronze, an alloy of copper and tin.

Like Spindler, Pedrotti had learned that ax blades shaped like the Iceman's were, with very few exceptions, made of bronze. The books on Europe's Bronze Age were filled with illustrations of axes that looked just like the Iceman's. They even had a name: Neyruz Type B. Their technical name was "low-flanged ax." The problem was that artifacts—and the people behind them—did not always obey the neat classification systems, based on the artifacts' shape, pattern, or raw material, that archaeologists had devised to make sense of them.

Experimental archaeologists often accused their strictly book-learned colleagues of being too concerned with typologies and of looking at tools in a static and formal way. They assigned functions to tools without checking to see whether the tool could actually perform in that way. If a tool had one shape, then they said it was an awl; if it was another shape, then it was an arrowhead. While experimental archaeologists appreciated typology as an organizational aid, they tended to think of artifacts, especially tools, as having life cycles. A tool might begin its working life in one function but go through various metamorphoses as it wore down or became damaged.

Not long after the Iceman's discovery, Annaluisa Pedrotti drove to the tiny provincial museum where the finds from the Remedello Sotto excavation were displayed. There, in an old-fashioned case labeled "grave 102," she found what she had come for. It was the grave of a man who had died about 2800 B.C.E. He was buried on his side in a fetal posture. Around his corpse, the people of his community had placed various items, including several flint arrowheads and an ax blade. Pedrotti studied it closely through the glass. Just as she had remembered, the blade looked remarkably like that of the Iceman. But it was made of copper.

Virtually the only difference lay in the length. The Remedello 102 blade was four fifths of an inch longer than that of the Iceman. The form itself was identical. The trapezoid-like profiles were narrow at the base and flared out very slightly at their cutting edge. The broad sides of the blade were slightly concave, and the narrow edges were faceted. Instead of pounding the edges flat, the coppersmith had hammered three narrow facets into that edge, lengthwise down the blade. That seemingly unimportant detail was, in fact, a subtle improvement in blade technology. This kind of blade was known as "flanged" because the edge of the concave and faceted sides created a rim that helped hold the blade in its wooden haft. Those flanges represented a considerable advance over the older flat copper axes, some of which were also found at Remedello.

Pedrotti stared at it through the glass case and let her mind run over everything she knew about copper in northern Italy. The low-flanged copper ax was rare, but here it was in a context that looked very much like that of the Iceman. Since she had driven so far, she swiftly passed through the rest of the displays, but her mind was on the ax. By the time she walked out of the museum, she was sure she was right. The Iceman's ax was made not of bronze, as Spindler thought, but of copper.

While work on the artifacts and clothing moved swiftly forward through the autumn of 1991, research on the corpse was put on indefinite hold while the scientists made sure their preservation efforts were working. Unlike in Mainz, where the artifacts were being conserved according to well-established methods, there were few case studies of frozen mummies, and the Innsbruck scientists were not immediately aware of their options. Werner Platzer had no experience in the preservation of human remains of archaeological interest, though he knew plenty about conserving corpses for anatomical research. Consequently, he based his decisions about the Iceman's well-being on principles he had worked out in his institute over the previous two decades.

In the early 1970s, Platzer had faced a vexing problem. He wanted to preserve samples of human tissue in precisely the condition in which they were removed, without the addition of any chemical preservatives. But when he stored them in the freezer, samples inevitably dried out and fell apart, destroying tissue structures. Before long, he hit upon the idea of raising the humidity in the freezers to prevent desiccation. The method worked splendidly. He had put the frozen Iceman in more or less the same conditions as his other samples: 70 percent humidity and a temperature just below freezing. From the many scientists who were already clamoring to get a piece of Ötzi, he learned that much interesting science depended on an unaltered corpse. If he was as well preserved inside as he seemed to be outside, then there might still be dried blood in the heart and parasites in the stomach or intestinal tract, not to mention food. All were potentially rich avenues of exploration for scientists interested in questions of prehistoric nutrition, health, and disease.

There was another consideration as well. This was, in effect, a borrowed corpse. At some point, it was to go back to Italy, and Platzer did not want the Italians or South Tyroleans to say that he had ruined it. Based on these considerations, he formulated a clear-cut mission for himself. He would conserve the Iceman in precisely the condition in which he was discovered. As long as the corpse did not decay, Platzer would be doing a good job.

Given his powerful position within the university, as well as the fact that he was actually in possession of the corpse, no one protested when Platzer assumed control of the preservation efforts. The responsibility for research on the mummy fell to him as well.

Since, unlike Spindler, he had decades of experience dealing with the country's bureaucracy, Platzer had also been the natural choice to chair the first hastily convened meeting with government officials in Vienna, which had since become a committee charged with Iceman affairs. At one of the committee's first meetings in early October, Platzer proudly announced that swab tests on the corpse had failed to turn up signs of a fungus. Since both tests were done after the Iceman had been treated with carbolic acid, they could not know for sure whether a fungus had ever existed. In the meantime, the dark bluish, wartlike bumps that had beset the mummy shortly after its arrival in Innsbruck were identified as vivianite, a harmless iron phosphate that turns blue when exposed to air and had also been found on fossilized bones from silt deposits.[4/5] Platzer assured everyone that the mummy was doing well. Given the critical questions still being directed at the university over Henn's recovery of the corpse, Platzer believed this was an important step forward.

Just a few days after the meeting, an Italian anthropologist named Luigi Capasso arrived at the Institute of Anatomy. Polite yet mysterious, Capasso was an official in Italy's Ministry of Cultural Treasures who had been appointed by the government in Rome to examine the mummy and report back on what he found. Press reports about the messy excavation of the corpse had alarmed Rome, and Italian politicians wanted to make sure that this great find made on their territory was being handled properly. The agency, which ran the country's multitudinous museums, possessed several hundred mummies, and Capasso was responsible for them all. None, however, was quite like the Iceman.

From the standpoint of the Austrians, the visit ran smoothly. But Capasso, it turned out, was not at all pleased with the situation he found. Once back at his office near Rome, he wrote a highly critical report to his superiors on the Austrians' management of the frozen mummy. Directly contradicting Platzer's recent claims, Capasso charged that algae and fungi were visible at several spots and were not being treated. The algae, he wrote, could proliferate even in the dark and below freezing. In these conditions, the algae would destroy the skin within a few months.

He also alleged that Platzer had neglected to follow "the most elementary and widely known rules for the preservation of mummified matter." The refrigeration system he called "pure song and dance," and he alleged that no guards against fire, short circuits, or blackouts were in place. He also decried the utter lack of security around the freezers. He alleged that the freezers lacked proper safeguards against contamination, and he criticized the way the mummy was being shown to people. Visitors were allowed to approach the mummy as closely as they wanted, possibly exposing it to contamination via the visitors' mouths. Not only did Platzer have no previous experience in the preservation of mummies, Capasso wrote, but he had not yet contacted people who did.

Finally, Capasso called for the immediate and permanent involvement of Italy's Ministry of Cultural Treasures, which had at its disposal "the most scientifically advanced technology, all the scientific competence and a network of international consultation necessary to begin at once the urgent program of preservation." Implying that the mummy should soon be moved, he also urged the ministry to prepare a system of refrigerated transport and a refrigerated cell in a separate institute.

As outlined by Capasso, the circumstances of the mummy's conservation looked dire indeed. Rome would have to do something.

Werner Platzer was not immediately aware of the report by his Italian colleague. Confident that the conservation issue was well under control, he had shifted some of his attention to the recent negative media coverage of the Iceman story. The video of Henn and the Alpine gendarme snagging the frozen corpse on the ice pick had been broadcast over and over in Austria and around the world. Anyone could see that an archaeological find should not have been excavated like that, but so far no one from the university, not even Henn himself, had come up with a solid explanation for why it had happened. At this stage, no one quite knew what had gone wrong, although rumors abounded that several tips and warnings had been ignored or overlooked during the epic five-day recovery. In one of the few media reports on the topic, ORF spared no harsh words in describing the excavation, calling it a "catastrophe" and a "systematic destruction of a find."[6] The network also interviewed a Viennese anthropologist who bemoaned the fact that the sensational discovery had ended up in the hands of the University of Innsbruck.

The problem, it was suggested, was not just Henn but the whole university.

Most reports were less focused on the bungled recovery and more interested in facts about the Iceman. Several researchers thought the university should just admit that mistakes were made and then go on. But the criticism, especially from ORF, stung Platzer. He complained that the ORF report failed to explain that Henn used a ski pole in the recovery only because he had been told the corpse had been already dug out of the ice. Though no one at the university knew precisely how many visitors had been on the site in those days, Platzer also claimed that the video made Henn's actions look like the desecration of an archaeological site when, in fact, it was already ruined before he got there. Had he been in the litigious United States, Platzer claimed, he would have sued the broadcast corporation and won millions for slander.

What seemed to concern him most was that the video embarrassed the university before its South Tyrolean and Italian partners. Though South Tyrol had already informally agreed to let Innsbruck take charge of the research, the university might have to wait months for the official treaty with South Tyrol and the Italian export permit. More negative press coverage might undermine the process.

Even as media criticism waned in the weeks following the discovery, Platzer's strategy was to circle the wagons around Henn and sacrifice those unconnected with the university. In one statement released by Platzer's federal committee, blame for the messy recovery was shifted from Henn to the two "amateurs" who first tried to dig the corpse out: Anton Koler and Alois Pirpamer. These earlier two attempts "are to be viewed as completely unprofessional. Thereafter followed the true, official excavation, which found before it a site that, from the archaeological point of view, was disturbed," the statement read.

Neither Pirpamer nor Koler ever publicly defended their work. But in the face of the sensational video of the recovery, the campaign to exculpate Henn was futile. For Platzer, the lesson was clear: If the camera had not been there, Henn's operations might have been shelved away with those of the other visitors to the site.

Platzer was especially irritated that ORF had made money by selling the tape of the excavation to networks around the world. That was standard business practice among broadcasters, but Platzer felt ORF was being exploitative. He said repeatedly that the university should try to hinder "third persons" from profiteering off the Iceman.

He did, of course, recognize the value of footage of the Iceman. Documenting the research undertaken on this extraordinary corpse was important and Platzer's Institute of Anatomy was equipped to do it. Over the years, the anatomist had made dozens of medical films, and he decided to have one of his technicians videotape all the work on the Iceman. As long as the university was documenting the Iceman, there would be less need for the media to get involved.

The next media issue was not long in coming. One of the few researchers to get a look at the Iceman so far was Dr. Dieter zur Nedden, a radiologist at the University of Innsbruck and an old acquaintance of Platzer. As a young doctor, zur Nedden had worked as Platzer's assistant and he had used his pull with Platzer to get the Iceman for a full set of X rays and CAT scans using his state-of-the-art facilities at the medical university. As chief of one of the university clinic's radiology departments, zur Nedden oversaw a team of doctors who handled everything from simple broken bones to the images required for brain surgery. He had worked hard to keep Innsbruck abreast of the rapid developments in the field and now, in his late forties, he had won the respect of his European peers and had strong connections to the companies that developed the rapidly changing imaging technology.

Both Platzer and zur Nedden realized that if the corpse decayed and could not be autopsied or examined directly, it could at least be preserved in images. The CAT scans delivered cross-sectional images of the Iceman's body at millimeter-wide intervals. These could be mined for information on injuries, disease, or physiological abnormalities. Exactly one week after the corpse's arrival in Innsbruck, orderlies wheeled the Iceman through an underground passageway from the anatomy building to the hospital.[7] Working quickly to avoid thawing the corpse, zur Nedden's team first snapped dozens of X rays. Then they readied the body on the CAT-scan table and sent him through the donut-shaped scanner, taking care that his outstretched arms did not catch on the sides.

As the first images emerged, a knot of doctors gathered around to look at the film. The chest X ray was one of the first out. Zur

Nedden held it up to the light and immediately noticed an odd skeletal asymmetry. He was not quite sure what to make of it.

He and his team would need many hours with these X rays. They would get outside advice, too. He had connections to a few forensic radiology specialists and he thought this would be a good case for them. He would not be willing to offer a public statement on the state of the mummy's bones for some time.

Since the media had learned he was X-raying the corpse, his department had been inundated with calls from journalists. Some made it clear that they were willing to pay for information. At this early stage of his evaluation, zur Nedden felt no compulsion to share anything with the press, and he told them so. But someone in the clinic leaked a little bit of news to one paper. The Iceman, the paper reported, had died of a stroke.

In fact, the report was wildly premature. Zur Nedden traced the rumor back to a comment by one of his neurologist colleagues. While reviewing the CAT scans of the skull, the neurologist had pointed out a dark area in the brain and opined that it might be a sign of a stroke. Zur Nedden agreed that there was something unusual about that spot, but it was too soon to make a diagnosis. When Platzer learned that the rumor was being used to sell newspapers, he was outraged. The X rays and CAT scans were full of information that the media would pay for, and the release of such information should be controlled if it was going to be made public at all. Platzer believed that if anyone cashed in on the find, it should be the university.

But even zur Nedden was surprised by Platzer's next step. The anatomist told zur Nedden to give him all the copies of the X rays and the optical disk containing the CAT-scan images. He locked the materials in a bank vault. Zur Nedden was not to see the images again for several months. He ordered the people in his department not to discuss their work with the press. Based on his quick assessment of the X rays, zur Nedden knew there would eventually be plenty to say. All had not been well with the Iceman.

The Roman-Germanic Central Museum was bound by its charter to inform the public, and Markus Egg's workshop was open to any colleague or journalist. Already in the artifacts' first month in

Mainz, dozens of archaeologists and other researchers stopped by for a look, and many made comments that Egg incorporated into his interpretations. Though he specialized in the European Iron Age, Egg was well connected in the continent's archaeological circles and personally knew many of the people who were eventually to collaborate on the research.

Through the fall, Egg and his team sent each artifact through a carefully orchestrated regime of preservation and study. Before he allowed archaeologists or other researchers to handle the artifacts, each one had to be X rayed, CAT scanned, and photographed, and then documented, cleaned, repaired, and preserved. Egg walked a difficult path between protecting and conserving artifacts for future generations and making them available for current scientific investigation.

Egg's most frequent visitor was Spindler, who throughout the fall commuted to Mainz. Spindler was impressed by the variety and quantity of equipment the Iceman had managed to carry into the mountains. Except for his unfinished bow, which the archaeologists still could not comprehend, the man seemed well equipped for a sojourn in the mountains. One of the most useful tools seemed to be the flint-blade dagger. The archaeologists had immediately recognized the blade. About three inches long (it could not be measured precisely because the tip had been broken off), it was made of a gray-flecked flint common in Europe. Archaeologists usually called such blades arrowheads, though they had not actually found them attached to an arrow shaft. In normal circumstances, wood decayed long before discovery. Archaeologists just assumed they were arrowheads because they seemed to have the same shape as arrowheads used today. Yet here, to their humbled surprise, was that same blade hafted instead into a very simple dagger handle. There was no arguing with this. The blade was being used as a dagger. And it must have been used, for it was also well-worn.

The edge of the blade was serrated. The serrations, every archaeologist knew, resulted from "retouching," a kind of sharpening in which tiny bits of the blade's edge were broken off using a bone or antler tool. Also visible to the naked eye was the peculiar polish on the edge of the blade that comes from using it to cut grass.

Egg had an idea of how large the blade might have been when it was new. Among the artifacts he had found a finely woven grass sheath, whose shape nearly matched that of the dagger blade. The blade fit loosely inside; probably the sheath had been constructed when the blade was larger, before its edges had been retouched so much.

A little grass string coming off the handle of the dagger hinted that the man might have tied it onto some other object, perhaps to carry it. Egg found the same string bound around the most curious and unexpected of all the artifacts. For lack of a better term—no one had ever seen anything like it in all prehistory—he initially called it a fanny pack.* Essentially, it was a leather pouch on a broad leather band. Whether the man had really worn it around his waist Egg did not yet know. The band's ends were torn, so he could not determine how the item had been attached. But the band was more than long enough to reach around the man's waist or hips, had he chosen to carry it like that.

It was a decidedly simple model. Access to the contents was through a three-inch-long gap in a seam along the top, which could be laced shut. When first recorded in the autopsy room at Innsbruck, the fanny pack already had a large tear in its center. Out of this tear poked a flint blade of a type well known to prehistorians. After first X-raying and CAT-scanning the pouch, Egg carefully opened it. Inside, he found a second flint with a pointed end, which looked like a drill bit, and a third flint, which was just under an inch long and had one razor-sharp edge. Each was distinctive and must have had particular functions. The largest was a scraper, while the drill-like flint could have been used to bore holes in wood. The tiny, razorlike blade could have been used to cut very fine things, like the feathers used in an arrow.

The fanny pack also held a piece of hollow goat or sheep bone with two pointed ends, both of which were now bent over but not broken. Egg suspected that it was used for punching holes in skins so they could be sewn together. The rest of the small space in the pack was filled by a curious mass of black material, now matted and soggy from having thawed. Since many of the tools seemed to have

*The term in German, *Gürteltäschchen*, is directly translated as "little belt purse."

been useful in making a bow and arrows, Spindler wondered whether this black stuff, too, was material for archery equipment. He suggested it might be birch pitch, a glue made of birch bark that could have been used to attach the feathers onto the ends of the arrows. A sample of the material would have to be sent to chemists for testing.

In other cases, identification could not be solved by simply sending the object off to a specialist. Two items in particular stymied Egg and Spindler. One was the leather tassel on the marble disk, which Egg thought might just have been the man's supply of leather strips. The other was a wooden object that looked like a very fat, short pencil. From one stubby end protruded a dark, dulled stone or bone point, just like an extra-thick lead in a pencil. Originally, Spindler had suggested that if the point was stone, it might give off a spark when struck against a piece of pyrite or marcasite, minerals used in prehistoric and historic times for that very purpose. This idea seemed particularly economical because two other artifacts, whitish, marshmallow-sized organic objects threaded onto strips of leather, were suspected of being *Fomes fomentarius,* a fungus commonly known as true tinder bracket because it is used as a kindling. The surfaces of both seemed to have been trimmed, as if the Iceman had cut off a section to use in starting a fire.

But Egg was unsure. In the meantime, he sent a sample of organic material to a mycologist at the University of Innsbruck and had the pencil-like object X-rayed. The image of the interior revealed that the little hard bit protruding from one end was just the tip of a long point whose sharp end had been inserted into the medullary canal of the wood. Archaeologists had found many such pieces in the past, but of course the wooden casing had decayed, so they had usually interpreted them as awls or needles.

Several months after the stubby pencil arrived in Mainz, an experimental archaeologist named Jürgen Weiner came by. Weiner had a lot of experience in stone toolmaking, so it did not take him long to see that this little tool might have a very practical use. He suggested it might be a retoucheur, the sharpening tool that made the little serrated bites along the edges of stone tools. When pressed forcefully against the edge of a somewhat dulled flint knife, the horn or bone tip of a retoucheur would break off a little flint flake in a fairly predictable fashion, creating a sharp new edge. Before Weiner bet any money on his guess, he wanted to re-create the little tool using the same materials, once the archaeologists knew what the point was made of, and test it out. He promised Egg that he would report back.

In the meantime, results from other researchers were also coming in. Spindler had assigned a graduate student named Elisabeth Zissernig to track down everyone who had seen the Iceman while he was still packed in ice.[8] Her interviews with people who had visited the site were turning up inconsistencies. Their recollections of what they had seen and where were not only vague but often contradictory. Even people who were at the Hauslabjoch at the same time recalled things differently. Worst of all, Zissernig had uncovered a theft. Gerlinde Haid had turned over a number of fragments of birch bark she had collected at the site on the day of her visit with her husband. After two months out of the environment that had preserved them for millennia, they were on the verge of disintegration. Dried and crumbling, the birch bark was immediately put on a preservation regime. The archaeologists were incredulous that Haid had not handed them over sooner, but no one inquired into her motivation. Still, they could not dismiss the possibility that known or unknown visitors to the site were in possession of other Hauslabjoch artifacts.

Based on the witness accounts, Egg now believed that the birch bark, some pieces of which had holes pierced around their edges, had once formed a cylindrical container. Though the interior bore no trace of the container's contents, Pirpamer and Koler told Zissernig that they had seen wet grass or hay inside. That reminded Egg of the bundle of leaves found during Lippert's dig and turned over to the botanists. He wondered whether it might have been part of the organic material that filled the container.

Zissernig's work had also uncovered a number of important photographs of the site. One, taken by Anton Koler shortly after his arrival to dig out the corpse, showed the rocky ledge laden with several artifacts. The image was dark and even-toned. But there, in the center of the photo, propped up among the rocks, was the ax. The picture showed clearly that the leather strip holding the copper blade in the haft had already come partly unraveled. Below the ax, the bow lay diagonally across the rocks. The picture did not show the bottom of the bow, where it plunged down into the ice. Just above the ax, where the ledge began to flatten out on top, were a number of other pieces of wood. Chunks of what looked like fur clung to the rocks underneath the wood and ax. When he looked closely, Egg could also make out a bit of string or rope amid the fur. Though Pirpamer had already touched and moved a number of these artifacts before the photo was taken, the placement of these items together was very interesting. If assumptions about the snow and ice were correct, then this photo showed the spot where the Iceman had decided to set down his belongings shortly before he died.

Another picture retrieved from Reinhold Messner's group showed him and Hans Kammerlander crouched next to the corpse and grinning up at the camera. Kammerlander's hand was propped up on what appeared to be a wooden crutch. But when the archaeologists looked closely, they recognized the crutch as a section of an artifact Egg now believed was a wooden, horseshoe-shaped backpack frame. In the photo Koler had taken, this piece of wood was lying on the rocks above the ax. The photo showed the stick in one piece, but by the time it reached the autopsy room in Innsbruck, it had broken in two. No one wagered an accusation about when or how the break had occurred. Zissernig had learned that this was the wood Kammerlander and perhaps others had used to hack at the ice. No other photograph so pithily captured the indignities inflicted on this extraordinary site.

Egg fit the two freshly broken pieces together and found two more from the same branch. Among the rest of the artifacts were two roughly hewn boards with notches on their ends that matched notches on the two ends of the horseshoe frame. Egg thought these two boards had probably been fixed across the bottom of the horseshoe to hold the bend in the wood. Using a microscope, he could see the impressions of string or rope that, he guessed, had been tied onto the frame, perhaps to hold a net or bag. This might have been the use of the masses of grass or bast string collected at the site, some of which had lain near the frame on the rocky ledge.

Egg and Roswitha Goedecker-Ciolek, an organic-materials specialist at the museum, thought some of the leather shreds might have formed a bag for the wooden frame. They assumed that the bulk of the leather had once clothed the man, since there seemed to be no other material that could have done the job. The leather was so badly tattered that they had not yet reconstructed any items of clothing. When they reviewed the entire video shot by ORF of Henn and the gendarme extracting the body, they were horrified. From the narrow perspective of archaeological methodology, the events at the Hauslabjoch had been one disaster after another, from the moment Helmut Simon picked up the birch-bark object to the moment when the recovery team had stood by while the passing hiker snapped the bow out of the ice. Many mistakes had been made, but now, thought Egg, the archaeologists just had to do the best they could with what remained.*

The South Tyrolean archaeologist Hans Nothdurfter was greatly distressed after reading Luigi Capasso's damning report on Platzer's conservation. As an official in a ministry that was responsible for hundreds of mummies, Capasso was highly credible. Yet Nothdurfter and his colleagues were not specialists, and they were not qualified to evaluate his charges.

The possibility that the scientists whom South Tyrol had charged with the preservation of their treasure were in fact destroying it mortified Nothdurfter. Was Platzer really incompetent? If so, there would be real political consequences. Capasso's report contained all the ammunition necessary for the Italian authorities to recall the mummy to Italy.

The very idea that this South Tyrolean mummy might pass to some university in Italy was deeply humiliating to Nothdurfter. Though both he and Capasso were on the Iceman committee South Tyrol had established to deal with the University of Innsbruck, Nothdurfter was sure his colleague did not have South Tyrol's best interests at heart. If the corpse had to be returned to Italy, there was a good chance that it would go right into Capasso's open arms. Nothdurfter was annoyed at how powerless South Tyrol appeared in relation to Innsbruck and Rome. He was sorry now that South

*Rainer Henn died in a car accident on July 25, 1992, on his way to give a talk on the Iceman.

Tyrol had not engaged its own experts to examine the Iceman. Now they were too late. Nothdurfter understood, however, that arrangements would have to be made to keep the mummy in South Tyrol.

Back in Innsbruck, still ignorant of the political storm about to strike from across the southern border, Werner Platzer was facing a deluge of advice and offers of collaboration from scientists the world over. Beside the radiologist zur Nedden, one of the few scientists Platzer had admitted to see the Iceman was Horst Seidler, who was determined to be involved. Austria's university system was rigidly hierarchic, and Seidler was literally at the top of the discipline. Not only did he head the University of Vienna's human biology faculty, but he was the only human biologist in the country to be an Ordinarius, the highest academic grade. Though he and many others privately ridiculed the hopelessly archaic university structure, that title, which put him on par with Platzer, was his ticket onto the project.

The day after the announcement of the discovery, he had caught a flight to Innsbruck and arrived breathless at Platzer's office. In tow was his teenage daughter, who became the first and, for many years, the only child ever to get a glimpse of the Iceman. The move was typical of Seidler, a balding and barrel-chested man with a salt-and-paprika beard. While his title and stuffy three-piece suits had the power to intimidate, his friends knew him as irreverent, impulsive, persuasive, and, above all, loyal to his family and friends. If he could get his only child a glimpse of the Iceman, then he would move heaven and earth to do it.

Seidler's first concern was to establish a few basic statistics on the man, such as his age at death. Many scientists maintain that because individuals' morphologies vary so greatly over time, geography, and culture, the most one can say is whether a person died young, as an adult, or old.[9] Despite the difficulties, some scientists regularly assign ages in years to archaeological finds. The index considered the most reliable is the type and condition of the person's teeth.

Seidler could not get a direct look at the entire set of teeth through the frozen mouth. But since the corpse's upper lip was pulled up and to the right, Seidler could see the several front teeth in the upper jaw. The most remarkable feature here was the gap, known as a diastema, between his two front teeth. The gums had shrunk considerably, which made the teeth look almost normal in size. But when Seidler looked closely, he could see that the front teeth were severely worn down. A combination of chips and uneven wear suggested that the teeth had frequently been used as tools. Seidler estimated an age at death of between thirty-five and forty years.[10] Seidler had little information on the life expectancy of people in the Alpine region in prehistory, but he suspected that this individual was approaching the later stage of life. When the researchers began looking for signs of the cause of death in the man's tissues, they would have to be aware of this relatively old age.

Two other human biologists had measured the Iceman's height. By today's standards, he had not been a big man. Since he had reached adulthood, however, he was as big as he was going to get. When measured from head to foot, he was about five foot three—shorter than modern populations in the area but similar to heights measured for his contemporaries in the Alps.[11] But like age, height is a surprisingly tricky thing to measure. The corpse had shrunk considerably—it weighed only about thirty-three pounds—so it must also have become shorter.

When the corpse had been rolled into the autopsy room, no one had doubted that it was a man. Normally, determining a person's sex is not terribly difficult. The primary indicator is genitalia. Breasts and body hair on the face and chest, though less reliable, are sometimes secondary markers. In his forensic report, Unterdorfer had described the genitals as "leaf-like, as far as can be determined most probably male, desiccated." No breasts were evident. Because the mummy had lost all its hair, hair growth—an uncertain indicator in any case—could not be used as a clue to the sex. The presence of the bow and arrows reinforced the scientists' assumption that the corpse was male. Based on what little evidence there was, it was not a bad assumption. The few representations of hunters in prehistoric art did seem to be of men.

But before long, Platzer and then Spindler released apparently new and surprising information about the body's genital area. Platzer said the scrotum was present but the testicles were not. "It looks like it's scooped out," Platzer told the German news magazine *Der Spiegel*.[12] The implication was ambiguous, but Platzer seemed to be suggesting that some human interference might have occurred in the genital region. The article did not pursue the question, and Platzer did not undertake any immediate research into the matter. But he was not the only one to comment on the absence.

In an article for an Austrian archaeology journal, Andreas Lippert and Konrad Spindler commented that the genitals seemed to be missing and suggested that they "fell victim to predatory animals," an idea that originated with one of Platzer's colleagues.[13] Later, recalling how much yanking and pulling the extraction from the ice had cost the corpse, Spindler suggested that the presumably frozen penis could have broken off during the excavations. The scientists did not attempt to explain why the penis would have been the special target of predators or would have been ripped off more easily during the excavations than other body parts.

Viewed against the background of the missing penis, the enigmatic tattoos that dotted the body's lower half seemed almost self-explanatory. They were concentrated on the lower back, right knee, left calf, and both ankles. They were bluish-black, and their basic form was a group of short, parallel lines, usually aligned vertically. Two, one on the inner right knee and the other on the lower left ankle, were in the shape of a cross about the size of a quarter. At first, the anthropologists believed that two parallel lines running around the left wrist were also tattoos. They looked something like a bracelet. But when the skin was examined more closely, the lines looked unlike the tattoos. Seidler speculated that something tight might have been wrapped around his arm there, even though no one could identify an artifact that might have left such a mark.

With just these few hard facts and many more questions, Platzer convened the first meeting of scientists interested in research on the Iceman's corpse on November 6, about six weeks after the discovery. Unlike at the earlier meetings in Vienna, where the discussion had centered on bureaucratic issues such as jurisdiction and competency, or a meeting a few weeks earlier in Mainz, where Egg had hosted a group of researchers interested in studying the artifacts, the focus here in Innsbruck was to be research on the corpse. Though Platzer and Spindler had stressed from the beginning that they would make the research international, only six of the twenty-six scientists at the meeting were from outside Austria. Among those present were researchers who hoped to study questions of health, disease, and diet involving the body itself: zur Nedden; Lippert and Spindler; Bortenschlager; and Seidler. Assistant professors such as Klaus Oeggl were not invited. The one Italian scientist present was Luigi Capasso. Though not formally invited, Nothdurfter also managed to slip in at the last moment.

With characteristic decorum, Platzer opened the meeting. Before long, Capasso indicated he wanted to say something. Speaking politely but adamantly in Italian as Nothdurfter translated, Capasso criticized the conditions of the corpse's storage and argued that both the temperature and the humidity should be greatly reduced. He reiterated the threat algae still posed to the corpse.

For many people in the room, Capasso's suggestion was the first indication they had had that there might be another way to conserve the mummy. They anxiously looked to Platzer. In his gravelly voice, Platzer insisted he had solid evidence that this method worked for his corpses, and he believed it would work for a prehistoric corpse as well. He firmly defended his choice of temperature and humidity level, and he noted that they were closer to conditions in a glacier. If the mummy dried out further, the cell structure, if still intact, might be damaged. At this point, Spindler commented that the Mainz conservators, too, were trying to keep the organic artifacts from drying out. Instead of being chemically conserved, the wood in the ax shaft, bow, and arrows had been placed in a water bath, where they would stay for as long as a year, before being removed and allowed to dry out slowly, wrapped in plastic. As counterintuitive as it seemed, moisture was sometimes part of the preservation method. But Capasso was insistent. When the group went down to see the corpse in the freezer, he pointed out drops of condensation that had formed on the corpse, and he said he feared they would penetrate the skin.

Back in the library of the Institute of Anatomy, the dispute continued. Capasso prescribed several urgent measures. The temperature must be lowered considerably, the humidity should be set at 30 percent, and the corpse should be kept in the freezer at all times. Humidity and temperature measurements should be recorded automatically at regular intervals and the results printed out. An isolation tent should be built around the corpse, and filters should be built into the freezer to clean the air of microorganisms.

Platzer was now growing visibly annoyed. He claimed that his institute had been free of contamination for years. There was no need to worry about tiny organisms colonizing the Iceman. Capasso did not budge. As an emissary from Rome, he wielded considerable authority, especially since South Tyrol had no comparable expert on conservation. The veneer of politeness was becoming increasingly thin. Though many of those present had known nothing of Capasso's criticism prior to the meeting, they were not naïve about the threat represented by his charges. The export license was hanging in the balance. This was not only about science, but also about who would control the Iceman, his conservation, and the years of research ahead. It was about who would be viewed as the spokesman and caretaker for the Iceman and who would, at best, be confined to the shadowy edges of research. But the issue was not resolved at this meeting. The group broke up without any consensus. Platzer had no idea what Capasso would do once he got back to Italy, but the answer was not long in coming.

Several days later, the South Tyrolean Commission, of which Capasso was a member, formally requested Platzer to follow through on several of the Italian scientist's recommendations. Platzer was incensed after reading the letter. He was to convene the research group the following week for another meeting, and there, again, he would ask other experts about his method of conservation. Nevertheless, since he had some stake in appeasing the mummy's South Tyrolean owners, he lowered the humidity in the freezer to slightly below 70 percent, as the commission had demanded. If the corpse suffered because of it, he would know whom to blame.

On November 19, Platzer convened a second meeting of the researchers, with preservation again the main topic. This time, four of the eleven researchers were not from Austria. Oddly, Capasso called in sick. Two scientists with experience in conservation, including a Danish archaeologist who had worked on bog bodies, attended. Her recommendation was unequivocal: The higher the humidity in the chamber, she said, the better for the corpse. Her assessment also accorded with that of a medical physicist at the University of Innsbruck who had studied conditions inside a glacier. According to a report he had written at Platzer's request, the temperature of glacial ice varied between twenty-three and thirty-two degrees Fahrenheit, with a constant humidity of 100 percent. If the scientists wanted to keep the body in the conditions that had apparently preserved it so well for millennia, then they would have to raise the humidity even higher.

Late in the meeting, the scientists paid another visit to the corpse, which, following another suggestion by Capasso, was now kept in a laminar-flow box, a type of isolation tent, when outside the freezer. The box was a coffin-shaped construction with clear sides and one open side. Sterile air was blown lightly from the back of the box, across the corpse, and out the open side to prevent contamination by the scientists.

Wearing surgical gloves and a mask, the Danish archaeologist bent over the corpse and closely examined the tissue. Yes, some damage was already apparent. On the left shoulder blade she spotted tiny tears in the skin that she believed resulted from dryness. When these had occurred she could not say, since this was the first time she had examined the corpse. However, she said, low humidity would only exacerbate desiccation and lead to further deterioration of the corpse. Any damage was already irreparable. She strongly urged Platzer to raise the humidity by 10 or 15 percent.

This was all the evidence Platzer felt he needed. Armed with this new testimony, he finally responded to the letter from the South Tyrolean Commission. Though he had not seen a copy of Capasso's report to the Italian government, some of its details had leaked through to him. He addressed many points in the report and the commission's letter, sometimes with a sarcasm that made his opinion of the Italian clear. He ended by citing the opinion of his experts:

> After unanimous agreement among about 30 scientists, except Dr. Capasso, 70 percent humidity for the corpse is the lowest permissible level, as was already determined in the meeting on November 6, 1991.* Nevertheless, since it concerned this unique

*In exchange for permission to quote from his letter, Dr. Werner Platzer asked that it be emphasized here that "according to the actual state of knowledge (July 1999), humidity higher than 90 percent is required for permanent conservation."

find, I effected (despite knowing better) a small decrease of a few percentage following Dr. Capasso's demand. At the next meeting and examination on November 19, 1991 this appeared to be wrong because there is a danger of too much drying out and the humidity should be kept at 70 percent. This was repeatedly emphasized intensively by Prof. Dr. Sander-Jørgensen (Denmark, previously University of Columbia [sic]) and Dr. Oswald (Swiss Provincial Museum, Zürich). This also accords with our experiences. All scientists except Dr. Capasso have until now emphasized the excellent accommodations and the excellent condition of the corpse.

Platzer was not going to give up the mummy without a fight. Not only was the Iceman's preservation at stake, but so was the reputation of his institute. Miraculously, he managed to keep the politically charged wrangle out of the public eye. When, in the last weeks of 1991, journalists asked Platzer what was holding up research on the corpse, he inevitably replied that he was still waiting for the "Italians," meaning South Tyrol, to sign the research agreement with the university. When pressed, he muttered something about how complicated it all was and how difficult it was to get anything accomplished with the notorious Italian bureaucracy. That he was struggling to hold on to the mummy, as well as his good reputation, he never let on.

In any case, more surprising news took the spotlight. In early December, the results from the radiocarbon dating of the botanists' grass samples at last came in. Both laboratories turned up an age more than a thousand years older than Spindler's estimate. They said the Iceman dated to about 3300 B.C.E.[14]

If they were right, then the man lived nearly a millennium before the development of the technology to alloy copper and tin to make bronze. It was a hugely significant gap. Spindler, who learned of the dating from a journalist, was chagrined. Could he have been wrong about the ax? In Mainz, Egg hurriedly prepared to take a closer look at it. Somewhere there was a mistake.

CHAPTER 5

EVIDENCE OF DISTRESS

MARKUS EGG'S ANALYSIS of the material in the ax blade revealed not bronze but almost pure copper with just 0.22 percent arsenic and 0.09 percent silver. Annaluisa Pedrotti, who had mentioned her hunch to Egg at a conference six weeks earlier, had been right. In form, the ax was an advanced design that archaeologists believed had become prevalent only around 2000 B.C.E. Yet it was made of the first metal people knew how to smelt: copper. Suddenly, much of what archaeologists thought they knew about this region was open to question.

According to archaeologists' standard time lines, 3300 B.C.E. was in the late New Stone Age, or Neolithic period, when people in the southern Alps still relied on stone for most of their tools. The few scattered copper items found there from this period were believed to have trickled in from peoples to the east, in the region later known as Yugoslavia, where copper metallurgy was already flourishing. Pedrotti had expected the radiocarbon dates to place the man around 2700 or 2800 B.C.E., since that would have made the man contemporary with the people at Remedello who had made the similar copper blade. The dating results said he was even older.

The Remedello people were believed to have been the first smelters of copper in northern Italy. The Iceman's low-flanged copper ax thus should not have been older than theirs. There was something wrong with archaeologists' conception of prehistoric Alpine life. Archaeologists in northern Italy immediately responded that Remedello must be much older than originally believed. Since the Remedello excavation had taken place more than a century earlier, they thought that perhaps the carbon-dating, which had been done relatively recently, was somehow skewed.

This was not a problem that could be solved immediately. Archaeology's paradigms had developed over decades, as new information and material from excavations slowly became available. When contradictory new information did turn up, it could not always be immediately accommodated in the bigger picture. Often, archaeologists just had to live with the contradictions. But this was a catalyst for further searches. Because archaeologists had not expected to find much, the valleys around the Hauslabjoch had never been systematically surveyed for signs of prehistoric life. This was the most logical place to start. In Trento and Bolzano, associates of Bagolini, Pedrotti, and Nothdurfter immediately began making plans to help survey the valleys to the south of the Hauslabjoch. At the University of Innsbruck, students in Konrad Spindler's department would do the same for the Austrian valleys to the north. If the Iceman had lived in the valleys near the Hauslabjoch, there must be some trace of his people.

Meanwhile, Egg's work on the artifacts had been turning up more ambiguous evidence about the state of the Iceman at the time he died. Less than two weeks after the carbon-dating results were announced, Egg, Spindler, and several other researchers gathered in Mainz for the official opening of the quiver, now recognized as the oldest surviving one in the world. Before its appearance, archaeologists had not even known with certainty that people used quivers. A rock carving from Spain that was slightly older than this man depicted hunters running after prey with a handful of arrows clutched in their hands.

Egg suspected that the Iceman's quiver had originally been made of fur, since a few hairs were caught in the side seam, but it was now bald skin. To hold the quiver's shape, the maker had stitched a wooden rod onto the side of the leather bag with a piece of leather. But this rod was now snapped, and the middle section was missing.

Part of the quiver's top flap, which apparently had closed over the feathered ends of the protruding arrows, had also been ripped off, so Egg could not yet figure out how the quiver had closed over the arrows.

The torn closure had exposed the ends of fourteen arrow shafts, two of which had feather halves attached. X rays and CAT scans taken earlier had given Egg a pretty good idea of the other contents. When the images first came back, he and Spindler had been surprised to see that all but two of the fourteen arrow shafts lacked arrowheads. The tips simply came to a blunt end where normally a stone or bone point would have been attached. Spindler's first tentative explanation was that the man had used these arrows to shoot birds; archaeologists knew of a few such examples of pointless arrows. When fired with tremendous force from a bow, they knocked a bird out. But this idea had a very short life. The pointless arrows had one fat end; one in the Museum of Ethnography in Vienna, for instance, had a broad end that had the flared profile of a trumpet horn. Ötzi's arrow shafts had more or less the same diameter all along their lengths.

Egg and Spindler were now eager to see precisely what the ends of these arrows looked like. As the two men looked on, a conservator seized the whole bundle of arrows and firmly pulled it a fraction of the way out of the quiver. Then they stopped and took a quick X ray. Egg's concern was that one of the pointed objects they saw in the initial X ray would slice open the delicate hide as the arrows moved by. But this X ray showed that everything was fine, and the conservator pulled the arrows out a little more. They monitored the progress from an existing tear toward the bottom of the quiver. They pulled, stopped, checked, and then pulled a little bit more. After one more X ray, it was all out.

As Egg had thought, just two of the fourteen arrows had feathers. The ends that had been sticking outside the quiver were smeared with a black material and set with three half feathers, parallel to the shafts. Both had apparently originally been equipped with flint arrowheads, but only one was still mounted. As they had already noticed in the X ray, the second arrowhead had broken in half, leaving its rump still embedded in the shaft, while the other bit was loose in the quiver. Flint, the standard material for arrowheads for tens of thousands of years, did not fracture easily, so the break was puzzling. But both these arrows, which at one time must have been ready to shoot, had more damage as well. As the arrows emerged from the quiver, Egg and Spindler saw that both wooden shafts were broken, too, one in two places.

Laid out next to the two arrows with feathers and arrowheads, the other twelve arrow shafts looked naked. They were branches from a tree—what kind Klaus Oeggl would no doubt be eager to determine—that had been stripped of their bark. All were remarkably straight, given the time they had spent under ice, and all but one were of the same length. The fourteenth arrow was notably shorter and appeared to have a broken end. All were also notched at one end, presumably for an arrowhead. Obviously, they were shafts in an early stage of production. Not only did this man have an unfinished bow, Egg thought, but not one of his arrows was ready to use either.

He and Spindler discussed whether the man had been intending to complete these arrow shafts with the material on hand. No more flint had been found in the quiver, but there was a bundle of four unequal pieces of stag antler, efficiently bound together. There was a little bit of this Iceman's personality in that job, a careful and thorough wrapping of these apparently precious antler points, using just a slender strip of bast, a fibrous material found underneath bark. Egg had no intention of undoing that bundle. He and Spindler agreed that those points probably had been destined to serve as arrowheads, since no other flint found with the man could have served that purpose. Whether this material was considered better or worse than flint, neither archaeologist could say.

Also inside the quiver was a longer, curved tool with one pointed end and one flat one. Carved out of an antler, it looked like awls known from other prehistoric sites. Probably it had several uses, including skinning animals. There were also two other little items inside, including a neatly wrapped skein of grass string. Egg marveled at this simple find. Spindler suggested that it had been intended as the bowstring, but Egg was doubtful. They decided not to unwind it—that would be irreversible—so they could not figure out for sure whether it was long enough to fit the bow. Egg pointed out that the string was not uniformly thick. Some sections had little bulges, and others were quite thin. Egg suspected—although he wanted to ask a bowyer to be sure—that a bowstring would have to be of a regular width to ensure the smooth departure of an arrow.

The final item was a pair of animal sinews, also held together with a piece of grass. Egg knew that sinew was the preferred material for a bowstring, but it did not look like there was enough there to reach from end to end. But the man had used sinew in other parts of his equipment, too, such as in attaching the feathers to the arrow shafts.

In the following months, Egg examined each artifact carefully and regularly shared the findings with Spindler, who was growing increasingly interested in the Iceman's apparent lack of preparation as well as the amount of damage to his equipment. In fact, almost all the artifacts displayed some break, tear, or other sign of rough handling. The birch-bark container was crushed, the tip of the dagger was missing, its handle battered, and the woven grass sheath ripped. The leather pouch was torn, and the pointed tool inside was damaged. The clothing was unrecognizable. Even the ax blade had come loose from its notch.

Little things seemed to be missing. Where was the carrying strap for the quiver? Where was its hood closure? The bag or pouch for the backpack? What had he carried in there? Had there been provisions attached to the backpack? What had been inside the birch-bark container? The bow was fractured, the quiver torn, and three arrow shafts and one arrowhead were broken. What was to account for this damage? When had it occurred? Archaeologists were used to finding damaged artifacts. Yet the assumption was that these artifacts had been locked in snow or ice since their deposition.

Spindler and Egg were especially intrigued by the damage to the wooden rod stitched up the side of the quiver. Somehow, the broken middle section of the rod had come unsewn and was not recovered at the same time as the quiver. In fact, it had come down the mountain *before* the discovery of the quiver, among the artifacts collected by Alois Pirpamer. Egg did not doubt that it was the missing piece, for its two broken ends matched those on the other two pieces of the rod. Apparently, it had been found several feet from the quiver, near where the corpse lay. However, the middle piece seemed to be too long to squeeze back in between the top and bottom pieces. At first, Egg did not want to believe it. Examining the top piece of the rod, Egg noticed that it seemed to have been removed from the quiver and then provisionally reattached. Perhaps, he thought, both the top and middle sections had broken off, and then the top piece had been reattached. But by whom? Patzelt's group said they hadn't done anything to the quiver but bring it down the mountain, and Egg was sure no one had fiddled with it since it arrived in his custody. That left only the owner himself.

The quiver rod must have broken when the Iceman was still alive. What they saw was the relic of an emergency repair. The explanation suddenly cast a new light over all the other equipment. Maybe other damage had occurred before the man's death. Why, after all, did the Iceman need a *new* bow? What had happened to the *old* one? Was there some connection between the broken arrows and the broken quiver? What force could have split that flint arrowhead in half? Did the broken equipment have anything to do with his journey over the high pass? What had happened to this guy?

University of Innsbruck botanists had known for two decades that Neolithic people had ventured into the high Alps, and they even thought they knew why. The evidence came not from archaeological sites but from Alpine bogs that had formed over the millennia since the end of the last glaciation and were now often covered with sedges, Alpine grassland, herbs, and mosses. Many lay above the tree line. In their depths, they were composed not only of the metamorphosed remains of the generations of plants that had grown on top of them but also of innumerable pollen grains that had landed on them. Pollen grains are borne in the wind, water, or in the coats of animals, but most never come close to their goals and land instead in unpleasant places like bogs, where their services are wasted.

Pollen grains, however, survived well in anaerobic peat bogs and so constituted a record of the vegetation that had grown there and in the vicinity. By counting the grains, analyzing the ratios of the various kinds of pollens, and carbon-dating the organic materials in which they were embedded, researchers could arrive at a picture of past environments. The work was extraordinarily laborious, since it entailed the methodical counting and identification of literally tens of thousands of microscopic objects. Yet the results were occasionally stunning.

After the Iceman was discovered, Sigmar Bortenschlager dug around in his old records and found a pollen profile from a bog high in the Ötztal, within view of the Hauslabjoch. The profile showed that for millennia following the last glaciation the area was covered by a natural grassland whose ecology was undisturbed by humans. But around 5,500 years ago, just a few hundred years before the Iceman lived, the local vegetation underwent a remarkable change. Bortenschlager found that plants belonging to the nettle, dock, and goosefoot genera, which thrive with an increased supply of a nitrate found in animal droppings, increased markedly.[1] Bortenschlager knew these were indications that people had begun to use the area as pasture for their flocks. At the same time, plants that grazing animals either do not like to eat or cannot easily eat also increased, which indicated that they were facing less competition from plants that animals grazed upon, which were often eaten before they could release their pollen. Not only were prehistoric people active in the area around the Hauslabjoch, but they were also altering their environment to serve their economic needs. For Bortenschlager, these results were especially noteworthy because they documented the origins of a grazing strategy that had endured to the present day. The Ötztal was one of the few places left in Tyrol where the sheep drive into the high pastures, called the transhumance, still survived.

The modern transhumance gets under way in mid-spring, when shepherds collect several thousand sheep in Vernagt, the tiny village at the foot of the path to the Similaun lodge in the Schnalstal. Over the previous weeks, the sheep have been grazing near the valley bottoms, where the snow melts first. By mid-June, the deep winter snows that flanked the southern slopes of the Alps have melted away, charging the creeks with chilly waters and revealing the fresh pastures of the high Alps. Early one morning, the shepherds begin driving the reluctant flocks up the steep mountain, over the international border and the main Alpine ridge, across a glacier, and into their summer pastures above the tree line in the uppermost Ötztal.

In the past, when the mountains were full of predators, several shepherds and their bands of dogs probably stayed with the animals through the summer, but nowadays just one shepherd remains behind. During the long summer days he tends to sick or wounded animals and helps others give birth. At night he retires to a tiny stone house built into a slope that has been used by many generations of shepherds before him.

In mid-September, just before the first snows threaten to close off the passes for the winter, the event takes place in reverse. The sheep owners arrive and help the summer shepherd round up and count the sheep. Until quite recently, when the practice was banned, the farmers used to set fire to the tract of pasturage after the sheep had left, in order to keep the land a pasture. The next spring, a luscious carpet of new sprouts—grasses and clover— pushed up through the blackened soil. Almost all high Alpine meadows had been managed, and even expanded, in this way.

As the sheep arrive in Vernagt, people in the village turn out to celebrate their return for the winter. Local historians had documented the Schnalstal transhumance to the fourteenth century, but Bortenschlager's pollen profiles suggested that it might be several thousand years old.

The paths linking mountain villages had long fascinated the glaciologist Gernot Patzelt. Not long after the Iceman's discovery, he conducted an experiment. Starting from Vernagt, on the South Tyrolean side, he headed up the mountain toward the Similaun lodge. His intention was to follow the natural path over the mountain into the Ötztal, by which he meant the path that was easiest and quickest. For a few hours, his path coincided more or less with the marked trail hikers use, a stone path built in the Middle Ages, and the very same one Helmut and Erika Simon, as well as the sheep, had followed up to the Similaun lodge. But after about ninety minutes, this marked trail veered off toward a relatively steep slope, at the top of which was the Niederjoch Pass and the lodge. A series of switchbacks had been built into the slope in the nineteenth century to make the going easier for the sheep.

Patzelt saw that this was not, however, the most logical way to go. To the left, high above, he could make out a little notch in the profile of the ridge. Common sense told him this was the best spot to cut across the ridge. Patzelt therefore headed that way. The ground grew steeper, and he had to lift his legs higher to step up the boulders that had fallen down from the ridge. But before long, without even having taken his hands out of his pockets, he was standing on the pass he had seen from far below. The terrain flattened out a little, and he looked around to orient himself. He was fewer than one hundred paces from the site where the Iceman had been discovered. Experience had led him the way that others experienced in the Alps had gone. The Iceman had died along what amounted to a prehistoric highway. He was almost certainly not lost, nor was he wandering around blindly. The Iceman had been more or less on the road itself.

The Pirpamers confirmed Patzelt's hunch. Alois told him that the pass on which the body had been found was known locally as the Tisenjoch, or "Tisen Yoke," though the name was not on any map.* Before the construction of the path to the Similaun lodge a century earlier, the local herdsmen had always driven the sheep across this pass because, though it was higher and took a little longer than ascending over the Niederjoch, the going was easier.

Patzelt's recognition that the Iceman was not in the middle of nowhere but on what was probably a well-traveled way did not surprise Bortenschlager. The people who had begun using the high pastures 5,500 years earlier must have had some established route up there. In fact, Bortenschlager suggested, the Iceman himself might have been involved in the pastoral economy. He might well have been in the mountains watching over a herd of sheep or goats. Perhaps he had been a herdsman who spent his summer high in the mountains and then returned to his village at a lower altitude once the winter snows came.

Spindler and Egg warmed to the idea as soon as they learned of it. Other new botanical results seemed to support it as well. During Lippert's dig, a sample from the ice that had enclosed the corpse was extracted for Bortenschlager, who analyzed the pollen suspended inside. He detected and counted ample amounts of pollen types from the late summer and the early fall. Assuming that the ice had formed at the same time the man died, then the results pointed

---

*The Hauslabjoch, in fact, lay three hundred yards to the north of the Tisenjoch and crossed not the main Alpine ridge but a side ridge that connected two parallel Austrian valleys. Patzelt later tried unsuccessfully to change the name of the find to "Tisenjoch Man." Most researchers continued to call the site of the find "Hauslabjoch."

to an early autumn death, the same time the animals were driven back over the mountain into the Schnalstal for the winter. If the Iceman had been in the Alps with his flocks, then his death could have occurred only in the months in which the sheep were grazing there—namely, from about mid-June to mid-September.

If the man had died at the start of the cold season, that might explain why his body had not decayed or been eaten. The Iceman's corpse would have been quickly covered in snow, protected from predatory animals and the rays of the sun. Suddenly there seemed to be a pattern. The evidence seemed to be falling into place.

Egg had entrusted the delicate bits of leather material to Roswitha Goedecker-Ciolek, the conservator who had accompanied him to Innsbruck to retrieve the artifacts. A rather enigmatic young woman who spoke only under duress, Goedecker-Ciolek ultimately logged hundreds of hours with the scraps, patiently attempting to match up the uneven edges and analyzing the regular stitches made by some tailor millennia earlier.

The very first challenge had been to get the leather into a condition where it could be handled without falling apart. The plan was to first soak it in a fatty emulsion to restore the lost oils. It would then be freeze-dried to remove the excess water. If successful, this method would return the leather to its former suppleness and make it possible to handle. The same process would be used on a portion of a net and large piece of a plaited mat or coat of grass, portions of which had been recovered from the boulder on which the body had been found.

Part of the conservation process was to clean the artifacts with distilled water and filter the runoff through three sieves of decreasing size to capture anything of interest: perhaps bits of organic matter, legs of parasites, or pollen. One day while cleaning the leather and fur pieces, Goedecker-Ciolek found a little piece of organic matter trapped in the dense hairs of one of the pieces of fur. Egg came down quickly to take a look and saw in a second that it was grain, almost certainly of the domesticated variety. Within days, it and a second grain Goedecker-Ciolek found in the fur were identified as einkorn.

Egg was thrilled and immediately called Spindler to tell him the news. Here was definitive evidence that the Iceman had been in contact with agriculture, and probably not long before his death, for otherwise the grains would have rotted in the fur. The discovery of the einkorn made it very unlikely that the man was some sort of outcast, banished to the perimeter of village life. Somewhere not too far from the Hauslabjoch 5,300 years ago, people had been planting crops, at the very least this variety of wheat. That entailed a settlement, which, if other Neolithic sites were any guide, was inhabited year-round by a community of farmers whose lives were strictly regulated by the seasons. There was also a nice symbiosis between agriculture and pastoralism, since in the winter the animals' manure fertilized the fields.

One visitor to Egg's conservation workshop that spring was Annaluisa Pedrotti. Like Egg, she thought the herdsman hypothesis had potential, even though the Iceman's equipment did not yet seem to bear out his direct involvement with animals. Recent work by an English archaeologist suggested that in many parts of the world the domestication of animals had occurred in two stages.[2] Until around the fifth millennium B.C.E., domesticated animals such as cows, sheep, and goats were kept solely for the products that became available when they were slaughtered: meat, hides, bone, and horn. But then, beginning in the Near East, farmers diversified and expanded their use of such animals. The implementation of animals for wool, milk, and work was called the "secondary products revolution" and occurred only in Eurasia and Africa. Pedrotti maintained that the revolution had already occurred by the time and in the place the Iceman lived. For centuries, the herdsmen of South Tyrol have raised their animals for milk, wool, and, occasionally, meat. The mountains were dotted with little stone houses where shepherds had collected milk to make cheese. But Ötzi apparently had nothing that suggested he was transporting milk. He had no pottery nor any other vessel that could have been used to carry liquids.

Since Pedrotti and her colleagues had assumed that by the time the Iceman lived, people of this region were also familiar with the practice of weaving, they were surprised that not a shred of woven material turned up among any of the man's clothes or other possessions. Weaving is defined as the interlacing of flexible threads on a loom.[3] This is not the same as plaiting, in which stiff materials such as grasses and reeds are braided together. The woolen or flax thread typically used in weaving was produced by twisting together short strands of wool, hair, or vegetable fibers known as bast.

The lack of woven material in the Iceman's equipment might have been a fluke, but it might also have meant that his people did not have weaving technology. If he had not kept his animals for their milk or their wool, then what?

One clue to the Iceman's local economy would be found in those eighty pieces of skin that Goedecker-Ciolek was poring over daily. If the Iceman had been a herdsman, then he almost certainly would have used the skins from his animals for his clothing. Pedrotti expected that when the analysis of the leather was completed, they would discover that he was using at least some hides from domesticated animals.

Whenever Markus Egg was asked to speculate about who the Iceman was, he was always careful to mention all the current possibilities. By the late spring of 1992, however, he had become partial to the herdsman idea. It made sense that the Iceman would have been involved in the predominant economy of the valley. The idea neatly satisfied several questions at once. Why had the man been so high in the mountains? Because the pastures were there. Why had he needed a bow and arrows? To protect his flocks from predators and hunt food for himself during the long summer. He had been dressed in leather and fur clothing because it was cold in the high Alps all summer long.

Egg had grown somewhat disillusioned with the idea that the man had been a simple hunter. Clearly, he had known how to hunt. But if he were strictly on a hunting expedition, then his bow and arrows should have been ready. The shaman idea had other problems. The Iceman's outfit and equipment looked too practical for a holy man who had come to carry out some ritual. The only artifact with possible ritual significance seemed to be the small white marble disk with the tassel of leather strips. There was something to all these ideas, but Egg thought they were too narrow, as if prehistoric people, like people in the twentieth century, had just one specific job or were defined primarily by their occupation.

The herdsman hypothesis was more flexible. Using it as a framework, Egg began considering new findings in terms of the life of a herdsman. One recent discovery was a mend in what Egg believed was the leather clothing. Throughout the spring of 1992, Roswitha Goedecker-Ciolek had been making progress with the leather scraps. Some pieces had fur on them, while others were plain leather; some were dark and some light. Apparently, the tailor had used not one large hide for the garment but many different pieces of all shapes and sizes, which he or she had then sewn together, perhaps in a patchwork design. That was what accounted for the large number of seams running through almost every scrap. Several pieces showed signs of wear and repeated mending. A few mends were in a fine stitch using doubled and twisted animal hair.[4] But one rip had been closed with thread made of twisted grass. It looked provisional and a bit sloppy. Goedecker-Ciolek doubted that the same person had mended both. One was designed to last; the single blade of grass probably would not have held up for much longer than a summer. That it had survived the rough handling until now was surprising enough. She wondered whether the man died before he or his tailor could do a proper repair on this new rip. What could have prevented him from doing the job right the first time?

Egg had a ready explanation. If the Iceman had spent all summer in the mountains with his flocks, then he would have had to do his own mending. Perhaps he had done this one in a hurry and intended to stitch it up neatly once he got back to his village for the winter. The hasty grass repair seemed to indicate that the man was, therefore, away from his permanent settlement.

The birch bark supported this idea as well. After receiving the new bits of birch bark from Gerlinde Haid, Egg and his team realized that the Iceman carried not one but two birch-bark containers. One of them still retained its natural light wood color inside, while the other was slightly blackened. That suggested to Egg that they had not held the same things.

He had recently heard back from Reinhold Pöder, the mycologist, and his team at the University of Innsbruck that at least one of the mushrooms, punched and threaded on the leather straps, was not, as the archaeologists had originally guessed, *Fomes fomentarius,* the true tinder fungus. Instead it was *Piptoporus betulinus,* otherwise known as the birch polypore or razor-strop fungus, a common type of mushroom that grew on birch trees.* Neither was it hallucinogenic, as some people had suspected, but was known to have antibiotic properties.[5] Pöder was not willing to guess what the Iceman had used the mushroom for, but he thought the antibiotic properties were worth testing.

This meant that the Iceman apparently had nothing with him to use as tinder. That was perplexing. Egg considered it unlikely that a man would have been out on his own in the mountains without some relatively easy means to make a fire. The point of the stubby pencil, originally taken for a spark striker, had now been identified as antler, which could not strike sparks. The tool was now considered to be a retoucheur, although the experimental archaeologist Jürgen Weiner had only just begun his investigation. None of the Iceman's flints seemed designed to strike sparks or showed the marks that such strikes would have caused.

Egg could easily come up with a scenario that explained the Iceman's death. The Iceman, he suggested, might have been a herdsman who had been spending the summer with his flocks when he had a little accident with his bow and arrows. Leaving his animals, perhaps with other herdsmen, he had quickly gone down into the nearby Schnalstal to fetch supplies for a new bow and arrow. On the way back, around the middle of September, he was crossing the Hauslabjoch when a bad storm blew up and disoriented him. He tried to seek shelter, but for some reason he had not been able to go on, and he had died right there on the pass, maybe of hypothermia.

Egg warned this scenario was speculative, and he told journalists that they should present it as such. Egg knew there must be dozens of ideas that could explain the Iceman's fate, but so far the cold, hard facts were very few.

---

*The second mushroom also turned out to be *Piptoporus betulinus.*

CHAPTER 6

THE MUMMY TO MARKET

WERNER PLATZER'S LETTER defending his preservation of the Iceman arrived in Bolzano just in time. The South Tyroleans had just learned that Rome was on the verge of demanding the immediate return of the corpse. Luigi Capasso's lobbying had apparently had results.

But Platzer's letter was convincing. Though sarcastic and defensive in places, it appeared to carry the endorsement of people outside the University of Innsbruck. Platzer was finally seeking the advice of international experts, and he had been quick to follow up on Capasso's concerns regarding microorganisms. He also showed a willingness to cooperate with Italian scientists.

Almost overnight, Rome's threat to withhold the export license evaporated. Hans Nothdurfter suspected that some conversation had occurred in the upper echelons of politics, perhaps between the governor of South Tyrol and the Italian prime minister. Given the sensitivity of the South Tyroleans about their autonomy, recalling the corpse to an Italian university would have damaged relations between Rome and Bolzano. In early 1992, following six more nerve-racking weeks for the Innsbruckers, the Italian government formally approved the "duty free" export of the finds. The permit was temporary and could be revoked at any time, but it gave the South Tyroleans the freedom to formalize the arrangement with the university.

By this point, three men had emerged as the official leaders of the project in Innsbruck. Platzer assumed management and coordination of the conservation and research of the corpse. Konrad Spindler oversaw the archaeological side of the project, including the evaluation of the artifacts. Lastly, the rector of the University of Innsbruck, a mild-mannered, earnest scholar of the German language named Hans Moser, took on an oversight and mediation role in the project.

On February 5, 1992, over the simmering objections of Capasso, the University of Innsbruck and the Province of South Tyrol signed a contract that handed over to the university the responsibility for conserving and researching the corpse and artifacts. The contract was valid for three years, but if the work was accomplished sooner, then the corpse and the artifacts must be returned at that time. The university would decide what research would be done and who would do it. The contract stipulated only that the "integrity" of the corpse be preserved, which precluded an all-out autopsy. Neither could the university undertake any research that would damage future scientific research possibilities. All steps would have to be approved by the South Tyrolean Commission, which included Capasso and Nothdurfter.

A fair portion of the contract had to do with the funding of what the two parties were calling the Iceman Project. The corpse was turning out to be an expensive guest. Werner Platzer calculated that his department would be spending ten thousand dollars a month just to store the mummy in one of two brand-new walk-in freezers he was acquiring expressly for that purpose. (The second one was kept running in case the first broke down.) Costs included electricity for the freezers, the on-site manufacturing of sterile ice, a sophisticated humidity- and temperature-control system, and a pager, carried at all times by one of the anatomy professors in case of an Iceman emergency.

These were just the costs of storage. Platzer estimated that research—everything from the illustration of the artifacts to the analysis of the stomach contents—would cost about ten million dollars over several years. That was not the kind of money the Republic of

Austria was willing or even legally allowed to shell out for a mummy it did not own. Platzer said that regular department funds could not legally be used to bankroll the project because the project was commissioned by a third party—namely, South Tyrol.

In the United States and most European countries, much scientific research is funded primarily by government bodies such as the National Institutes of Health and the National Science Foundation. Such a government fund also existed in Austria, and it was sure to be one source for various research projects. To get these funds, a scientist had to write a detailed grant request. The agencies usually sent the proposal around to other scientists in the field for review and evaluation. If the peers found merit in the project, then it might be funded, although not always as generously as the scientists wished.

From the start, apparently in response to criticism of the corpse's messy recovery, the project leaders had emphasized that the world's top scientists would be invited to participate in the high-profile project. They also said that each research project would be done by two independent teams. The policy had caused disconcertment among some of the Innsbruck researchers, who believed that it would create a competitive rather than a collaborative atmosphere. Among the researchers already enlisted were Don Brothwell, the British anthropologist who had led the studies on the bog body known as Lindow Man; Svante Pääbo, a Swede who was a pioneer in the field of molecular archaeology, the study of ancient DNA; and William A. Murphy, Jr., an American forensic radiologist. Normally, scientists of this caliber had no problem obtaining their own grants for research. Given the interest in the unique Iceman, they would almost certainly be able to find funding for this work. Much of the basic science involved in the research, such as material analysis, could probably be done using funds from general laboratory expenses.

But in the months leading up to the signing of the contract with South Tyrol, the project leaders had discerned a potentially even more lucrative source of funds for the Iceman project: the media. In the weeks following the discovery, Platzer had noted with disapproval that people he believed were only marginally involved in the Iceman's story were already cashing in on their luck. ORF, Rein-

hold Messner, and Helmut and Erika Simon had all sold their videotape and photographs of the corpse in the ice. Among the media,
these sales were viewed with utter indifference, since most photographs are bought either from photo agencies or from amateurs.
The sales simply demonstrated that the university's archaeological
treasure was also a real commodity. If others were profiting off their
coincidental involvement with the Iceman, then why should the
university not do the same? In fact, the money and attention heaped
on Messner and the Simons were a pittance compared to the huge
sums being offered to the university and the three professors running the project.

Generally, paying a source for information or interviews violates
journalistic ethics. The reason is simple: If a source sees a market for
his information, he might make something up just to be able to sell
it to the highest bidder. Yet several publications did not hesitate to
try to grease the palms of the Iceman scientists in the hope of landing an exclusive. Quietly, so as not to be accused of checkbook journalism, the National Geographic Society offered the university an
astounding $100,000 for exclusive North American rights to the
story. Another collaboration offer came from the BBC, which
wanted to film the corpse, the artifacts, and the various researchers
at work. The BBC was prepared to pay an access fee and allow the
university to retain the copyright to all the film they shot in exchange for transmission and book-publishing rights.

These offers gave the Iceman project leaders the impression that
the media's appetite for Ötzi was enormous. Just how much was the
Iceman worth? Was $100,000 enough, or could they get much,
much more? Most important, as long as the possibility existed to
make easy money off the media, then why bother with the peer-
reviewed science funds? If they wanted something done, they would
just commission the work. This would also allow the project leaders
to keep a tight rein on what research would be done.

The first attempt to earn a little cash off the Iceman had already
occurred in December 1991, even before the contract with Bolzano
was signed. With several collaborative offers from the media still
pending, Spindler endorsed what for a scientist was an unusual idea.
He suggested charging the media to attend the press conference following the opening of the quiver at the Roman-Germanic Central

Museum in Mainz. The museum's director was not amused by the suggestion. Like the University of Innsbruck, the museum was a public institution, financed by public tax dollars. The museum's charter mandated that it keep the public informed about its many projects, so it could not be in the business of selling its results to a public that had already paid for them, even if the media would profit financially from the information it gathered.

Nevertheless, Platzer, Spindler, and Moser persisted in their plans to commercialize the Iceman, and these plans were enshrined in the contract signed with South Tyrol. The province gave the university the right to earn money off the project in order to pay for the research. According to the contract, money for the project was to be provided from the proceeds from commercial rights, "especially publication of written, photographic, film and other types of documentation [of the finds], and . . . the scientific research and studies as well as their commercial uses," as well as "all other proceeds garnered from the commercial uses of the finds or which can be raised for the scientific work." Additional funds could come from a "third party," such as a corporate sponsor or a government.

The project leaders enlisted an Innsbruck lawyer to help develop a marketing strategy. Part of the plan was to hire a public-relations firm to find financial sponsors for the research and manage communications with the media. The university would then sell various kinds of rights. The goal was ten million dollars. This, Platzer later said, was the "elegant" way of doing science.[1]

Overall, the project leaders were pleased with their contract with South Tyrol because it had few specific restrictions. Technically, the South Tyrolean Commission had a say only over how the conservation and marketing were done, not the research itself. But before research could proceed, one final bureaucratic step still needed to be taken. Platzer, Spindler, and Moser foresaw that their university departments might be too inflexible to coordinate the intricacies of the Iceman project, especially its finances. So, in a highly unusual move, the men successfully lobbied Austrian officials for the establishment of an entirely new institute with full responsibility for the project. The institute's mission was to extend beyond the Iceman project to include research on "man and his environment in the Alpine region from prehistory to the Middle Ages." This Research

Institute for Alpine Prehistory could hire its own lawyers and public-relations firms and administer the monies taken in by the commercialization of the Iceman. As a regular university institute, it would receive some federal Austrian funds for personnel and material. South Tyrol and Austrian Tyrol also each pledged to pay the institute approximately $100,000 a year for costs related to the Iceman. The new institute's directors were Platzer, Spindler, and Moser.

By the early spring of 1992, the stage was finally set for the Iceman to start earning his keep. In order for the commercialization to succeed, the project leaders had to have complete control over the information about the project. They assumed that any potential sponsor of the research would demand certain rights to or exclusivity over the results. Obviously, no one would pay for information available to everyone for free.

Accordingly, on March 31, 1992, Moser, Spindler, and Platzer issued a four-page contract to all researchers who had expressed interest in the project, including a few who already had projects under way. Though innocuously titled "Principles for Activity in Connection with the Tyrolean Ice Man and the Objects Found with Him," the "principles" constituted a binding contract between the researchers and the university. For the sake of protecting the rights of potential financial sponsors, the contract restricted the scientists' freedom to discuss or publish their work. It also turned almost every permissible contact between the scientists and the public into a potential revenue generator for the research.

According to the contract, all research results were to be made public only at press conferences in Innsbruck. Researchers who wished to publish their findings in professional journals or books could do so, but the date of publication had to be approved by the university, in order to avoid scooping the press conferences. By contrast, researchers who wished to write for nonscientific journals, such as popular magazines or newspapers, had to get explicit permission from the university, which would decide what to charge for the information and also receive the money.

"Proposals regarding . . . interviews [with scientists] as well as a declaration of the topic must be disclosed to the university," the contract stated. "The university reserves the right of assent over the holding of the proposed interviews and decides a timely occasion together with the participants in order to avoid reducing the importance of the regular press conferences or impairing or endangering sponsor or marketing rights."

The contract also saddled the scientists with the task of telling the media that they had no rights to the material they published and could reproduce or broadcast it only once. They were also supposed to tell their interviewers that three copies of the published material, or one copy of any video, had to be sent to the University of Innsbruck within one month of publication or broadcast.

To many scientists who read the contract, the "principles" seemed exaggerated and possibly irrelevant. But even the most easygoing or absentminded researcher reading through the list of dos and don'ts was stopped in his tracks by point eighteen: "The participants will refrain from anything that impairs or endangers the sponsoring or commercialization rights of the university and in doubt will consult the university. By breach of these principles, the participant will on one hand be liable for damages in the amount of the damages caused, and can on the other hand be eliminated from the research, effective immediately." None of the scientists had ever seen anything like it before.

Yet the concept behind the contract was not out of line with the recent trend, especially in the United States, for corporate investment and regulation in science. Such involvement can take many forms; most commonly, companies that have commercial interests in protecting their research results from competitors often bar their scientists from going public until the company's financial interest in the project is secured. Even in academia, where research is sometimes supported by taxpayers' money, researchers on a multidisciplinary project sometimes agree formally or informally on guidelines for publishing, citation, and authorship. Not a few researchers have been annoyed by colleagues who published results they considered premature. Sometimes a researcher signs an agreement giving partial or even exclusive publication rights to the sponsor. But usually public interest in a project is not great enough to guarantee much of a profit off information about it, and media relations are left to the judgment of the scientists. Where money changes hands, however, the question of ethics arises.

Since no sponsor had yet been found, the scientists did not know how their findings might eventually be used, and the contract granted them no say in the matter. While the research was supposed to be multidisciplinary, decisions about the commercialization were left largely to the three men running the new institute. Moreover, the whole strategy was developed behind closed doors. The Austrian and South Tyrolean publics, which had been paying for most of the research and the salaries of all the professors, heard only the vaguest rumors of the commercialization plans.

While surprised by and not entirely supportive of the university's tactics, most scientists already engaged in the project were eager to work on such a unique specimen and signed the contract without protest. But at the university itself, the contract soon encountered opposition. The glaciologist Gernot Patzelt and the prehistorian Andreas Lippert refused outright to sign it, claiming that it limited their academic freedom. The botanists Sigmar Bortenschlager and Klaus Oeggl also had problems with the contract and declined to sign.

Over the next several months, Moser, the university rector, pressured the men for their signatures while at the same time trying to keep their insubordination quiet. Patzelt, whose independent nature was known and admired, steadfastly refused. Despite the fact that he had worked previously with the archaeologists in Spindler's department on prehistoric environment issues, he was not invited to join the Research Institute for Alpine Prehistory. This exclusion of the man who had rushed to the site and so tenderly aided in the recovery of the quiver did not escape the attention of other Innsbruck scientists. In omitting Patzelt, the researchers also deprived themselves of potentially important revisions in the glaciologist's first assessment of the site, including the condition of the trench at the time the Iceman arrived there.

In October 1992, under continuing pressure and outright threats from the president, Bortenschlager finally signed a greatly modified version of the agreement. In a one-page letter, he outlined his position:

First of all I beg your pardon that my answer comes so late, but the principles still cause me great difficulty, especially the second part, which contains many things that a researcher cannot accept.

Since I am not alone with my thoughts, but know I am in good company at our department, I would like to make the following remarks.

1. I assure collegial and correct behavior for the work on the research project, as is natural and usual for scientific research.

2. Furthermore I will strive, through my work, to bring every advantage and avoid every damage to the Leopold Franzens University [University of Innsbruck].

Bortenschlager went on to say that he could sign the contract clauses that provided for the university to make his results public first but, twisting the university's use of the word *principles* against it, that "precisely out of considerations of principle and also legal dubiousness" he could not sign the parts having to do with the protection of marketing rights. He concluded: "If both creators of the principles are of the opinion that I thereby can no longer take part on the research project 'Homo Tirolensis,' then I just have to acknowledge that."

Given Bortenschlager's sterling reputation, his conscientious objections discomfited Moser, who had had reservations about the commercialization from the start. His signature on the greatly truncated document would just have to do. At least he was not threatening to violate the contract outright, as had Lippert, who now headed the Department of Pre- and Early History at the University of Vienna. The agile archaeologist who had led the first excavation of the Hauslabjoch was also scheduled to lead the second dig, planned for the summer of 1992.

By now Spindler had made it clear that he was going to write a book for a popular audience about the discovery. Given his central standing in the project, no one objected. But Lippert, too, had been considering a book. When he was approached by an ORF producer in Vienna to undertake such a project to accompany a film on the topic, he accepted. He also invited his old friend Lawrence Barfield, an English archaeologist who specialized on the northern Italian Neolithic period, to join him as a coauthor. Given Barfield's familiarity with both German and northern Italian prehistory, he was a wise choice. Indeed, Lippert believed he should be invited onto the project in any case.

But the University of Innsbruck's contract allowed for no such renegade projects. Lippert had opposed the marketing program from the beginning, and he knew he would have to refuse to sign. In June 1992, he instead signed a contract for his book.

When Spindler learned of Lippert's actions, he was furious. By this time, Innsbruck had already officially nominated Lippert to do the second excavation of the Hauslabjoch, which was scheduled to take place in August. Under pressure from Spindler, Moser telephoned Lippert in Vienna and threatened to withdraw the nomination if Lippert did not sign the university's contract, which would contain a special stipulation prohibiting Lippert from writing anything in his book about the results of the excavation.

But why, Lippert asked, should he do the work and let Spindler get all the credit in his book? Though he had known for many months that Spindler was planning to write a popular science book on the Iceman, he did not see why that should prevent others from doing the same. He thought many voices were better than one. But Moser's threat to take away the second dig was real. Concerned that he might really lose the chance for a big discovery, Lippert tried to work out a solution.

Lippert had high hopes for the Hauslabjoch dig, and he wanted the media to be there when they were realized. His emergency excavation the year before, a few weeks after the discovery, had been cursory, focused mainly on the top of the boulder upon which the man presumably died. He had not found much, but it was enough to convince him that more clues to the man's circumstances at the time of his death must be buried beneath the ice and snow in the trench. Given the way the man's possessions had been spread about, Lippert thought he was likely to find more of them. There might even be another corpse up there. Already Lippert had developed a hypothesis that explained the pattern of the artifacts' deposition, and he was eager to see how it would hold up. He began by plotting out the location of each individual artifact at the site. Since neither he nor any other archaeologist had actually seen the finds in situ, he had to rely on the memories of people who had, such as the Simons and Markus Pirpamer, as well as the few photos that documented the site. His prime assumptions, based on Patzelt's analysis of the Hauslabjoch, were that the man entered the trench when it was free of snow and ice and that his corpse and the artifacts had barely budged, if at all, since they had been deposited. The situation presented to the first witnesses was, therefore, a snapshot of the scene of the man's death.

From his own experiences as a camper and hiker in the mountains, Lippert had noted that modern hikers choose resting spots carefully. When a hiker intends to stay at a site for a while, he or she might stake out a bit of ground. When Lippert looked at where the body lay relative to the artifacts, he noticed such a pattern. Ötzi seemed to have used the low ledge around the trench as a table, depositing his backpack and ax on top of it. He had leaned his unfinished bow against the ledge. Some ten yards away, he had placed the quiver on the rocky floor of the trench. The boulder on which he was found and on which he had apparently died formed the third point of a triangle. He was not hunkering down with all his equipment around him. He was not cowering. He had not just dropped everything. He had taken some time to arrange his things. Perhaps he had even had time to make a campfire.

But why on earth had he stopped there at all? Lippert doubted that the man had stopped willingly, and he was eager to see what he could turn up to explain the man's predicament. Given all the preparations he had gone to, as well as the prospect of finding something that would shed more light on the man's final hours, Lippert was loath to give up his chance to lead the excavation, which was likely to proceed even without him. Just a few days before the excavation was scheduled to start, he caved in and signed the contract.

Getting their scientists to sign the contract was only one problem on the minds of Platzer, Spindler, and Moser early that summer. Their lawyer was also scrambling to find a public-relations firm to handle the project's marketing and communications. The hesitancy of established firms to take on the project should have sent up warning flags. By June 1992, at least two firms had withdrawn from considering the project because their potential sponsors got cold feet.

While that search continued, the project leaders tried to stave off journalists' hounding the scientists engaged in the research. In early June of 1992, Spindler and his colleagues at the Department of Pre- and Early History organized a three-day conference called "The

Man in the Ice: A Find from Tyrol's Stone Age." Only scientists working on the project were invited to attend, and all media inquiries were initially referred to one press conference. But when several journalists complained, Moser allowed them to listen to the participants' papers, as long as they made no sound or video recordings of the event.

In July 1992, the university's lawyer finally hired a young, enthusiastic public-relations firm called Ethik & Kommunikation (E&K) to take on the project. The goal of the firm's flashy director, Charlotte Sengthaler, was to raise about one million dollars within six months and a total of ten million within three and a half years. She also recommended that public relations be removed from the stuffy and amateurish halls of academe, where they had been managed informally by Spindler and Moser, to her ultrachic offices on Innsbruck's main avenue. Sengthaler was a savvy and commanding woman, and her tight and colorful designer suits combined with rock-star eye makeup were on the opposite end of the spectrum from the more traditional habits and styles of Spindler and Platzer.

Sengthaler knew the job would be difficult. A year had passed since the discovery, and many Austrians said they were already tired of hearing about the find. Though Platzer had kept the Iceman away from the lenses of the world press since the day of the very public press conference in the autopsy room, so many pictures of the shriveled corpse had been taken that day and sent into circulation that potential sponsors wondered whether there was anything new to show the public. All exclusivity had by now been lost.

Sengthaler recommended aggressively countering the "myth" that there was nothing left to research or market. In her plan for the project, she quoted Spindler as saying that "just 5 (five!) percent of the questions scientists had asked about the archaeological find had already been answered. In any case, many of the proposed theses will have to be revised."[2] The "strategic message" of the marketing plan, she wrote, was that the Iceman was a "gift to all humanity." Not only would the study of the Iceman contribute to the fundamental knowledge of humankind, she said, but it would also contribute to the solving of actual problems in such fields as medicine and climatology.

Before she could embark on her grand scheme, Sengthaler

wanted to get comprehensive research proposals from all the scientists who would be involved in the project. She envisioned that her main task would be to sell film and publication rights to the media and also to apply for national scientific-research funds, a chore the scientists normally did themselves. She also wanted to send out a mass mailing to targeted groups such as doctors and scientists in Europe and the United States, asking for their contributions to the project.

E & K kicked off its project about a month after being hired with a fund-raiser to celebrate the Iceman's first "birthday" at Innsbruck's civic center. Proceeds from the sale of tickets, which cost just ten dollars, were to benefit research. The program featured a lackluster roundtable discussion of the newest results with Spindler, Moser, and two representatives of Platzer, who normally kept himself away from the public eye. There was also an interview with Helmut and Erika Simon. Ever since the geographers had decided that the corpse had been on Italian territory, the Simons' claim to the Iceman had been stymied. Their Innsbruck lawyer insisted that the Simons were owed up to one fourth of the Iceman's value, and he had already asked South Tyrol to pay them six thousand dollars toward that goal. But the Simons seemed less interested in the money than in their association with the Iceman, and they were obviously pleased to be acknowledged, especially by Moser, who had graciously kept them abreast of research developments and invited them to the recent conference. The dubious climax of the anniversary celebration was the presentation of the first volume of research papers on the Iceman to the Simons and the governor of Austrian Tyrol.

The celebration was a flop. So few people attended that the university ended up losing five thousand dollars. In effect, the organizers were asking Austrians, whose taxes had in the last year at least partly funded the research, to pay again for the privilege of hearing the results which, for the most part, were already public. The commercialization effort was off to a cool start.

In July 1992, a crew of shovelers arrived at the Hauslabjoch to clear the way for Lippert's second dig. The plan for the excavation was to remove all the snow and ice from the trench in which the corpse and the artifacts had been discovered. But the four Innsbruck meteorology students and the professor who had volunteered to shovel out the trench, which nine months earlier had been virtually emptied of snow and ice, now found it packed solidly with more than eleven feet of weather-hardened snow.

Over the last year, despite his differences with the project leadership, the glaciologist Gernot Patzelt had been trying to piece together the factors that had led to the emergence of the corpse in September 1991, presumably for the first time since his death. The climate in 5300 B.C.E. was much as it was in 1991, and the two periods were separated by a long, slightly cooler period. Evidence from this century documented a very slow warming trend. Old maps of the area, along with temperature and accumulation data from the weather station in Vent, told most of the story. After World War I, when the region was surveyed with an eye to drawing the border, the pass on which the corpse lay had been covered in several meters of ice. Patzelt found a 1938 map that also showed the area still under snow and probably glacier as well. But by 1950, at least one rocky outcropping had melted out. Between 1965 and 1980, the situation remained relatively stable, but then the melting picked up quickly. All across the Alps, the glaciers began to melt at an almost astonishing pace, and the situation on the Hauslabjoch changed rapidly. In the years after 1980, the new snow that accumulated each winter melted completely by the end of the summer, and more of the glacier ice beneath the snow melted away.

Patzelt found that records from a nearby weather station confirmed that the most recent period had been warmer than the beginning of the century. According to the data, the warmest decade of the century was 1982–1991, with an average temperature of −5.6°C, while the coldest was 1907–1916, with an average temperature of −6.5°C.

The July weather was even more indicative of the warming trend. In the decade leading up to the corpse's discovery, the average July temperature was two degrees Celsius above zero, while in every other decade the July temperature stayed below freezing. Though rising temperatures definitely played a part in the mummy's appearance, Patzelt thought they could not be the only factor. Other warm periods had occurred in the last five thousand years, for example in the third and fourth centuries and when the Vikings had settled Greenland in the ninth and tenth centuries.

Patzelt concluded that the extreme melting in the summer of 1991 was due to a fluke of the weather that spring. In early March, more than a thousand miles away in the Sahara, a storm tossed up masses of sand and carried it north and east across the Mediterranean and over Europe, where some of it was deposited on the snow covering a large section of the high Alps. The golden sand was soon enough concealed by more snow and lay buried until the hot sun of July melted off the snow above it. Once the sun hit the relatively dark sand, the melting proceeded even faster. The warm and sunny days continued even into September. At the Hauslabjoch, the tops of the rust-colored rocks and boulders along the ridge began to melt out, although the snow and ice still filled the lower-lying areas and the spaces between the rocks. In the trench where the Iceman lay slumped across a boulder, the sun steadily eroded the snow and ice, and the melted water drained slowly from the northeastern corner, beginning a bumpy journey that eventually took it down through the Ötztal into the river Inn. Patzelt estimated that just two or three days before the Simons' visit, the back of the Iceman's head had emerged through the slush and water.

Over the next day or two, as the sun continued to blaze down on the pass, the melting proceeded and the man's shoulders and upper back appeared. While Patzelt could not say with absolute certainty that the man had never been exposed since his death, he thought it unlikely, given what the forensic doctors said about the nearly perfect state of preservation of the corpse. The exposure of 1991 could have been very short-lived. In five thousand years, Patzelt believed, the corpse had been visible for just six or seven days. By astonishing coincidence, the Simons happened to pass by in precisely that blink of time. Just four days after their discovery, new snow fell again and concealed the site, which was why the ORF team had had trouble spotting it.

Yet that light dusting of snow was nothing like what faced the crew of shovelers preparing for the excavation. For three weeks, under a strong sun, the young men shoveled and shoveled, breathing in air that had much less oxygen in it than they were used to.

With half the trench cleared, they estimated that they had moved some six hundred metric tons of snow.

Lippert had wanted to eliminate all the snow and ice from the trench to allow a picture of it as it was at the time the man died. But there was just too little time and too little manpower. Regretfully, he decided that they would have to focus just on the side where all the artifacts had been found. Another difficulty was that water melting off the ground slightly above them kept running into the trench. The team, which included archaeologists from both Austria and Italy, experimented with a network of pipes and channels and gutters to divert the water. Later on, a generator and pump had to be rigged up to ferry water away from the site. Before it could be drained, the water had to be filtered.

They used a mesh that caught hundreds of bits of organic material and human hair and flesh, probably from the jackhammered part of the Iceman's hip. One day, a tiny white, plasticlike object landed in the screen. The archaeologists realized to their delight that it was a human nail, probably from a finger. It was placed in a small plastic bag, labeled, and eventually passed on to Luigi Capasso, the point man for several Italian researchers involved in the project.

The archaeologists soon noticed that the bits and pieces of artifacts, presumably all from the Iceman, were turning up beyond the locations where the first visitors had reportedly seen them. Mainly grass and hair, these remains seemed to be spread throughout the part of the trench they had cleared. If a pattern was here, it was not immediately recognizable. Still, the excavators did note areas of higher concentrations. One was under the ledge on which the ax and backpack had been found. The bow had been leaning against that ledge, so the archaeologists were not surprised when, a few days into the excavation, they found the broken end still stuck in ice there. Its end was in contact with the floor of the trench, and Lippert guessed it was the exact spot where the man had planted it. It had not budged in more than five thousand years.

The man had set it down with the flat side facing the ledge. Like the other end, this one was tapered and had no notch or other indication of ever having been strung. Neither did the team uncover any sign of a bowstring. Near the eighteen-inch-long piece were also tiny fragments of wood, more grass, leather, and fur, and one piece of wood with a bit of fur sticking to it. This he interpreted as a third cross board for the backpack. They also discovered a small fragment of horn and more small animal bones. This material had probably washed down the ledge toward the bottom of the trench in earlier thaws.

One day, while excavating about four feet to the west of the boulder, in approximately the area where Helmut Simon had first picked up the birch-bark container, the archaeologists began uncovering bits of charcoal. At first, Lippert thought this might be the remains of a campfire, which he had been hoping to find. But the rocks at the base did not show the typical discoloration of those exposed to great heat, and there were very few charcoal remains. If the man had made a fire in this trench, they expected it to be close to where he had lain down. But no such fire was evidenced.

Since several artifacts were found lying directly on the rock in the trench, Lippert agreed with Patzelt's assertion that they had not moved since they had been deposited. He assumed this deepest layer of ice had not melted at all since it had formed in the late Neolithic period. At the request of the botanists, several samples were taken from the deepest pockets of ice in the trench; with luck, the pollen in them could be analyzed.

As in the first excavation, Lippert paid particular attention to the large boulder on which the man had lain. As the archaeologists fastidiously cleared away the snow around it, its peculiar angles emerged. The side across which the body had been found was rather steeply and unevenly sloped. How or whether the Iceman had managed to find a comfortable position across it was by no means obvious. Its only distinction seemed to be that it was the largest boulder in the immediate vicinity. It was also poised near the ledge, which may have provided extra protection from the wind.

Once the snow was removed from around the sides of the boulder, the team melted away the several feet of ice around its base in the sole of the trench. At the base, just below where the man's head had rested, the archaeologists came upon a singular find. A fur cap was pressed, frozen, against the bottom of the boulder, as if it had slipped off the man's head and tumbled down the side. It was made of several sections of fur sewn neatly together in a bowl shape. The fur was thick. But like so much of the man's equipment, it was not in perfect shape. A chin strap was still attached to two sides of the cap, and in the middle it had been knotted neatly. He must have died with his hat on. However, at one place the strap had broken between the knot and the end attached to the hat. Lippert supposed that it had happened as the man lay dying or after he died. Losing a hat in bad weather was not good. Had the man noticed as it slipped from his head, or was he already unconscious or asleep? Or had it happened only after he was dead, as his frozen corpse shrunk and the weight of the snow-encrusted hat pulled it from his head? Lippert did not know, and he guessed no one ever would. The fur hat seemed to be just further testimony to the man's helpless death.

Nearly five weeks after the first hardy students and their professor arrived with their shovels, the archaeological team finally packed up their equipment. In all, they had catalogued more than four hundred items. Despite the incredible effort, Lippert, whose last official contribution to the Iceman project would be the excavation report, was a bit disappointed. He had hoped to find more obvious clues to explain the man's death, yet nothing of the sort had turned up. There had been no companion or faithful dog in death, no campfire, and, indeed, no firm outline of a campsite. Instead, most of what they found was mud, grass, hair, water, and ice—the dregs of the trench. All of this stuff, weighing several hundred pounds, was to be turned over to Klaus Oeggl. But no archaeologist, not even Lippert, quite realized at the time just how much a botanist could learn from such muck.

Oeggl needed a clear head for research, and he felt he could not get it under the constant urgent scrutiny of the media. Even a year after the discovery, he frequently was overwhelmed by the speculation, hearsay, and exaggeration that accompanied every new bit of information. Though he continued to give the occasional interview, Oeggl asked Bortenschlager to handle most journalistic inquiries so that he could concentrate on research, including developing contacts with a number of scientists whom he believed would be interested and helpful.

In the summer of 1992, Oeggl's mind was on a series of discov-

eries that had emerged out of a fist-sized package of organic material that Egg had passed along to him the previous December. When
Oeggl peeled back part of the sample, he had instantly recognized
the five-pointed structure of a maple leaf. Parts of it were still completely intact, while other parts had decayed, leaving only a delicate
web of veins.

Oeggl had found a second maple leaf folded inside that first leaf,
and inside that was a third one, closed into each other like pages of
a book. Ultimately, he unwrapped fourteen maple leaves. Once they
were separated, Oeggl had noticed that all the stems, as well as the
rump of the leaf where the stem was attached, were missing, though
when leaves are shed in the fall, the stem comes off with the leaf.
When he put a few fragments of them in alcohol, it turned green-
ish. Incredibly, after thousands of years, the leaves still had chlorophyll in them. That meant the Iceman had not gotten them off the
ground. They had been plucked—harvested from a maple tree—
while still green. Oeggl was astounded. These were green leaves
from prehistory, the first he had ever seen.

While unwrapping the leaves, Oeggl had made yet another curious discovery. As he pulled open the leaves with a tweezers, tiny bits
of charcoal, about a thimbleful altogether, as well as a few spruce
and juniper needles and birch-bark fragments, rolled out. The leaves
seemed to have been rolled up together intentionally, and Oeggl
wondered whether the charcoal bits were meant to be in there. He
noted it all carefully, and passed the results via Spindler over to Egg.

The discovery had set Egg thinking. He recalled reading that
some Native Americans had transported glowing embers from one
camp to the next in order to facilitate starting a fire. Might the Iceman have been doing the same thing? The man could have used a
little pad of maple leaves to pick up a glowing ember, and then pack
it inside the birch-bark container. As the embers burned down, they
would have been covered in a thick layer of gray ash, but inside they
would still have glowed. Upon reaching his next campsite, he could
have removed the leaves and the ember and then placed tiny bits of
kindling on it. Then he would have blown gently, coaxing the glow
into little licks of fire, which would have ignited the kindling.
Within minutes, he could have made a fire.

Given that the Iceman did not otherwise seem prepared to make

a fire, the idea seemed quite practical, and Egg's colleagues immediately liked it. It seemed to suit the wandering life of a herdsman.
If he had been spending the summer away from his village on the
high Alps, as the modern shepherds did, then he would not have
had easy access to fire. If Egg was right, then Oeggl expected to find
evidence of exposure to extreme heat—scorch marks perhaps—on
the leaves. However, he had not.

In May, Oeggl had taken a break from a conference he was at-
tending in Kiel, Germany, to take a walk with a Swiss wood expert
named Werner Schoch, who had quickly become an indispensable
adviser and collaborator. As he and Schoch passed under a maple
tree, Oeggl impulsively grabbed a branch and let his hand slide
down as they moved by, pulling the leaves off. Still walking, he
glanced down at the catch in his hand. The spiked leaves had broken away from their stems in the same way as the Iceman's maple
leaves had.

"Aha!" Oeggl thought. This was probably how the Iceman had
ripped off his leaves: not one by one, but fast and economically, by
running his hand down a thin branch. The accidental research
amused Schoch, and the two men continued their discussion. Oeggl
was not prepared to dismiss the whole ember-container hypothesis.
Cold embers also worked extremely well for kindling—so well, in
fact, that several kinds of natural-wood charcoal for conventional
grills were made of cold embers. Lighting them with a flame was
easy. The problem was still that the Iceman did not seem to have a
spark maker with him.

Back in Innsbruck, Oeggl continued his analysis of the composition of the charcoal he had found wrapped in the leaves, as well as
of another sample that had washed out of some remains in Mainz.
This work was part of his project to plot out the habitat of each of
the woods found in the equipment. Other researchers planned to
do the same thing for the mosses and fungi found on the organic
material. In many fragments he was still able to discern the outline
of the tree rings, and their tight curvature suggested that the wood
came from twigs or branches, the kind of wood often used to get a
fire going. Eight different varieties of wood were present in those
little crumbs of charcoal. With one exception, all came from trees
that grew well below the spot at which they were discovered. The

one bit of wood represented in the charcoal that grew at a higher altitude, all the way up to the tree line, was the dwarf willow, which accounted for just 0.8 percent of the sample. Oeggl thought that if the man kept adding embers from many different fires into the container, that might account for the mix. But the composition suggested that the Iceman had spent much time, perhaps even shortly before his death, at an altitude at least an hour or two below the Hauslabjoch.

Oeggl wondered about how this fit with the shepherd hypothesis. For if the man remained high in the Alps with the sheep all summer, then he probably wouldn't have had easy access to all the trees represented in this charcoal. Fires lit in the area of the pasture should have had a higher composition of Alpine species, woods that grew toward the forest limit, such as the dwarf willow.

If the Iceman had been found on the Midwestern plains, where the same environmental and climatic conditions stretch for hundreds of miles in either direction, then it would have been unlikely that botanists could have traced his exact movements through his surroundings. But because of the extremes in altitude, soil, and climate, the Alpine mountains and valleys were home to a large diversity of life. Within twenty miles of the Hauslabjoch were a number of ecological niches, from the warm and humid Vinschgau, where fruit for all of Europe was grown, to the Alpine glaciers of the Ötztal.

Naturally, the botanical landscape had been altered over the millennia. By far the biggest change was that farmers had cleared vast tracts of forestland for crops and cut trees at the upper tree line to create more pasture. They had planted nonnative trees they liked, such as ash, which provided fodder for their animals in the winter, and neglected others that were not useful to them. Patzelt said that the climate, however, was about the same as it had been five thousand years earlier, and the topography of the land had not changed much. Using information from pollen profiles and data on soil, Oeggl tried to reconstruct a picture of the floral landscape at the time the Iceman lived.

Oeggl realized most of the woods the man used could be obtained within a day's walk of the Hauslabjoch, but not on both sides of the main Alpine ridge. To the north were the glacier-filled valleys of the Ötztal, where larch and pine stretched for miles. On that side, most trees represented in Ötzi's equipment had probably grown within a day's hike away. However, not until the Ötztal joined the Inn, some sixty miles to the north of the Hauslabjoch, would the Iceman have been likely to find a yew tree. Maple trees were almost as far away. If the Iceman got his material from the north, then he had made quite a hike. The botanists' guess was that the nearest source for all the trees and plants found in his equipment was to the south, in the Schnalstal or the warm and humid Vinschgau. But Oeggl still wanted more information. If he got a piece of the Iceman's gut contents, he might be able to find pollen there. This would provide a snapshot of the man's last hours or days. Then, as soon as he had identified all the species of plants found on him, the botanist could begin trying to match up the species to their habitats. With enough data, and maybe some luck, Oeggl thought he might be able to specify where the Iceman had spent most of his time.

Nobody had gotten a really good look at what Ötzi was wearing before he was ripped out of the ice, and that had made the conservators' work very difficult. When the Simons spotted the corpse, his shoulders were already naked, and the gendarme who had tried to hammer it out of the ice had not encountered any clothing as he worked down the back to the hips. Those people who had noticed clothing were a little vague on what they had seen. No one had seen anything covering the torso. But the few people who had looked closely at the legs reported some intriguing clues: The legs appeared to be wrapped in leather. Whether this was a garment for the legs, they could not say. The only recognizable feature was the nice, even seams sewn through them.

After successfully cleaning and freeze-drying the leather pieces, Roswitha Goedecker-Ciolek set to work trying to fit them together. One obstacle to her work was that she did not yet possess all the pieces. The fur and leather bits that Patzelt and his friends had seen in the water and that Silvano Dal Ben had then retrieved, were stranded in Bolzano, waiting for another export permit.

The work was rather intimate. She was sorting through and matching up bits of an outfit that this man had pulled on his body each morning. In fact, she wondered whether he had ever taken them off. Goedecker-Ciolek had immediately noticed a particular odor arising out of the skins. It reminded her of an animal. It was not the scent of decay but more earthy. Possibly it was the animal whose furs were used to construct the clothing. Maybe it was even *his* scent.

Goedecker-Ciolek had quickly established a few guidelines. Since the leather was of varying shades, she began by collecting all the pieces of the same color. The seams served as a guide. She slowly managed to put together a good portion of them. Ultimately, she segregated the material into four distinct garments. The biggest was about the size of a large beach towel, roughly rectangular in shape and composed of wide strips of alternating light and dark fur in a clear pattern. Whoever had made this garment had been thinking about the aesthetic of it.

The second garment was also rectangular but smaller and relatively narrower. It was the only one made of leather instead of fur. The last two pieces were tubular, but when laid out flat on the table, they formed rhomboids. Given that shape and the fact that there were two of them, Goedecker-Ciolek assumed that they were either sleeves or legs. If they were sleeves, then they had to attach to something. If they were pants, then they had to be held up. Yet she could not identify any pieces that would have served to connect them. Until more pieces came from Bolzano, she would not rush to any conclusion.

Goedecker-Ciolek also realized that the artifact that had been described as a "grass mat" was really part of a long grass cape that had stretched past the man's knees.[3] It was constructed of long bundles of grass, aligned parallel to each other, with the roots still intact at the bottom, and then bound together at $2\frac{1}{2}$- to $3\frac{1}{5}$-inch intervals by two lightly twisted grasses plaited through horizontally. Very little of the cape had survived, but one piece that did was from the upper edge, at the neck. There, Goedecker-Ciolek found the remains of two twisted grass ties, which she assumed had been used to bind the two sides of the cape together at the chest and neck. She could not determine whether the cape had armholes. The lower part of the cape was not plaited, so the grass blades hung freely in a long fringe, which probably had allowed the man to walk and climb freely.

The man also had a second plaited item, a small dagger sheath, made of strips of bast. The design was simple, and the technique was a straightforward plait, but even in the simplest craft there is room for error. Along the upper rim of the sheath, Goedecker-Ciolek spotted a tiny mistake. Instead of catching up two bast strips in one part of the plait, the maker caught only one, which caused a little glitch in the pattern along the rim.

Goedecker-Ciolek was also in charge of restoring the shoes, which, strictly speaking, were the only artifacts whose ownership was beyond question, since the right one had still been on the corpse's foot when it arrived in Innsbruck. After photographing it, Goedecker-Ciolek had carefully maneuvered the shoe off, sliding a piece of cardboard inside to take the place of the foot. When she looked inside, all she could see was grass. The man had stuck his foot right into a mound of grass, which obviously had served as insulation.

The remains of the second shoe had been found among the piles of grasses and leather pieces carried down the mountain in the plastic garbage bag. Goedecker-Ciolek could make out a leather sole and what looked like part of an upper. Before she could handle these, they, too, had to undergo the conservation process. This accomplished, Goedecker-Ciolek set about trying to understand how the man could have traveled through the Alps in a grass-stuffed shoe, which she thought probably required considerable maintenance.

The shoes appeared to consist of three main parts: the grass insulation; a net that held the grass snugly around the foot; and a leather or fur sole and upper. Made of twisted grass knotted together loosely in a technique still used today, the net on the left foot was virtually intact, and she could see that at one time it had been tied around the ankle. To aid in the reconstruction, she carefully drew every visible bit of string and leather. She soon realized that the nets in the two shoes were constructed differently. Whereas the right foot net was tailored to the form of the foot, the left one was constructed as a band and appeared to have wrapped around the circumference of the foot. Its secure fit around the foot was achieved through the particular way it was pulled tight by laces rather than by its form alone. She wondered whether the nets were made by different people or whether one was an experiment or recycled from something else.

The bottom edge of the net, which followed the outline of the foot, and thereby the sole, had loops. These caught up a strip of leather woven around the edge of the leather sole. Here she detected a trick of the prehistoric cobbler. Since the grass net was not attached directly to the sole itself but to the strip of leather, the string did not have contact with the ground. The loops were thereby protected from friction against the ground.

Across the bottom of the sole, at the level of the ball of the foot, was a strip of leather. This, Goedecker-Ciolek decided, was a feature much like a modern tread, designed to reduce slipping. The fur side of the skin was worn on the inside of the sole, which probably made the going easier and kept the foot warmer. But the little bit of the upper part of the shoe, which was sewn around the bottom of the sole, had the fur on the outside. Several holes around the area of the instep appeared to have served as eyelets. The tops of the net were drawn through here and held not only the grass in tightly but the shoe's upper as well.

One day, months after her work started, Goedecker-Ciolek was examining the lace area of the right shoe when she found something that did not seem to fit. Tucked under the laces was a loose swatch of fur, about the size of a shoe tongue. One end was ripped. It did not seem to be part of the shoe. It was made of two bits of fur sewn together, in the same patchwork style as part of the clothing. Returning to the remains of the clothing, she spotted a similar tongue-like tab sewn onto the edge of one of the garments. That was interesting. The little tab was small, but she suspected it was important, so she carefully set it aside.

A major difficulty in her reconstruction was that she had virtually no information on how prehistoric people had dressed. The reason, of course, was that clothing made of organic material rarely survived. In lakeside settlements in Switzerland, archaeologists had found remnants of woven textiles they believed had been part of clothes, but they could only guess at how these had been put together. Leather did not survive in the chilly waters where the discoveries were made, so archaeologists did not know the extent of its use among those people.

The best items of comparison available were the garments recovered from people buried in oak coffins in Denmark.[4] The standard men's dress seemed to be a woven undergarment, cloak, cap, and footwear. Sometimes the undergarment consisted of nothing more than a woven loincloth, held at the waist by a leather belt. But there were also gownlike garments that were tied at the shoulder with leather straps and then again around the waist with a leather or woven belt. Men apparently tucked their daggers into the belts, while they wore the swords in leather straps across their shoulders. The typical shoe was a large, square-shaped piece of leather that had been cut at one end so that a lace could be pulled through it and then cinched up around the foot.

The women had a woven woolen jacket that had to be pulled, poncho style, over the head. They also wore a belt and an above-the-knee corded skirt, constructed of a dense curtain of fringes connected to a woven band at the waist and another at the lower hem. Some cords were even wrapped in bronze-leaf tubes, which would have caught the light of the sun and perhaps also attested to the wealth or status of the bearer.

Archaeologists believed that many of these garments were based on older models of clothing made of fur. Though the Danish garments were much younger than those of the Iceman, they were almost all Egg and Goedecker-Ciolek had to go by. They pored over photographs of the garments and their patterns, looking for similarities with the Iceman's furs. Whatever else he wore, the Iceman must have had some covering on his torso, so the conservators were particularly intrigued by the variety of skin capes that had been recovered from bogs. Both men and women had worn these garments, which were not simply hides thrown around the shoulders but carefully designed garments with collars and different types of fasteners, such as loops and wooden pegs. Normally, the skin side was worn on the inside.

The Danish clothes were surprisingly similar to modern clothing, though made from different materials. Was prehistoric Danish clothing any more relevant to the Iceman than, say, that of nineteenth-century Mexican cowboys? Some archaeologists resisted consulting clothing worn by other peoples through the ages. Others allowed that clothing and other tools and equipment known from living people or historical accounts might be useful in interpretations of artifacts, but only if they came from the same region.

Egg embraced the idea that clothing from all cultures and times might prove helpful in understanding the Iceman's clothes—and tools, for that matter. He thought it was ridiculous to suggest that the Iceman's clothing should be compared only with other European clothing, as if there was something about European clothing that was constant through the ages and distinct from that of other parts of the world. He was open to inspiration wherever he found it.

One day, not long after Lippert's dig, the South Tyrolean archaeologist Hans Nothdurfter dropped by to see how work was going on the restoration of a tiny fifteenth-century church in the village of Laces, about twelve miles south of the Hauslabjoch in the Vinschgau. Nothdurfter had excavated and restored dozens of medieval churches in the province and he knew what to expect. When the archaeologists began peeling up the tiled floors, they entered an architectural palimpsest. Almost always they discovered the ruined foundations of earlier chapels embraced in the walls of the newer church. Once Nothdurfter found the smashed remains of a beautiful pastel-colored medieval fresco. Materials from the earlier constructions were usually recycled into the new ones, but the location of the churches never budged. The ground itself was hallowed, and often had been for time immemorial.

Nothdurfter had come to secure a few items against the thieves who stalked provincial churches. Those undergoing restoration were at particular risk because they were often left open during the day while workmen came and went. While he was there, Nothdurfter wanted to check the altar, which probably had a hidden niche containing a page or two of liturgical text and a little relic, a bit of bone or hair from the saint to whom the church was dedicated.

Chatting with one of the painters, Nothdurfter pulled away a lace cloth covering the altar to reveal a flat wooden surface. Cut into the top was a square niche fitted with a marble plate about the size of a book. That was what he had been looking for. He pried the marble plate up and withdrew a pretty copper etching, probably a few centuries old. But before he could really study it, the painter was interrupting him excitedly.

"Look," he said, "there's an old tombstone under here." He indicated the niche from which the marble plate and the etching had come.

Nothdurfter's heart took a wild turn. Through the square hole in the wooden tabletop, he could make out strange markings carved into a gray stone. He knew immediately that it was not a tombstone, but one of the rarest and most precious of Copper Age artifacts in northern Italy. It was a statue-menhir.

In great excitement, the two men removed the rest of the wooden cover from the surface of the statue-menhir. Carved into the massive stone were dozens of symbols and other representations. Like other northern Italian statue-menhirs, this one had originally been sculpted into a rather boxy, humanlike shape. But it had been through a lot of recycling. The head section was cut away, and the sides and the bottom were also shaved down. All that remained was the chest region of the figure, bound at the waist by a band of wavy lines. Clusters of dots and concentric circles had also been chiseled into the rock. But what most intrigued Nothdurfter was the carving of a long-handled ax in the upper left corner on the statue-menhir's pectoral area. The blade protruded at a familiar angle, and its edges flared out the slightest bit. Nothdurfter recognized it at once. This statue-menhir depicted a man with an ax that looked like the Iceman's. And it was in his neighborhood.

Located within a day's hike of the Hauslabjoch, the statue-menhir was the first new indication of prehistoric human presence in the mountains since the Iceman's discovery. It had been intentionally embedded inside the wooden altar table. If local church authorities had just needed a table, they could easily have gotten a marble platter from the nearby quarries. From old church documents Nothdurfter learned that a bishop had consecrated the altar in 1465; he must have been aware of the statue-menhir. Though the bishop could not have understood the original meaning of the slab any better than modern archaeologists did, he nevertheless thought it important to include within his church, perhaps as a symbol of the ancient and enduring holiness of the spot or of the mysteries of life and faith. In a similar acknowledgment of its importance, this statue-menhir would probably end up in a museum, the place where modern people contemplate the past.

Though the stone statue-menhirs were now recognized as being younger than the Iceman, archaeologists still thought they were relevant for the period in which he lived. Lawrence Barfield believed that the stone statue-menhirs might well have been preceded by carved and painted wooden statues that the Iceman probably would have known.

Statue-menhirs were erected in other parts of the world for a multitude of reasons: to mark a battle, a boundary, or an individual. But Barfield was partial to one use in particular. In his decades of study and excavations in northern Italy, he had noted that many statue-menhirs turned up in association with burials. Importantly, however, they did not show up as far south as Remedello. Because of the association with death, Barfield suggested that the statue-menhirs might represent ancestors, who exercised some control over their descendants' fertility. The fertility symbolism in the statue-menhirs was rife: Their shape was generally phallic. Likewise, the suns and plowing scenes depicted on them frequently referred to the cycles of growth and life.

More important, the statue-menhirs found throughout northern Italy depicted a lot of copper, even though very few copper artifacts themselves had shown up in the region. The Iceman's ax was one of the few copper artifacts found between the main Alpine ridge and the Remedello culture on the Po plain. Barfield knew it might take years of excavations and lucky finds to determine the relationships among all these facts. But he was convinced that much more copper had been produced in these Alpine valleys than had so far shown up in the archaeological record.

CHAPTER 7

A CASTRATED EGYPTIAN

THE FIRST HINT that the Hauslabjoch man might not have been in good health when he died came from the doctor who X-rayed him. What Dieter zur Nedden thought he had detected in those first X rays of the Iceman's chest was a series of broken ribs. In early 1992, when he retrieved his X rays from Platzer's safekeeping, he called his staff doctors into his office, where they began going through the images, one by one. One of the first things they looked at was the condition of the chest cavity.

On the Iceman's right side, zur Nedden again spotted a faint crack. He traced the white outline of the third rib with his finger. Halfway around, the bone broke off, there was a narrow black gap, and then the bone resumed. Zur Nedden looked at the ribs above and below the fracture. They also appeared to have tiny fractures running through them, all in the same plane, as if they had all been broken at once.

Intuitively, zur Nedden began looking for indications that the healing process had begun. When a bone breaks, the area swells up, and a purplish bruise forms. As healing gets under way, swelling decreases, and the bruise turns yellow. The surface of the man's body revealed no sign of the rib breaks, probably because the corpse was so dehydrated and the skin darkened. Neither could zur Nedden detect a callus, the new bone that starts to form immediately after a break and normally shows up in an X ray about twelve days later.

This gave him pause. If he found no sign of healing, then they could not be sure the breaks occurred while the man was alive. This corpse had been enclosed in a bed of ice for millennia. Almost anything could have happened in that time. If the fractures did date to the man's lifetime, however, then they represented a serious impairment. They might not have killed him, but zur Nedden did think they could have severely weakened him and thereby contributed to his death. He and the other doctors were soon speculating on the timing and cause of the fractures.

Often, rib injuries result from a bad fall. As a person tumbles, his arms fly out in an attempt to break the landing, leaving the ribs unprotected. A strong punch or blow, from a weapon or another person's arms or legs, can also cause serious damage. With every breath, the lungs expand, exerting painful pressure on the broken ribs. In particularly bad breaks, part of the rib can puncture the lung. But even though this looked like an extremely serious injury, the broken ribs were more or less in alignment and had probably not caused the Iceman severe difficulty in breathing.

As zur Nedden and his colleagues were exclaiming over the fresh rib breaks, he noticed signs of yet another injury: On the man's left side were several healed rib fractures. The fracture sites appeared in the X rays as slightly bulged where new bone had developed. They were at about the same position—just under the arm—as those on the right, and all in a row. The man was certainly no stranger to pain, zur Nedden thought. The healed fractures were the aftermath of a very serious injury, which would have laid up a modern person for at least a month. From what zur Nedden could see, however, the breaks had healed normally and had probably not caused the man any limitations.

There were several other irregularities in the chest cavity. Normally, people have twelve ribs, but Ötzi had only eleven. The condition was not very common but it would not have hurt him, and he probably was not aware of it. Zur Nedden's team also noticed that the two halves of the rib cage were asymmetrical; the upper right part of the rib cage was strangely deformed, as if it had been smashed in from the top of the shoulder. The top ribs, which normally curve around the body in a tight arc, were bent almost at a right angle in one place. They looked as if they had been subject to some pressure. The most likely culprit, zur Nedden thought, was the glacier, which might also have snapped the ribs.

The idea that the man had broken ribs at the time of his death was, admittedly, a very attractive explanation for his need to stop on that frigid pass. But zur Nedden could not confidently claim that the fresh rib fractures had occurred before the man's death. As far as he could see, there were three distinct possibilities for the timing of the breaks. (1) The ribs might have broken as long as twelve days before the man died. (2) The breaks might have occurred while the man was buried in the ice, perhaps under the shifting of the glacier. (3) They had broken during the recovery, as the corpse was being pulled out of the ice.

As zur Nedden had recently learned, damage from the recovery efforts could not be underestimated. Not only had the left hip, buttock, and thigh area been largely obliterated by the gendarme's jackhammer, but the upper left arm had also been snapped in two. This zur Nedden had heard from the forensic doctors, who said the arm fracture had occurred when the corpse was stuffed into the coffin. The break showed up clearly on zur Nedden's CAT scan.

He doubted his instruments would be able to determine the timing of the fresh rib breaks, but his clinic was scheduled to receive new digital radiography that would give them better resolution in their images. Possibly this would give them a cleaner look at what was going on at the ends of those fractures. But before he knew more, he was not going to publish anything or make a press release. Zur Nedden liked to think of himself as a "dry" scientist, a man who went quietly about his work and published when he had something to say. Of course, he did tell Platzer about the breaks, and he supposed the news got passed on to Spindler and other researchers in an informal way. Though the project was multidisciplinary, no formal exchange network had been established.

Zur Nedden's closest intellectual and spiritual ally among the many scientists working on the Iceman project was Horst Seidler, the professor of human biology from the University of Vienna. The two men, who had known each other vaguely years earlier as students, had become reacquainted at Platzer's first meeting of researchers in the fall of 1991. They shared a critical view of Austrian history and current politics and were aware that narrow parochial concerns could easily skew science. But in personality and style, they could hardly have been more different. Zur Nedden was considered rather dashing, and dressed in carefully tailored suits. He had a full head of gray hair and a large mustache that drooped over the corners of his mouth. Seidler was balding and stockier and cared little about labels. While zur Nedden approached everyone with a studied indifference, Seidler was charming and emotional. Zur Nedden barreled through the narrow streets of Innsbruck in a big, fancy BMW. Seidler hadn't driven in decades. Zur Nedden smoked Davidoffs and Seidler Marlboros. Zur Nedden and his woman companion, who was the province's minister of health, juggled demanding careers with a packed engagement calendar and a bustling household of teenaged girls from their previous marriages. His friends were well-heeled, and attractive.

Seidler kept company until late in the evening with a bawdy group of Viennese politicians and celebrities. He managed on only a few hours of sleep a night and was often at his office at 6:30 A.M. on Sundays. Zur Nedden liked to spend his weekends at his second house in the mountains. Seidler was known for rushing down the street, speaking rapidly and unself-consciously into his cell phone. Zur Nedden had no problem putting his calls on hold.

Curiosity had driven both men to become involved in the Iceman project, and their preexisting relationships with Platzer guaranteed that they would have roles. But both understood too that the Iceman was an opportunity to profile themselves and their work. Zur Nedden, whose clinic was generally admired in Austria and Germany, neither wanted nor needed another big project on his plate, but there was work to do, so he invited specialists to join him in analyzing the Iceman's images. In the fall of 1992, he began exchanging visits with Dr. William A. Murphy, Jr., a celebrated American radiologist, then at the Washington University School of Medicine in Saint Louis, who had participated in other prehistoric forensic cases.*

For Seidler, however, the Iceman was a godsend for him and his department, which was not particularly well known. Seidler felt in-

*Murphy subsequently moved to the University of Texas M. D. Anderson Cancer Center in Houston.

tellectually isolated, even though he thrived on being a little bit different from most of his colleagues. Whoever did good research on the Iceman would find an international audience. Inevitably, that would lead to international connections for him and his graduate students. Seidler found himself spearheading research and encouraging other scientists, mainly at the University of Vienna, to get involved. Though he vigilantly controlled access to the Iceman, Platzer seemed uninterested in conducting much research himself. But Seidler saw the Iceman as a gold mine of interesting projects, and he thought the obvious first step was to try to get an article on the Iceman published in *Science*. If he succeeded, it would be a first for him and most of the other authors. With Platzer's blessing, Seidler initiated several lines of research into the man's life and death. The most pressing was the one that was hardest to answer: How did he die?

The forensic doctors had not been able to pinpoint a cause of death, but they had eliminated the assumption that he had fallen into a crevasse and perished. The body bore little resemblance to corpses swept down mountains in glaciers. Moreover, the glaciologist Patzelt had reported that the site was probably free of ice at the time the man died. Virtually every researcher now accepted the assumption that poor weather had forced the man to seek shelter in the trench, where he had died right on top of the boulder on which he was found.

The corpse showed no apparent external injuries or sign of fatal infection. Since no standard autopsy was going to be done, the scientists had hoped that zur Nedden's images might uncover some obvious cause of death, but they were barely more informative. The X rays and CAT scans did reveal that the man's heart, lungs, stomach, intestines, liver, and kidneys had shrunken to almost nothing. All that showed up in the first images were the spine, the ribs, and a lot of wispy material in the cavity. The organs were so desiccated that zur Nedden's team initially had a hard time identifying them. Whereas CAT scans on a normal human might reveal signs of pathology, the desiccation meant that researchers would probably have to take samples of the organs in order to learn anything about them.

The brain had shrunk to the size of a large orange, and it rocked around in the skull, anchored only by the large bundle of nerves that ran into the neck. The CAT scans revealed that the brain was fractured along several lines, just as a frozen and brittle object would shatter. Zur Nedden speculated that these fractures had occurred during the recovery, when the man's head had repeatedly struck the ice as people tried to lift it out. The brain's shrinkage seemed to be less severe than that in the rest of the body. Zur Nedden guessed that it might be because the skull was a better preservative than the skin.

Zur Nedden was particularly interested in sampling the slightly darker part of the Iceman's brain that one of the neurologists had suggested might be a sign of a stroke, where a weakened blood vessel bursts and hemorrhages into the brain tissue. Strokes do not always lead to death, though they usually result in impaired function. It was an idea worth pursuing, and zur Nedden indicated to Platzer that when the time came to take samples from the brain, he would like to get one. That procedure was, however, not yet on the agenda.

Zur Nedden noticed other potential warning signs about the man's general health as well.* The CAT scans revealed a heavily calcified region in what was probably the man's abdominal aorta—the largest artery in the body, at the point where it breaks into the main vessels that go to the legs—as well as in the carotid artery, which carries blood from the heart to the neck. This was a clear sign of arteriosclerosis—hardened arteries—a condition that occurs when plaques adhere to the walls of the arteries, partly blocking the flow of blood. Once that happens, the heart must work ever harder to push the blood, since the once flexible arteries are now hardened and cannot help push it along. As people age, their arteries inevitably harden, and smoking, eating too much red meat, and exercising too little tend to speed the process. But the Iceman was not very old, and zur Nedden was amazed at how much plaque had already accumulated. Possibly he had some metabolic disposition toward hardened arteries. As curious as the condition was, however, it was not enough on which to build a theory.

In the fall of 1992, a year after the discovery, Seidler's paper, written with Platzer, zur Nedden, Spindler, and others, was published

---

*Zur Nedden's images also revealed at least one sign of good health: The Iceman's teeth had no caries.

in *Science*. The researchers endorsed a commonsense hypothesis about the Iceman's cause of death. The man, they wrote, "was in a state of exhaustion perhaps as a consequence of adverse weather conditions. He therefore may have laid down in a small depression, fallen asleep, and froze to death."[1]

Evidence for this was circumstantial and came mainly from the left side of the man's head. Seidler had noted that the skin on the forehead there was scarred with deep, pebbly impressions. The flap of the ear was turned sharply over along a more or less straight line, as sometimes happens when it is slept on. Seidler figured that the man, exhausted and confused, in a hypothermic state, might simply have lain down on his left side, with his head on the boulder. The man's arms would have been in front of him, pointing toward his legs. The bumpy surface of the rock had pressed into his face and left impressions that eventually froze into place. Apparently, he did not shift his head so that his ear was not trapped. Seidler guessed that the man's strength was so depleted that he was not even capable of that.

Zur Nedden had found another indication in his X rays that Ötzi was no stranger to extreme cold. In the small toe of the left foot, zur Nedden spotted signs of frostbite: The space between the end and middle bones of the little toe was much smaller than normal, and there was a three-millimeter-wide hole in the bone of the middle toe.[2] Zur Nedden interpreted this as damage from recurrent frostbite. This did not mean that the man had been suffering from frostbitten toes when he died, but it did suggest that he had experience with extreme conditions. The most recent episode of frostbite probably had occurred not more than six months before his death.

Seidler also liked the hypothermia hypothesis because of the Iceman's position on the rock: He was not huddled up protectively with his back against a rock. He was lying facedown, and his arms were stretched out, as if struggling to pull himself onward. There had been one attempt to explain this position. Early on in the research, two Innsbruck scientists who had studied many glacier corpses suggested that the Iceman might have partly disrobed just before he died, which explained why his torso was naked during the recovery. "Often before death by hypothermia, the victims para-

A CORPSE IN THE ICE

The first picture of the Iceman. On September 19, 1991, while hiking in
the Alps along the Austria-Italy border, Helmut and Erika Simon
stumbled upon a corpse melting out of glacial ice.

HELMUT SIMON

A MISSING HIKER
OR AN ARCHAEOLOGICAL FIND?

The day before their discovery, Helmut and Erika Simon hiked to the summit of the Similaun, less than two miles from the spot where the Iceman lay.

COURTESY HELMUT SIMON

Curious artifacts lay on a rocky ledge above the corpse's head. From lower left to top right: a whittled stick, later identified as the bow; an ax; and wooden remains amid string and fur.

ANTON KOLER

September 21, 1991. The first, unsuccessful recovery attempt by an Austrian gendarme uncovered the corpse's hips and revealed strange tattoos on the lower back.

GERLINDE HAID

September 21, 1991. Celebrity mountaineer Reinhold Messner *(right)* suspected that the corpse might be hundreds of years old. His climbing partner, Hans Kammerlander, unwittingly used one of the artifacts from the site as a prop.

COURTESY PAUL HANNY

Alois Pirpamer, Hans Kammerlander, Reinhold Messner, and Hans Haid, photographed at the Similaun Hütte on September 21, 1991, were among a dozen people who saw the corpse while it was still packed in the ice. Messner alerted the media to the strange discovery, and it quickly became front-page news.

COURTESY PAUL HANNY

THE RECOVERY OF
AN "UNIDENTIFIED CORPSE"

September 23, 1991. Despite warnings that the corpse might be of archaeological significance, no archaeologist was present as gendarme Roman Lukasser *(foreground)* and Rainer Henn, a professor of forensic medicine from the University of Innsbruck, dug the corpse out of the ice using an ice pick and a ski pole.

ORF/TONE MATHIS

Rainer Henn *(left foreground)* and the local undertaker load the corpse into a coffin for transport to Innsbruck.

WERNER NOSKO

THE FIRST EXAMINATION

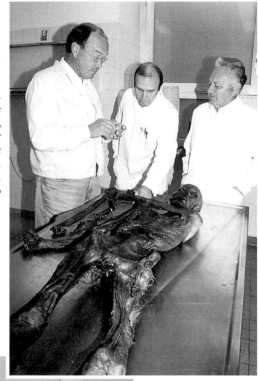

September 24, 1991. Summoned to the office of the medical examiner in Innsbruck, archaeologist Konrad Spindler *(left)* estimated that the corpse was four thousand years old. Rainer Henn is at right.
WERNER NOSKO

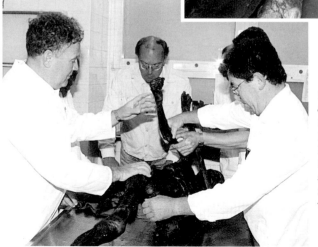

Inadvertently contaminating the Iceman with their own DNA, medical examiner Hans Unterdorfer *(left)*, Konrad Spindler *(center)*, and others examined the now-thawed corpse.
WERNER NOSKO

UNIQUE EQUIPMENT
FROM A PREHISTORIC LIFE

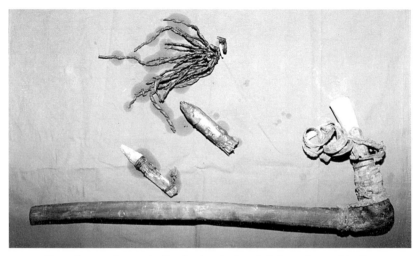

Top to bottom: the tassel of leather bands threaded through a marble disc, the retoucheur, a flint-bladed dagger, and the ax, the first of its type ever found with the blade attached.

WERNER NOSKO

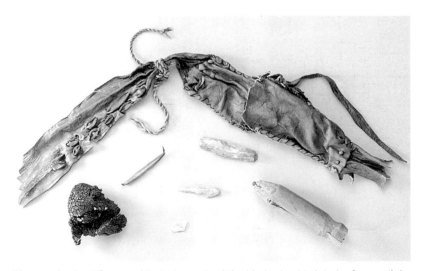

The torn leather "fanny pack" *(top)* contained the black, shredded tinder fungus *(left, bottom)* and the three flint tools *(center right, top to bottom)*. The slender antler point with the bent tip *(center left)* was inside the quiver. At lower right, the retoucheur.

CHRISTIN BEECK/ROMAN-GERMANIC CENTRAL MUSEUM

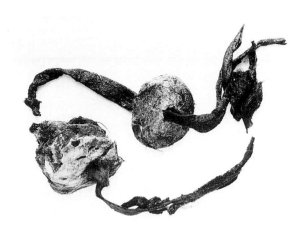

Two mushrooms threaded on leather straps.
CHRISTIN BEECK/ROMAN-GERMANIC CENTRAL MUSEUM

The bearskin hat, recovered during Andreas Lippert's second excavation, summer 1992.
CHRISTIN BEECK/ROMAN-GERMANIC CENTRAL MUSEUM

THE SCIENTIFIC TEAM IS ASSEMBLED

Innsbruck anatomist
Werner Platzer kept the
corpse in a freezer and
controlled access to it.

B. FOWLER

In Trento, Italy, archaeologist
Annaluisa Pedrotti suspected that
the corpse's ax might be made
of copper rather than bronze.

B. FOWLER

Anthropologist Horst Seidler
of the University of Vienna
suggested that the Iceman
may have died of hypothermia.

B. FOWLER

X rays by Innsbruck radiologist Dieter zur Nedden revealed that the Iceman had several broken ribs.
B. FOWLER

Following a dispute with Spindler, archaeologist Andreas Lippert was blacklisted from the project.
COURTESY
ANDREAS LIPPERT

THE MYSTERY OF THE UNFINISHED BOW AND ARROW

At the Roman-Germanic Central Museum in Mainz, Germany, prehistorian and conservator Markus Egg found damage on the artifacts that he believed had occurred during the Iceman's lifetime.
B. FOWLER

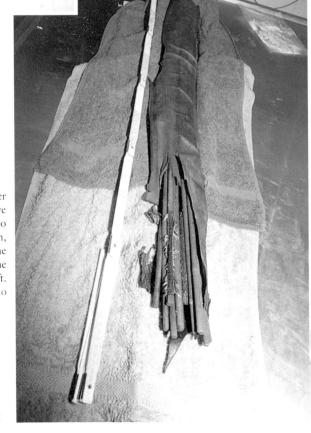

The damaged quiver was packed with twelve unfinished and two finished, but broken, arrows. Note the feathers visible on one end of a broken shaft.
WERNER NOSKO

The tips of the two finished, broken arrows.
CHRISTIN BEECK/ROMAN-GERMANIC
CENTRAL MUSEUM

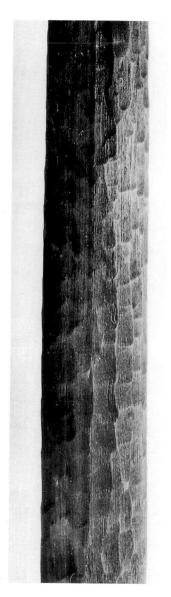

Whittle marks visible on the longbow surface
hinted that it had not been completed
at the time of the Iceman's death.
CHRISTIN BEECK/
ROMAN-GERMANIC CENTRAL MUSEUM

IS THE ICEMAN A FAKE?

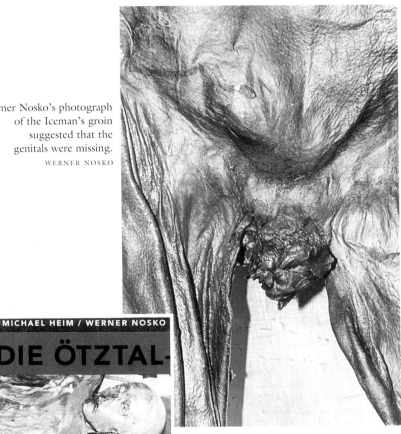

Werner Nosko's photograph of the Iceman's groin suggested that the genitals were missing.

WERNER NOSKO

The Ötztal Forgery: Anatomy of an Archaeological Farce, by Michael Heim and Werner Nosko, claimed that the Iceman was a castrated Egyptian mummy that had been planted in the ice.

ARCHAEOLOGISTS TURN UP AMBIGUOUS CLUES TO THE ICEMAN'S LIFE

In the tiny village of Laces, archaeologist Hans Nothdurfter discovered a stone statue-menhir with carvings that resembled the Iceman's artifacts.
KARL GRUBER

The statue-menhir from Laces depicted numerous axes similar to that of the Iceman.
HANS NOTHDURFTER

WHAT THE BOTANIST SAW

Botanist Klaus Oeggl's team at the University of Innsbruck sifted through hundreds of pounds of organic material found at the site.
B. FOWLER

Reassembled from the smashed pieces found in the ice, the birch-bark container apparently held embers wrapped in leaves.
ROMAN-GERMANIC CENTRAL MUSEUM, CHRISTIN BEECK

Shortly before he died, the Iceman plucked fresh maple leaves; the pattern of the leaves' tear was a clue to the season of the Iceman's death.
SOUTH TYROL MUSEUM OF ARCHAEOLOGY, A. OCHSENREITER

THE PROBLEM WITH THE BROKEN RIBS

American radiologist William A. Murphy, Jr., doubted that the rib breaks had occurred before the Iceman's death.

B. FOWLER

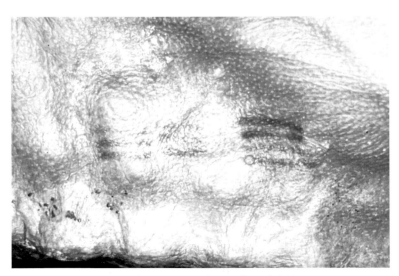

Were these tattoos a therapy for arthritis?

SOUTH TYROL MUSEUM OF ARCHAEOLOGY, M. SAMADELLI

A FINAL RESTING PLACE?

The Iceman on display in the museum built for
him in Bolzano (South Tyrol).

doxically remove part of their clothing because of a sudden feeling of warmth," wrote Edda Ambach and others in a letter to the British medical journal *The Lancet*.[3] "In addition, mental confusion often leads to uncoordinated movements, such as crawling. . . . We believe that paradoxical undressing in the cold and the discovery of the victim in the prone position as a consequence of uncoordinated movements are additional clues that the ice-man died of hypothermia and not of a natural cause, such as myocardial infarction." None of the other researchers rushed to embrace this idea, but neither had they come up with a better explanation for his state of partial undress.

The authors of the *Science* article backed the idea that the mummy was found in his death pose. But they also granted that the ice had moved him slightly since his death. For while there were pebble impressions on the man's left temple, Helmut Simon's photograph showed the corpse facedown. Neither his left temple nor his left ear was pressed up against the boulder at the moment of the Simons' discovery. The dozen or so people who had seen the man embedded in the ice described him as lying across his left arm.

Seidler suggested that the awkward position resulted as the body was turned from its left side to the stomach. The turning also explained the few deformations on the corpse's face. The man's upper lip was pushed up and to the right, and his nose was pressed up in the same direction. His left arm seemed to be at such an uncomfortable angle that they assumed it, too, had shifted under steady pressure from the ice.[4]

The article also provided new information on the man's age at death. The initial estimate, based on the analysis of the wear on the man's teeth, had been between thirty-five and forty, but, using zur Nedden's CAT scans of the skull, Seidler arrived at a significantly different estimate. At birth, a child's skull is not a seamless bony shell but rather a collage of separate bony plates that expands as the child grows. The plates finally grow together by adulthood. Though the method's reliability is often questioned, Seidler used it to determine that the sutures between the plates were closed but still visible, which was typical of someone between twenty-five and thirty years old. By either results the man had definitely reached adulthood. By the standards of his age, he was hardly young. Only

2 percent of the population of that time ever reached their fortieth year.[5]

The new information on the man's age at death seemed to fit well with another of zur Nedden's team's findings. The Iceman apparently had osteoarthritis, a slow degeneration of the joints, in his neck and especially in his right hip. In normal people, arthritis showed up on CAT scans as a narrowing of the joint space between the bones. But because the Iceman was so desiccated, his cartilage was thinner, and the doctors had to look for other symptoms— namely, lighter areas of bone, known as lucencies; little bumps of bone, known as spurs; and extra dense areas of bone, known as sclerosis. All three were present in his neck and hip. Generally, this kind of arthritis, which is believed to be genetic, shows up in places where the cartilage between the bones is subject to extra wear and tear, often because of the activity a person is engaged in. A person with a certain genetic predisposition who operates a jackhammer, for example, may develop it in his arms. Arthritis is common, but in a man younger than forty, it was rather unexpected. However, the rigorous lifestyle of a prehistoric Alpine inhabitant might have tried the joints. Zur Nedden refused to speculate about whether the man had been in pain. There was an enormous discrepancy between clinical findings and patients' complaints, he liked to say. Sometimes doctors could find nothing wrong with a person who was in constant pain, and on other occasions a person who seemed well was discovered to have what was normally a debilitating illness.

One of the last issues the researchers took up in the *Science* article was the question of the missing genitals. There was other damage to the corpse—the destruction of the left hip area, for example—but one of the article's footnotes discussed the touchy topic of the missing penis and testes. Whereas earlier speculation had centered on the possibility that predators had nibbled at the man's genitals, the scientists now speculated about an accidental removal: "During the earlier recovery attempts the corpse was lifted out of the glacier ice in such a way that the trousers were torn," they wrote. "Currently the most probable hypothesis . . . is that the prominent genitals, which were frozen to the clothing, were detached during the earlier manipulations."[6]

The authors did not wager a guess as to how the testes had gotten out of the scrotum. During Andreas Lippert's second excavation, he had collected a significant amount of human tissue. If the penis had been shorn off, there was a good chance that it would eventually be identified among those remains.

Though the loss was viewed as somewhat comical by the media, the scientists kept a straight face when talking about it. It was not a meaningless loss. The scientists might have investigated, for example, whether the man was circumcised. The removal of the penile foreskin has been practiced since ancient times, usually to denote membership in a certain group, and it must have had roots in prehistory.

Seidler believed that the results presented in the *Science* article were just the tip of the iceberg. Even a year after the discovery, Platzer reported that he was still sifting through requests from scientists around the world who wanted a piece of the Iceman. One imminent project involved Svante Pääbo, a young Swede who was a pioneer in the study of ancient DNA. The marketing effort, though it still had not picked up much speed, depended on a steady flow of fascinating inquiries like these. Still flush with the public attention this man had brought to their work, the scientists were confident that they would be delivering results for years to come.

When Lawrence Barfield was a student, the course of European prehistory could be summed up in just three words: *Lux ex orient,* the light comes from the east. The Fertile Crescent was believed to be the birthplace of civilization, the source of all new technology and writing. Over the millennia, civilization gradually swept across less developed Europe. One of those new technologies was copper metallurgy.

Like all the archaeologists of his generation, Barfield was taught that the metallurgy that showed up at early Italian Copper Age sites such as Remedello had come from copper-using people of the eastern Mediterranean and Anatolia, either by a simple diffusion by traders or by the immigration of these Eastern people themselves. The same process was said to explain the spread of agriculture. The evidence for this diffusionist view, as it was known, was in the supposed cultural and technological parallels among widely separated geographical regions. One such parallel was the one between the Remedello axes and those from the East.

But with the development of radiocarbon dating in the 1950s and its application to archaeology in the next decade, researchers could for the first time date sites in absolute terms. The results were not only surprising but revolutionary. The same technologies were discovered to be relatively contemporaneous in different parts of Europe. They suggested that copper metallurgy either was developed locally or spread from the Balkans, where it developed much earlier than in the Aegean. The new method spelled the end of the diffusionist view. Increasingly, the development and decay of certain technologies were viewed as having multiple sources and complex histories. The idea that all metal technology in northern Italy flowed out of the Remedello culture might well be incorrect. The person who made the Iceman's ax might have been influenced by developments in the Balkans or even north of the Alps. The technology might even have been native to the region.

Since the discovery of the Iceman's ax, archaeologists had been contorting the accepted chronologies of the northern Italian region to accommodate the unexpected low-flanged copper ax. One had suggested pushing back the date of the start of the Remedello culture from 2800 B.C.E. to 3300 B.C.E. Konrad Spindler's department, which was trying to coordinate a few archaeological projects following the discovery, also tended to emphasize the Iceman's connection to the Remedello culture. As far as Barfield could tell, the connection was based almost wholly on the similarity in the ax. But what, Barfield asked, was the Remedello culture?

The entire Remedello complex amounted to little more than 119 graves and their contents. In fact, archaeologists had very little information about the people who were buried there or about how far their influence extended. They were not even sure how long that cemetery had been in use.

Annaluisa Pedrotti's early recognition of similarities between the Hauslabjoch ax and the copper version from Remedello was useful because it demonstrated that the Iceman's low-flanged copper ax was not unique. But Barfield, and Pedrotti herself, had quickly grown doubtful that the Remedello cemetery could reveal much about the Iceman, not least because of the hundreds of years that separated them. They doubted strongly that the similarity of the axes indicated a direct cultural link between the Hauslabjoch and Remedello. The simple fact was that for hundreds of years copper axes throughout the region, even over the mountains in Germany, did not differ very much at all—one could see that plainly in the statue-menhirs, in which they all had virtually the same profile. A higher flange here or there or a straight neck rather than a curved one might not be all-important indicators of cultural brotherhood after all.

Barfield understood, however, that technologically advanced copper axes such as the Iceman's did not just turn up in a vacuum. Whoever made the Hauslabjoch ax knew a lot about metallurgy. Markus Egg's team in Mainz had reported that the Iceman's ax was made of cast copper. An X ray of the blade had revealed a lentil-sized hollow in the neck, a typical casting mistake. That meant that the maker had not just taken a lump of native copper, as naturally occurring pure copper is known, and pounded it into the desired form. Neither had he simply heated up the native copper, a process called annealing, and hammered it into the shape. Instead, the creator of the Iceman's ax had used the more complex technology of smelting and casting, which entailed melting down copper or copper ores, such as copper oxide or copper carbonate, in a crucible. Not until casting was invented did copper become an important part of the economy. A normal campfire did not get hot enough to start the desired reaction, so oxygen had to be pumped in through bellows, blowpipes, or some other method.

Using tongs, the smith then lifted the crucible out of the fire and poured the molten material into a mold. Archaeologists have found various kinds of molds. Sometimes they were just open forms, like cupcake pans. Others were constructed of two mirror-image pieces of carved sandstone that, fitted together, created a mold between them and were filled from a hole in the top. While filling the mold, the smith who made the Hauslabjoch ax had had a little problem. As the mold, probably the two-piece type, filled up, the metal cooled quickly, and near the top a tiny air bubble became trapped inside. Egg noted that the smith had realized the fault, for after the ax had cooled and was removed from the mold, he had tried to hammer it in, perhaps to close up the hole. But this set off a little epidemic of cracks from the hole into the ax, none of which was visible with the naked eye.

The ax then had to be hammered into shape. The smith had pounded up the long edges of the blade so as to create the low flanges, forming a slightly concave surface along the length of the blade where the wooden haft would be snugly inserted. The cutting edge of the blade had also been hammered, and this had caused it to flare out a bit. The X rays revealed a second small hollow near the blade edge and another, rather large, crack, which Egg assumed had happened during hammering. The last step before hafting was to polish and sharpen the blade, and for this the smith had probably used a stone. Even if the Iceman had not made his own blade, he must have known how to sharpen it on a stone. When freshly sharpened, it would have been an impressive tool or weapon. During the Iceman's life, it was probably bright reddish-orange.

If such ax production was happening in the region around the Hauslabjoch, Barfield thought, why had archaeologists not found more evidence of it? He wondered what had become of all the other copper that must have been there. Years earlier, Barfield had noted that the northern Italian statue-menhirs were spread across approximately the same region in which a certain type of collective burial was practiced. At a collective burial site he had excavated known as Manerba del Garda, about halfway between the Hauslabjoch and Remedello, he found that individuals were left at exposed communal gravesites with a few grave goods, often of copper, beside them. This burial practice differed sharply from Remedello burials, further to the south. Once their flesh had decayed, the Manerba bones were gathered up and placed inside an ossuary constructed against the rock face. The bones of the dead thus became mixed up together. Built of large boulders, smaller rocks, and paving stones, the ossuary received the bones of the dead as well as offerings from the living, such as beads, pottery, and possibly objects made of metal, such as daggers or axes.[7] At some time, probably after the abandonment of the graves, people had just picked up the valuable copper and taken it away, he concluded. The copper was then recycled. At another excavation in the 1980s, Barfield found a copper rivet that had been part of a dagger handle, which he guessed was the remnant of an offering left for the dead. He took that rivet as evidence that these people *did* have copper, but it had been picked up and taken away. Possibly the metal had survived at Remedello because people had either forgotten it or believed it was sacrilegious to open up graves. Just because archaeologists had found so little copper in northern Italy was no reason to believe that it had not been around. Barfield would not be surprised that the copper tradition in northern Italy might be even older than that at Remedello. After all, most parts of the Alps—the Ötztal was an exception—were full of copper and copper deposits, and they were relatively easy to mine.

According to Gerhard Sperl, an Austrian expert in metallurgy, the ore for the ax probably had come from malachite, copper carbonate that appears naturally as a bluish-green efflorescence on rock and cliff sides throughout much of the Alps. Prehistoric people first mined it by scraping and flaking off the layers that developed when chalcopyrite reacted with water. Since the reaction kept occurring and thereby replenished the malachite, a miner could visit the same spot again and again. Sperl estimated that one ax required a section of malachite of about one square meter and two or three millimeters thick.

When malachite is smelted, it yields a very pure copper, like that found in the Hauslabjoch ax. Occasionally, trace elements in copper can provide information on where the copper came from. The composition of the copper in the Hauslabjoch ax, however, was utterly common, Sperl said, and could have come from anywhere.

Partly due to the general difficulty in understanding the structure of Copper Age societies, Barfield had little idea about who the metallurgists in a community were. In ancient Rome, the smiths were slaves, while in other societies they held a quasi-religious status. In other societies, certain families or even classes of people were the smiths, or they were specialists who went from village to village offering their services. Barfield wondered whether those who mined the metal also worked it, or whether a division of labor existed between miners and smiths.

The Iceman's possession of the ax had initially suggested to the archaeologists that he might have been hunting for copper deposits in the region. But when it became clear that the Ötztal was one of the few places in the Alps with no copper source, the idea appeared to be doused. If metallurgy had been practiced in the Iceman's home village, then archaeologists would expect him to have more items made of copper, such as an awl, perhaps, or some kind of amulet. As it was, he carried just one copper item with him that, based on its prominent depiction in the statue-menhirs, might also have been a prestige object. Barfield knew the archaeologists needed much more data from the region before they could say more about the origins of that precious ax. But one thing seemed certain: While the Iceman might well have known firsthand the wonders of metallurgy, no one believed that a simple herdsman had made his own ax.

As research continued in Innsbruck, Vienna, and Mainz, the South Tyroleans were slowly starting to make plans to retrieve Ötzi once the scientists had finished their work. In the minds of those responsible for the cultural and political life of the province, there was never any doubt about what was to be done with the frozen mummy upon his return. "*Homo tirolensis*," as the province's governor, as well as a few scientists, persisted in calling the man, had not only become a symbol of South Tyrolean autonomy but also promised to be the tourist attraction ne plus ultra in a region where tourism was a mainstay of the economy.*

In the elaborate tourist brochures issued by virtually every hamlet and valley in the region, South Tyrol was portrayed as a land inhabited by pretty blond girls romping through mountain fields of wildflowers and by toothless farmers in traditional blue smocks and feathered loden caps. The message was that in South Tyrol problems and pleasures were both simple and local, and little had changed in the last century or so. Daily life for most South Tyroleans was, of course, more complex. Many farmers had moved to the cities. Those who had stayed on the land had learned that earn-

---

*Despite the fact that it was not a true scientific designation, the name *Homo tirolensis* began showing up in publications, including the volumes of scientific papers issued by the University of Innsbruck. Once, during a visit to the United States, in the middle of an interview with a reporter from the *Chicago Tribune,* Horst Seidler and Dieter zur Nedden briefly broke into German to discuss whether they were supposed to be calling the Iceman *Homo tirolensis.* They decided that it did not matter.

ing a living solely from farming was nigh impossible, so they had turned to tourism to add to their income. A nice symbiosis had emerged between the two industries. Both required their practitioners to be at home most of the time. Many rural Tyroleans in both countries had built extensions onto their picturesque farmhouses or ran restaurants or snack bars. Villages that just a few decades earlier had been nothing but a few farmhouses hugging a church now bulged with little tourist shops, hotels, restaurants, and parking lots filled with fancy tourist buses that somehow could manage even the narrowest and steepest mountain roads. Paradoxically, tourism both depended on and threatened the good, clean agricultural landscape.

The Iceman fit easily into the stereotypes promoted by the tourism offices. The leather clothes he wore were reminiscent of the region's lederhosen, and his wooden backpack frame was similar to a kind of Tyrolean backpack that had survived into the early twentieth century and was known as the *Kraxe*. Like the grandparents of many Tyroleans, this prehistoric man was perhaps a pastoralist who had eked out a living herding sheep or cows and planting crops on the steep mountainsides. Though South Tyroleans nowadays enjoy Europe's generally high standards of living, the history of extreme poverty and hardship of life in the mountains forms part of their ethnic identity. They seemed to share with the man a sense of place. He must have trod the same rocky Schnalstal and Ötztal paths modern people did and had his own names for the snowy peaks and valleys of the region. Even the man's death was familiar. Tyroleans know the awesome ferocity of the Alps.

A few years after the discovery, Walter Leitner, Konrad Spindler's right-hand man and a specialist on the Neolithic period, was hired by the Tyrolean Office of Tourism to speak about the Iceman at a convention of American tour operators. At that point, the touristic offerings were few, since none of the artifacts was on display. A few guides did offer hikes up to the site from either side of the mountain. The point was rather that the Iceman was a nice thing with which to be identified. Tyrol as the home of Ötzi, the Iceman, was an obvious formula.

Within a year of the discovery, both Vent, Austria, and Unser Frau, Italy, had begun planning exhibitions on the man. Vent's right to the representation of the Iceman lay in the fact that the corpse had been delivered there after its recovery. Unser Frau, meanwhile, was in the province that rightfully owned the corpse and had also been the starting point for Helmut and Erika Simon's hike. Tempers flared when officials in each village realized that the other was also organizing an exhibition. Though separated by just a few miles as the crow flies, Vent and Unser Frau were more than sixty miles apart over hazardous mountain roads passable only for a few months a year. Their regions—the Ötztal and the Schnalstal, respectively—though similar in their offerings were distinct and competing tourist destinations. Tourists might conceivably choose which side of the Alps to visit based on where the exhibit was. Since most visitors stayed more than one night, a community without an exhibit could face a loss of at least a few hundred dollars per group. After a few heated exchanges, organizers agreed to have two exhibits with a joint brochure and posters.

Of course, the ultimate tourist draw would be the frozen man himself. Early on, when scientists voiced doubts over the technical feasibility of such a display, one Austrian official quietly proposed to the South Tyroleans that copies of the corpse and the artifacts be made out of plastic. One would go to Austria and the other to South Tyrol, and each province could display theirs as they wished. He reasoned that limiting the number of copies would preserve their value and attraction for the public. But the South Tyrolean officials had no interest in diluting the real thing by making copies. Indeed, they were ever more aware of the treasure that had dropped into their laps. An exhibition of photographs, replicas of the man's artifacts, and a plastic copy of his corpse, no matter how good, would not have the appeal of the authentic 5,300-year-old flesh-and-blood Iceman.

They were not the only ones pondering the Iceman's display value. Aware of the possibly significant revenue to be earned off a display of the corpse, Helmut and Erika Simon rejected a onetime reward of six thousand dollars offered to them by South Tyrol and, via their lawyer, asked for ten times that amount as well as 10 percent of sales earned off the corpse. In response, Governor Luis Durnwalder questioned whether the Simons were, in fact, the first to find the corpse. Nevertheless, he repeated the initial offer. The

Simons were enraged that their status had been mocked. Accepting the paltry six thousand dollars was now out of the question. Instead, they were considering taking the matter to court.

Meanwhile, South Tyrolean officials were listening carefully to the companies that came to them with proposals that would make an exhibition of the corpse itself feasible. While some of the province's archaeologists were ambivalent about a display, some for reasons of technical feasibility, the politicians ardently pursued the possibility. The cultural affairs adviser for South Tyrol, Bruno Hosp, argued that if the corpse could be shown without damaging it, it should be. Hosp was viewed as a respectable and intelligent spokesperson on cultural affairs and one who did not shy away from opinions that might offend. His criterion was that the display have scientific and educational merit. He was also an elected official, and his sense was that his constituency wanted to get a look at the Iceman.

One of the first to emerge publicly against the idea of a display was Hans Rotter, a priest and theologian at the University of Innsbruck. Rotter argued that people care what happens to their corpse, even long after death. The fact that the Iceman died without a proper burial made it all the more important that his mortal remains be treated respectfully. While Rotter saw nothing wrong in autopsying the man or allowing scientists free rein in their studies, he called on the scientists to protect the man from the "irreverent curiosity of tourists" and not to "sacrifice considerations of reverence to economic interests."[8] "Precisely the fact that the Iceman from Hauslabjoch is so well-preserved and his human features are so clearly visible does call for a certain piety," he wrote.[9]

The South Tyroleans certainly did want to head off charges that the corpse was going to be used like a Mickey Mouse in a prehistoric Disneyland. The charge of crass commercialization implied by a comparison with the American theme park was a favorite one among European critics. The challenge was to keep something that truly was a sensation from appearing too sensationalized. One early plan was to allow the mummy to be displayed only indirectly, on a video monitor linked to a camera continually recording the corpse. Because normal light would eventually destroy the mummy's tissues and could potentially catalyze other degenerative processes in the soaked corpse, the company proposing the project would design a system that used special lighting. To house the display, a former bank in the center of Bolzano was suggested as a site for a museum of prehistory.

As the South Tyroleans' plans for the museum developed, Spindler and Platzer surprised many of their colleagues by coming out squarely against an exhibition of the corpse, agreeing with Rotter that it was unethical. Though guidelines for museums advised curators to consider local tastes before displaying human remains, many European museums freely exhibited human corpses. The Danish showed their many bog bodies, and the British Museum's Lindow Man was one of its most popular displays. European churches and crypts also contained the occasional saint's skull and other skeletal parts, and a few of these even had fleshy remains. There had been little if any debate on whether these things should be shown, and neither the politicians nor the archaeologists of the region, who, after all, made it their business to dig up graves, expected that people would object to the display of the Iceman's corpse, even if the province did make money off it. Notwithstanding the Innsbruck scientists' protests, the preparations to display the Iceman in South Tyrol moved slowly forward.

Like Spindler, Werner Platzer had quickly grown sensitized to the integrity of the Iceman, and yet that meant something very different for him. When Platzer spoke about the scientists applying to do research on the mummy, he sounded like the corpse's protector rather than a leader of an international and interdisciplinary investigation into a curious scientific phenomenon. If he had let them have their way, Platzer often said, nothing would remain of the corpse.

Much research would indeed require samples of the flesh. The Research Institute for Alpine Prehistory had received many research proposals that required tiny samples of skin, hair, or organs in order to answer questions of diet, nutrition, genetics, trace elements, and disease. There was no way to do the science without cutting into and removing tiny bits of the corpse. But there was not nearly enough of the Iceman for everyone to get a piece. Samples would be destroyed or greatly altered in the course of the research. In meetings and conversations with researchers, Platzer repeatedly emphasized the need to go forth cautiously, step by tiny step, and to ensure that no procedure jeopardize future research. At the same time, he claimed that this was a responsibility he would rather not have. He himself voiced no research interests in the Iceman, and he occasionally spoke wearily of all the planning ahead.

His primary interest and his early success lay in the Iceman's preservation, for which he and his colleagues had quickly developed an apparently effective, if cumbersome, system. Lying on a stretcher cushioned with a custom-fit foam pad, Ötzi was wrapped first in a sterile cloth, which was then covered with crushed ice. This bundle was next wrapped in a plastic sheet, topped with ice packs, and then wrapped in a second plastic sheet. This combination of cold and humidity kept the humidity next to the skin at between 96 and 98 percent. This was monitored by a sensor inside the innermost wrap. Cartons of crushed ice were placed on a shelf beneath the stretcher to help keep the humidity in the freezer itself at about 75 percent.[10] Unwrapping the mummy took at least five minutes, a considerable portion of the thirty total minutes Platzer allowed the corpse to remain outside the freezer during research episodes. Each time he was removed, all the ice and the sterile cloths had to be changed. Though the room in which the work was done was kept chilled, the body still thawed out a little bit every time it was removed.

The anatomist's first cautious move toward research involving tissues was to order special tools for the removal of tissue and organ samples. Platzer feared that normal stainless-steel surgical equipment might leave trace elements behind that could jeopardize the results of other studies of trace elements. He enlisted the help of a Massachusetts company called Acufex to manufacture the tools out of titanium, a very light and brittle metal that does not react with the body and is therefore used in such things as artificial joints. But the company was going to need at least many months to make the tools. A few scientists doubted the need for such instruments, noting that Platzer just had to be aware of what trace elements regular stainless-steel tools might leave behind. But Platzer, always mindful that the corpse belonged to another country, wanted no problems with the Italians or the South Tyroleans, and since he alone had the ultimate say on what got done, everyone would have to wait for the special instruments.

In the first year or so after the discovery, both the South Tyrolean

Commission and an informal group of international conservation experts occasionally convened in Innsbruck to discuss the latest in conservation and research. But as time went on and plans to sample the interior of the Iceman's body failed to materialize, the meetings were held less often, and communications became less frequent.

Moreover, because of the rigid division of the project between Spindler and Platzer, as well as the centralization of the entire project within the Research Institute for Alpine Prehistory, not even colleagues such as Markus Egg and Horst Seidler, who had several small projects running in Vienna, had good overviews of the project. While Spindler was thriving in his position as a spokesman, even while withholding certain results for use in his book and closely monitoring other researchers' contacts with journalists, Platzer, still angry over what he called the negative reporting about the Iceman's recovery, limited his own contact with the media and the public.

Asked directly by a journalist for information on the scientists involved in the research, Platzer sometimes balked, insisting that most scientists did not want to be bothered. Citing the contract, he refused to reveal the results of ongoing research and inexplicably dodged direct questions about who was doing the research. When the questioning turned in a direction in which he did not want to go, he simply called a halt to it. If, however, a journalist did ferret out a researcher, Platzer granted him or her permission to discuss the work.

Ironically, Charlotte Sengthaler, the public-relations representative, also had trouble getting information out of him. After creating a photo archive for the media and the corporate sponsor she still hoped to find, she asked Platzer for photographs and some video tape, but no material at all arrived from him. Sengthaler never got the thumbnail outlines of all the proposed research projects that she had requested either. If she was asking potential corporate sponsors for ten million dollars, she would have to provide a strict accounting of what the money would be used for.

On several occasions, Hans Moser asked Platzer for a comprehensive research plan. He was curious to see how the various proposals could be accommodated. But no plan ever surfaced. Until results were actually published, the only clue was a list of interested researchers and the titles of their proposed projects. Abetted by the contract, both Spindler and Platzer were able to indulge their own particular, if both restrictive, styles in public relations.

Platzer's predilection for control even extended to those few researchers who had received samples from the surface of the Iceman's body. In the winter of 1993, more than two years after the discovery, a team from the University of Munich laboratory of Svante Pääbo had arrived in Innsbruck to watch while their sample was removed from the Iceman's exterior. On that day, Platzer had scheduled not only the removal of samples for the DNA researchers but also a photo shoot by a German news magazine, which, under a deal not brokered by Sengthaler's firm, had recently paid the university a handsome sum for exclusive rights to photograph the corpse and to serialize part of Spindler's forthcoming book.

As the technicians removed the corpse from the freezer, one of Pääbo's researchers innocently began to take a few photographs of it from the hallway, where everyone not directly involved in the procedure was asked to stand. From inside the room, Platzer, muzzled with a surgical mask, said something to the man, but no one could understand him. The man continued to take occasional shots. Suddenly, Platzer stormed out into the hallway and, in a rage, grabbed the startled man's camera, opened it, yanked out the film, and threw it on the ground. Everyone stood around dumbly, amazed by his fury. Only the magazine photographer was obviously pleased.

Platzer later apologized for his reaction. But the incident had made an impression on the young researchers. In many ways, Platzer and Pääbo represented opposite ends of the spectrum of European science. Pääbo was a young Swede who had come of age in the competitive and open environment of an American lab, which he had, to some extent, replicated in Munich. His graduate students were not much younger than he was, called him by his first name, and, when he was not out of town, often sat down with him as a group for a typically healthful lunch in the lab. Conscious of how the study of human genes interested and concerned the public at large, Pääbo was a frequent contributor to popular publications such as *Scientific American*. He was also attentive to the ethical aspects of his work, such as the danger of reducing all of human behavior and history to the business of genes.

Platzer's department, in contrast, was stocked with a few trusty collaborators who were not allowed to overshadow their boss. Most of all, Platzer required deference. The people in Pääbo's lab had signed the project contract, and Platzer's outburst was a grim illus-

tration that the man in charge took it very seriously. Leaks were simply not to be tolerated.

Considering the popular and scientific expectations of DNA research, there was good reason to believe that the media would be
hot on the trail of those scientists exploring the Iceman's DNA. The
almost fantastic success of DNA studies in the previous decade suggested that the very key to the Iceman's identity might be unlocked
from the mysterious codes contained inside his cells. Ever since scientists had succeeded in developing a quick and easy method of
reading the chain of base pairs that make up DNA, the results had
been pouring in. Human health, history, and behavior (even
whether a person had been present at the scene of a crime) might
be read in the enigmatic sequence of base pairs. This "blueprint," as
scientists often call it, seemed to have no limits in its potential to reveal information about all forms of life.

Pääbo, a lanky fellow with a big grin, had already won a considerable reputation as a pioneer in ancient DNA studies, or molecular
archaeology, as it had quickly become known. In his short career, he
had initiated or participated in some of the field's defining moments. In the early 1980s, while a graduate student at the University of Uppsala in Sweden, he had an idea that no one else had
apparently thought of. Was it possible, he wondered, to retrieve and
clone DNA from an ancient source? Since he was also something of
an Egyptologist, Pääbo thought first of the DNA in the many
Egyptian mummies stored in museums across Europe. He suspected that if their DNA could be retrieved and examined, it might
provide some information on the relationships among Egyptian
rulers. Ancient DNA might be able to illuminate the course of history or prehistory.

With some difficulty, since curators were understandably cautious
about allowing samples to be taken from their precious charges,
Pääbo obtained tissue from several ancient Egyptian mummies.
After a few attempts, he believed he had succeeded in extracting
2,400-year-old DNA from one sample.* The strands were highly
degraded, broken into small pieces, but he was nevertheless de-

---

*Pääbo now believes that the DNA he retrieved was not, in fact, that of the
mummy.

lighted. Before he could finish his work and publish it, however, a group at the University of California at Berkeley led by Russell Higuchi and Allan C. Wilson announced that they had extracted DNA from the 140-year-old skin of a quagga, a zebralike animal of southern Africa that had become extinct a century ago. Comparing the quagga's DNA with that of other living members of the horse family, they found that it was much more closely related to the zebra than the horse. Although both Pääbo's and the Berkeley scientists' results later turned out to have problems, at the time the results were seen as doubly significant. Not only had they shown that DNA was still retrievable and identifiable long after an organism had died, but they also believed such procedures could answer questions of evolution and history. The field of molecular archaeology had been born.*

One elementary problem facing Pääbo and other DNA researchers in the 1980s was how to get enough copies of the section of the strand they were interested in studying to be able to measure and analyze it. The existing technique of molecular cloning was te-

---

*DNA (deoxyribonucleic acid) is a complex molecule that encodes the information required to create and operate the organism in whose cells it is found. The molecule is constructed of two parallel chains, each composed of four nucleotides—adenine, thymine, guanine, and cytosine—strung together in a variable sequence. Scientists believe that the particular sequence of nucleotides accounts for many differences among all living things, as well as among individuals of the same species. But few believe that genes alone determine how an organism will look and behave. No matter what the genes seem to say, the environment in which an organism lives still affects the outcome. The two parallel strands are held together by chemical bonds between complementary nucleotides. Adenine on one strand always pairs to thymine on the parallel strand, and guanine always pairs to cytosine. Every such union is called a "base pair."

Human DNA is located in two regions of the cell. Nuclear DNA, which makes up by far the largest amount—more than six billion base pairs—is contained within forty-six chromosomes in the cell nucleus and is responsible for the running of the organism.[11] A genome is one complete set of DNA instructions; half the nuclear DNA in a typical cell comes from the mother's genome, and half from the father's. Mitochondrial DNA (mtDNA) is found in the cell's mitochondria, organelles whose function has been analogized to that of a battery. Each mitochondrion—as many as five hundred are found in each cell—contains approximately 16,500 base pairs. Unlike nuclear DNA, mitochondrial DNA is passed to offspring intact from the mother. A gene is a particular sequence of base pairs—often several thousand base pairs long—that directs the production of one or more proteins, mainly enzymes, which manage the basic workings of an organism.

dious and almost impossible to replicate, a fatal flaw in a discipline where each hypothesis must be repeatedly subjected to experimental verification before it can become an accepted part of a theory.

But in 1985, a Californian chemist developed a relatively easy and reliable method of creating almost infinite quantities of any particular sequence of DNA.[12] Known as the polymerase chain reaction (PCR), the procedure fishes out a particular sequence of the genome and then directly multiplies it many times right in the test tube. The process works by heating DNA until the double strands break in two. A nucleotide soup is then added together with polymerase, an enzyme that rebuilds a complementary strand for each of the separated strands out of the loose nucleotides in the mixture. When the process is run once, the number of copies of the targeted section is doubled. With each run, the number grows exponentially.

The simplicity and relative reliability of PCR put sequence analysis of DNA within reach of many scientists, and soon there was hardly a biology laboratory in the United States that did not make use of it. In 1987, Pääbo moved to Berkeley for postdoctoral work in Wilson's lab. In 1988, Pääbo amplified mtDNA from the eight-thousand-year-old human brain from a bog site in Florida. Pääbo's efforts marked the first time PCR had been applied successfully to ancient tissues and kicked off a battle among several labs to see who could amplify the oldest bit of DNA.

While Pääbo had been getting started on the PCR work, other scientists in Wilson's lab had been investigating whether modern DNA might reveal information on human evolutionary history. In 1987, scientists in Wilson's lab announced that by analyzing the differences in mtDNA from people around the world, they had traced a small bit of mtDNA back to a woman who lived two hundred thousand years ago, probably in Africa.[13] Since mtDNA passes intact, except for random mutations, from mother to child, the researchers calculated the rate at which these mutations occur and from that how long it took modern-day mutations. The results suggested that the mtDNA of the Africans in the sample had begun diverging first, and that Europeans and Asians later diverged from some of these African branches.

Though the researchers later had to work out some bugs in their results, the usefulness of mtDNA in studying genetic evolution has been validated repeatedly in studies since then. The Berkeley researchers' conclusions also backed up those of another genetic researcher, Luigi Luca Cavalli-Sforza at Stanford University, who for decades had been plotting the frequency of hundreds of different gene sequences throughout the world. By examining the patterns of certain sequences, he sought to explain not only the origins of human populations but also the migrations of people around the globe.

The Iceman's place along the evolutionary time line was not in question: He was a very recent ancestor, a member of the *Homo* genus and the *sapiens* species. Pääbo was interested in his DNA for another reason. If, for example, the Iceman had a combination of genetic markers that have been observed only in a certain population, then the probability that he was related to that population would be quite high. With luck, they just might be able to say something about the Iceman's relations.

To Dr. Michael Heim, a producer for Bavarian Television in Munich, the University of Innsbruck's secretive attitude about the Iceman project seemed very fishy. He could not believe that they exercised such discretion just in order to make money. He wondered why no independent photographer had been allowed to take photographs of the corpse since the day of the press conference and why the names of the scientists working on the project were being kept from the public. Heim thought there was good reason to suspect that the university was hiding something, and he was determined to get to the bottom of it.

His earliest suspicions had come in November 1991, when he was reviewing footage of the year's big events in preparation for a year-in-review special. Like everyone else, Heim had initially marveled at the preservation of the prehistoric man and his curious equipment. As he pored over the video footage of the rescue and the press conferences, however, Heim detected inconsistencies. He had been raised in the mountains of southern Bavaria and served as a volunteer mountain rescuer for several decades. He knew the power of glaciers and had seen what bodies looked like when they came out of them. This man looked too good to have come out of a glacier, even one that was said not to have moved much. Something about the story just did not ring true.

In his search for more pictures, Heim had contacted Werner

Nosko, an Innsbruck photographer who had taken some of the earliest shots of the Iceman. Nosko was a young man with boundless nervous energy who worked out of a smoky office just five minutes from the university. He photographed news wherever and whatever it was, from corporate head shots to celebrities on Austrian ski vacations. On the wall of his office hung a framed front page of an Austrian tabloid with his photograph of Princess Diana on a ski lift. For a while it had been one of Nosko's most successful shots. But in September 1991, Nosko had happened to be in the fabled right place at the right time.

On assignment for the Austrian tabloid *Kurier,* Nosko had driven to Vent, arriving just in time to see Henn's recovery helicopter make a brief stopover there on the way to fetch the corpse. Ever alert, he had noticed that only three of the four seats in the helicopter were occupied. But when he asked whether he could ride along for the recovery, the pilot politely refused, citing concerns about the additional weight at the high altitude. After a little pleading from Nosko, however, he did agree to take Nosko's camera and take a few shots.

Ninety tense minutes later, the recovery crew landed safely in Vent with the corpse strapped to the bottom of the craft. Nosko quickly retrieved his camera from the pilot, who assured him he had taken pictures of the recovery, and then he raced back to Innsbruck to get them off to his paper. The next day, because of a tip from Hans Unterdorfer, the forensic doctor who also happened to be a family friend, Nosko and a colleague had been the first photographers allowed to shoot the mummy itself. His close-up of the corpse's face had appeared in countless publications around the world and earned Nosko a handsome sum. He called it his Ötzi "portrait." The work was thrilling and consuming, and he did not notice anything unusual about the mummy or the people involved. His first doubts arose only when Heim called him up and talked at length about the contradictions in the scientists' stories. His questions were good, and they began to kindle doubts in Nosko's mind.

The scientists had been saying that the corpse had been dried by the wind as it lay exposed on the pass. But Nosko wondered how the corpse could be mummified so evenly if it had been in the same position for all those years. Together, he and Heim pored over every photograph he had of the mummy, looking for inconsistencies. On one they discovered a little water droplet running down the corpse's skin. That seemed odd. Why would the skin not soak the droplet up? Perhaps, they thought, it had been treated with some preservative or chemically tanned, so that it might actually repel water. Was this evidence that the Iceman might not be a case of *natural* mummification?

The behavior of some of the scientists also struck them as odd. Why had Henn and the others refused to allow Nosko to fly with them in the helicopter that day? Was the seat reserved for someone else, possibly someone they had intended to pick up along the way, before discovering that ORF was already waiting for them at the site? What was the real story behind Henn's and Spindler's phone calls on the morning of the recovery? Why was the university being so secretive about their results now? Could it be that the corpse was an elaborate forgery?

They were not the only ones who had considered this possibility. Every responsible news editor in the world had asked his or her reporters to ask the scientists the same question. Even at that time, the Innsbruck scientists' answers had sounded a bit glib. Spindler spoke of the persuasiveness of the whole context of the find. He and others suggested such an elaborate forgery would have been impossible. When the radiocarbon results came in with more or less the same age for the body and grass, most journalists and researchers were satisfied that the man and his artifacts must be real. But Heim was cautious. Some of the scientists themselves could be behind the hoax. It certainly would not have been the first time that people had conspired on an archaeological fake.

Piltdown Man, a skull said to represent the evolutionary "missing link" between apes and man, had fooled scholars for decades. Assembled in 1912 from fragments found in a gravel pit by an amateur scientist named Charles Dawson, the skull displayed most of the features of a modern human except for the jaw, which was distinctly apelike. It was just the kind of skull that early paleontologists believed they would find to fill in the gap. Yet the Piltdown skull, which was said to be up to five hundred thousand years old, also caused great confusion over how to arrange fossils on the human family tree.

Over the following decades, some scientists challenged the authenticity of the skull, but not until 1953, when researchers noticed that the teeth had been filed down, was it conclusively proved to be a forgery.[14] The mastermind behind the scheme was never identified definitively. The two early proponents of the skull had died within two decades of the discovery. But whoever it was knew a great deal about fossils and how they were studied. He had chosen an unusually thick human skull to suggest similarity but not equality with the modern one, stained the cranium to make it look old, and filed down the molars of the jaw to make them look human. The skull was ultimately identified as that of an ape, probably an orangutan. In hindsight, of course, the forgery looked rather crude. But at the time of its discovery, the half-human skull had precisely fulfilled scientists' expectations.

The motivation of the forger or forgers was more difficult to understand. Certainly, money had played no role. The forger could have been an amateur fossil hunter disgruntled over his treatment by establishment scientists. Or the aim might simply have been to substantiate an English claim to the cradle of humanity. Piltdown Man had given England a place in evolutionary history that matched those of France and Germany, where several fossil finds and other important traces of early human life had been discovered in the preceding decades. Might someone have had similar plans for South Tyrol? Heim wondered.

By the summer of 1992, Heim and Nosko had collected ample evidence for a short film for Bavarian Television about incongruities in the Iceman story. In addition to scrutinizing the photographs, they had interviewed scientists and flown up to the Hauslabjoch to investigate the site. In a confrontational interview with Spindler himself, Heim made it clear that he seriously doubted the university's version of events and the results presented thus far. Spindler reacted calmly to the charges and defended the university's work. But a few weeks after the interview, the legal department of Bavarian Television received a letter from the Iceman project's lawyer, who had drawn up the marketing contract.

"The information discussed [with Spindler] was provided solely for the purposes [of the broadcast]," the lawyer wrote. "As we have been informed, this information is now going to be commercialized by Dr. Heim in a book to accompany the broadcast. As you know, the university's financing of the research project . . . is dependent on proceeds from the commercialization of its own publications. This goal would be endangered by the actions of Dr. Heim. We therefore ask you to check and inform us if such plans by Dr. Heim conform to the facts and what steps will be taken by Bavarian Television in this connection."

Heim was enraged when he read the letter, which he viewed as an attempt to intimidate him and his employer. It fueled his hunch that the scientists had something to hide and were just trying to make money off the Iceman to pad their research coffers. They must have known he was onto something.

In an impolitic response, he denied that there was a book accompanying the broadcast.

What is correct: In conversation with Professor Spindler, I protested that the University of Innsbruck has seized the "corpse in the ice," which is the common property of mankind, for commercial purposes through the fabrication of a world copyright. I protested Professor Spindler's allegation that I wanted to swallow up information for a book, but told him that I reserve the right to publish a book at a later time after agreement with my employer, BR [Bayerischer Rundfunk, or the Bavarian Broadcasting System]. I am a journalist and a writer and write whenever and whatever I want and, as a journalist, protest the regimentation of my profession by the University of Innsbruck.

That was the last formal contact between Heim and the university. Less than eight months later, on April 1, 1993, Heim and Nosko's book arrived in European stores. Published by the prestigious house of Rowohlt, it was called *The Ötztal Forgery: Anatomy of an Archaeological Farce*. The shocking thesis of the compact volume was that the corpse was not a Neolithic Alpine inhabitant at all but rather an ancient Near Eastern or Mediterranean mummy that someone had planted in the ice. Heim staked the connection to the Near East on the Innsbruck scientists' statements that the Iceman's penis was missing and presumed amputated during the recovery. In fact, Heim claimed, it was not missing but castrated. Since there was no tradition of castration in the Alpine region, he wrote, the mummy must have come from a place where it did exist, such as Egypt. Egyptian mummies were often castrated, and getting hold of one was relatively easy. Over the last centuries, hundreds of mummies had been brought to Europe, where they had been put on display and even, for a time, used in certain medicines. Possibly the Iceman came from a cache brought from Central Asia at the behest of the Gestapo leader Heinrich Himmler, who wanted to see them used in research on racial differences. But Heim did not exclude the possibility that the University of Innsbruck doctors could have made the mummy themselves by simply freeze-drying a corpse.

Precisely who was behind this archaeological hoax Heim and Nosko did not say with certainty. They saw enough suspicious activity to inculpate almost everyone involved, from the Simons to Charlotte Sengthaler and Konrad Spindler. But the figure who aroused the most suspicion was Reinhold Messner. In their preface, Heim and Nosko stated flatly that they were not alleging that Messner himself placed the corpse in the ice, but they did allow for the possibility that others had done it on his behalf. Messner's presence at the site just two days after its supposed discovery was just too great a coincidence to be ignored. Messner was a public-relations wizard who made money for his expeditions by publishing his adventures and who had made the front pages with his claim to have seen the Himalayan Yeti. What wouldn't a prehistoric South Tyrolean do for his career?

Heim and Nosko suggested that the Iceman had been planted in the ice so that Messner could then "discover" it during his highly publicized tour of South Tyrol. The plan went awry, however, when the Simon couple naively stumbled across the man first. Messner was thus reduced to simply visiting the site and reporting the find to the press.

Heim and Nosko believed they had uncovered several contradictory statements in Messner's own story. Messner told one interviewer that he had been able to see through the ice that the corpse was shod in a grass-stuffed boot. Yet other witnesses described the ice as brown and opaque.[15] Did he know the type of footgear because he had already seen the corpse before it was buried? Could it really be just a coincidence that Messner, the man behind the idea of a strong, independent South Tyrol, would discover a prehistoric Tyrolean on his tour? Could Messner, or someone working for him, have been trying to create an ancient symbol that would serve as a rallying point for the people of South Tyrol?

Messner was not the only one Heim implicated in the plan. Heim uncovered a bizarre set of connections between Messner, Spindler,

Helmut and Erika Simon, Charlotte Sengthaler, and a California-based "cult" called Paramahansa Yogananda, whose followers, through meditation and other practices influenced by Hinduism, were said to be seeking nonmaterial paths through life. It was strange, he suggested, that the group had a branch in Itter, the Austrian village where both Spindler and Sengthaler resided. Heim implied that many of the actors in the conspiracy were working to save Paramahansa Yogananda's Itter branch from financial ruin.

Before he went public with the book, Heim accepted an invitation from Svante Pääbo to run his conspiracy case by the people in his lab. They had just gotten the sample of tissue from the Iceman in order to study his DNA, and Pääbo wanted to make sure that they were not going to be wasting time by studying something that was not five thousand years old. Heim had marshaled together some contradictory facts, and he was a convincing orator. By the time Heim had finished talking, everyone had serious doubts. Was it a fake or not?

The general public was ready to believe it was. Because of the university's virtual information embargo, very little news about the Iceman had made it into the media in more than a year. The frequent press conferences Charlotte Sengthaler had envisioned had not materialized largely because she did not know who was doing what. But here, at last, was something concrete. Every newspaper in Europe ran the news that a German journalist and an Innsbruck photographer had unmasked the Iceman as an archaeological fake. Most articles included only a short sentence about the University of Innsbruck denying the charges.

Just as Heim and Nosko's book was coming out, when the university most needed public-relations advice, it severed its ties with Sengthaler's firm, E & K. To the three leaders of the project, the marketing and communications effort as originally conceived now looked like a huge error, one that had even cost the university money. Sengthaler complained bitterly that the Iceman project leaders' recalcitrance made it impossible for her to do her work, but the professors maintained that her inexperience doomed the project. She had managed to raise virtually none of the ten million dollars Platzer thought the project would cost. Apart from the conservation at the Institute of Anatomy, almost all the research was being paid for out of the researchers' general lab funds—that is, by the Austrian public.

The final straw had come in early 1993 after Sengthaler's return from New York, where she had contacted several American universities and the Museum of Natural History in Manhattan. She presented the university with the names of some American foundations that funded scientific research. Scornfully, Platzer replied that they already knew the names of such prestigious foundations—the National Science Foundation and National Institutes of Health—and that they could have gotten the addresses themselves. Several weeks later, her contract expired.

Despite the fact that she had been let go, Sengthaler urged Moser and Spindler to respond strongly to the forgery charges in a press release or interviews. The book had apparently convinced a lot of people; if the university really stood by the authenticity of the Iceman, it had to say so emphatically or it would never get any funding.

The project leaders preferred, however, to dismiss the book out of hand. In Spindler's mind, the book was just another bizarre effort by people who he believed had no business in the project to make themselves important or at least make some money off the Iceman. His department had collected a big file of such people and their interests and labeled it "Ötzi curiosa." Included in it was the case of a Swiss woman who claimed that the Iceman was really her long-lost father, who had disappeared in the vicinity of the Hauslabjoch in the early 1970s. This claim had been laid to rest once the carbon-dating results had come in.[16] There had also been the Australian woman, among others, who wrote to Innsbruck to inquire whether she could be impregnated with Ötzi's sperm. Unterdorfer got a chuckle out of the letter, but Platzer seemed uncomfortable acknowledging that such a letter existed and refused to talk about it.*

The same went for the report in a Vienna-based gay newspaper that the scientists had found sperm in the Iceman's anus.[17] Among the general public, the report sounded plausible. Would anyone really be shocked if, even before the Greeks, men had been sexually

---

*The British press, by contrast, had a field day with such reports. An editorial writer for *The Sunday Times* of June 21, 1992, suggested that the women might be after the money and the sensation. "However, there are one or two setbacks to the aspirations of prospective mothers, who, if they were to succeed in this dubious medical experiment, might produce a child with dark hair and eyes (his father's colouring) and horribly hirsute limbs." The fact that Stone Age people were not necessarily hairy had not yet, it seemed, seeped through to this editor, who, moreover, failed to explain what was wrong with a lot of hair.

engaged with one another? So far the scientists had not responded to that one either, even though it was easy to address. The Iceman's anus and rectum had been lost to the gendarme's jackhammer during the recovery.

One elderly Tyrolean man claimed he could channel Ötzi, and a German woman named Renate Spieckermann claimed she was his reincarnation. To Spindler's annoyance, she, too, was writing a book. The provocative title: *Ich war Ötzi* (I was Ötzi).

Spindler and Platzer viewed all these reports critically, insisting that they had nothing whatsoever to do with the Iceman or the project. *The Ötztal Forgery* deserved only slightly more regard. Shortly after the book came out, the Research Institute for Alpine Prehistory released a short statement. "With some astonishment, but also amusement, we have just read the new book from Rowohlt Publishers by Dr. Michael Heim and Werner Nosko," the statement began, before going on to lambaste Heim for shoddy and insufficient reporting. They nitpicked at inconsistencies and errors in Heim's book, noting, for example, that he had referred to the Institute of Forensic Medicine as the "pathology" department. "What is certainly even more surprising in the issue at hand is the spitefulness of attempting to degrade the reputation of noted scientists," the statement went on. "The brochure [book] . . . contains attacks which would justify legal steps. But such steps would possibly be seen as an undeserved upgrade of the book and the authors. . . . Even for a purely journalistic engagement with a prehistoric find a certain measure of basic knowledge would not have been harmful. Then, for example, it must have been recognized that the Professor Dr. Konrad Spindler's post-doctoral dissertation . . . was not about the Middle Ages but rather the Stone and Bronze Ages."

Strangely, however, the statement did not explain why scientists were sure that the Iceman was indeed authentic. Neither did it address the one fact on which so many of Heim's suspicions were based: the missing penis. Given that the scientists themselves had already publicly expressed their own puzzlement over this, they could not so easily ignore it. Just before it was released, the book had, in fact, motivated a little in-house research. Platzer had decided that it was time to check the genital area one more time.

CHAPTER 8

SPINDLER'S STORY

Werner Platzer had scheduled the examination of the genital region for April 1, 1993, the very day Heim and Nosko's book arrived in bookstores in Austria and Germany. Spindler later insisted that this was the long-scheduled date for the genital exam and had nothing to do with the book, but among the scientists on the project that argument brought only a chuckle. Everyone knew that the removal of the mummy from his cavelike freezer was no simple affair, and Platzer did not take it lightly. Like all the investigations on the Iceman, the time and purpose were closely held secrets. Normally not even the other leaders of the Research Institute for Alpine Prehistory knew when the Iceman was taken out for checks. Given the delicacy and urgency of the situation, however, Platzer had invited Spindler to observe the procedure.

As Platzer finished gowning up, his assistants rolled the Iceman out of the freezer and removed the plastic, ice packs, and sterile sheet. Apart from the removal of a few tiny tissue samples from the surface of his corpse, little research had yet been done on the man, and the corpse was virtually unchanged from the moment when Platzer had assumed responsibility for him. The mysterious fungus that might have plagued the corpse during the press conference had not recurred, and the storage at high humidity, just below freezing, was apparently working. As the videotape rolled from the doorway of the examination room, Platzer approached the examination table and leaned in for a look.

At first glance, the area between the man's legs was quite disorienting. Where a penis and testicles might be expected to hang was a curious geography of lumpy, smashed, and folded tissues. Except for a few random dark-brown strands, all the man's body hair, including the pubic hair, had fallen out in the ice. Whereas much of the Iceman's skin was pulled tight over his body so that the bones were clearly visible, the pubic area was oddly bumpy. More than a year earlier, in an interview with *Der Spiegel*, Platzer had been quoted as saying that the scrotum looked as if it had been "scraped out." The region where the anatomist normally expected to find the scrotum did indeed look somewhat concave. But on closer examination, Platzer now noticed something that must have escaped him the year before. There, below the pubic bone, was the seam that ran down the middle of the scrotum. Using a pair of long tweezers, Platzer carefully probed along the edges of a flap that extended off one side of the seam. Then he did the same for the other side. These looked like the outlines of the scrotum. Except for some slight cuts on the bottom, the organ was in fine shape.

"Here's the scrotum," he said calmly for the video, as if there had never been any question of its whereabouts. The camera zoomed in as Platzer gently lifted up a flap of tissue.

Next Platzer probed around a long, thin bit of dried flesh that was frozen across the scrotum. Gingerly, he separated it from the skin underneath and examined the point where it remained attached. This looked like the penis. He could feel the urethra inside the organ. Apparently it was all there. It was just desiccated.

"And here's the penis," he said brightly.

The video did not record the reaction of those in the room, who must have been astonished at the presence of an organ long assumed forfeited. Because anatomists are forever measuring body parts, Platzer next took out a small measuring device and attempted to gauge the shrunken appendage. He quickly discovered that the device did not function at temperatures below zero. He would have to guess. Platzer estimated that the penis was about two inches long, measuring half an inch thick at the base and narrowing to just one-eighth of an inch at its tip. The shrinkage was considerable.

Unterdorfer, the forensic doctor who had described the genitals as "leaf-like" and "desiccated" the day the corpse had arrived on his autopsy table, had been right all along. Yet somehow this initial opinion had been subverted, and for nearly eighteen months the lead scientists had been saying that the penis had either been eliminated by animals or torn off during the brutal excavation.

Heim and Nosko had enshrined the fact in their book. Yet now the penis turned out to be exactly where it belonged. The examination had been straightforward and yielded immediate, unequivocal results. People were bound to ask why Platzer had not thoroughly examined the genital area sooner.

Yet even now Platzer did not immediately make the news public. For the next three weeks, *The Ötztal Forgery* basked in the limelight. The university's dismissal of it was barely noticed. Then, on April 20, Spindler and Sigmar Bortenschlager were invited to appear with Heim and Nosko on an Austrian talk show called *Club 2*. The format of the prime-time program was an open, sometimes chaotic, discussion moderated by a well-known Austrian journalist. Several minutes into the program the journalist turned the discussion to the topic of the missing penis.

"May I now segue into a further theme that also appears in your book. What I'm showing now," he said, holding up Nosko's photograph of the genital area, "here, this part, are the remains of the male sexual organs of Ötzi . . . so the organs are missing, that means the testicles are missing, the penis is also missing, is that right, is that correct?"

Looking dead serious, Spindler cleared his throat, shifted in his seat, and prepared to address Heim. "Well now, I must say, Mr. Heim—" But he was not quick enough. Before he could get his next words out, he was interrupted by the moderator and then by Heim himself. In the next few moments, everyone spoke at once until finally the moderator managed to wrestle the contestants back into order. Then Spindler launched a question.

"Mr. Heim, I must ask you again, who told you that the corpse was castrated and the testicles scooped out? You emphasized in your book very correctly that in our first scientific publication there was no information on the genital region, because this investigation was going to be carried out at another point. You pull out of thin air . . . that he was serving the mother goddess, that he sacrificed his genitals. You must have gotten that out of some tabloid, where they also printed that there was sperm in Ötzi's behind. . . . Almost half your book you spend riding around on this topic. Of course now in the meantime the first examination of the genital region took place—"

Again he was interrupted, this time by Nosko. "Then you've established that Messner is not responsible for the missing genitals."

Spindler replied that Messner had asked him for a confirmation that he did not take the penis, and he had given him that confirmation. "He didn't remove the penis. No one did," he said, finally managing to make his point. Suddenly everyone began speaking at once, and when a solo voice again rose above the noise it was Spindler's.

"The penis is there, and in the scientific publications you'll see that," he said.

"Where is it?" Heim snapped again.

"It's there where it belongs, and if you don't know where that is then—"

Then what? Heim was not a man? Bortenschlager's booming laugh sounded, and then Spindler spoke up loudly and clearly. "Please, yes, of course it's there, you see it here because it's dried up like a leaf. Seventy percent of the water is gone, so it's dried like a leaf, but the penis is there, you can touch the urethra from the root to the glans."

Werner Nosko suddenly piped up with the same reaction many confused viewers must have had. "Then it surprises me that you didn't see that immediately. And that Dr. Henn and Dr. Unterdorfer didn't see that either," he said.

It was the obvious path to pursue. Why were the scientists saying one thing one day and a different thing the next? Spindler and the other researchers had not claimed the Iceman was castrated, but they had published scientific articles in which they had claimed that the penis was missing. What had changed? Where was the new proof?

Spindler did not offer any explanation for this discrepancy, and television did not require one. There was a built-in credibility to things said in the mass media from which Heim had profited, and now Spindler was using the same trick. To the public unversed in the scientific method, there was not that much difference between the rhetoric of a scientist and the rhetoric of a journalist.

But instead of challenging Spindler, Heim appeared taken aback at the revelation and tried to move to another topic. A bit nervously, he launched into an ill-prepared attack on how the university had handled his requests for information and interviews.

"In early 1991 I sent you a complete catalogue of questions which included the question—" he began, before Spindler interrupted.

"Early 1991, that cannot be."

"Ah, early 1992, ah, I also addressed you regarding questions of castration in August, I spoke to you regarding the castration, I asked whether this corpse from Hauslabjoch was a hermaphrodite."

"As you . . . the remains are not perfectly identifiable."

"But I did ask you," Heim pressed.

"Such questions we don't even answer. What kinds of requests do you think we get! Women come to us and ask whether they can get sperm from Ötzi, and then people come and ask if Ötzi was a hermaphrodite. Do you think that we as serious scientists answer such ridiculous questions? You came with an extraordinary alcohol breath and that was the reason not to have an interview with you."

"Alcohol breath is a matter of discretion," Heim said.

"We had to air the place out after—all the staff in the Institute can confirm this."

It was a damning volley, aimed not at Heim's ideas but at his very person. To have the castration hypothesis shot down was one thing. To be charged with a drinking problem on live national television was quite another. Still holding a meek smile, Heim sank into speechlessness. It was all over for him. The conversation skidded toward some of the other guests.

For the people who saw the confrontation, there was little doubt that Spindler and the other scientists had won an important battle. The common opinion among the Iceman scientists now was that Heim and Nosko had written their book just to profit financially off public interest in the Iceman. It was, as Spindler had charged, not "serious science." For the results of real scientific inquiry, the public would have to await the publication of Spindler's book, which he had been working on fervently for the last nine months. Serious science, presumably, would not bow to popular tastes.

T he results from Svante Pääbo's DNA lab were sobering. Oliva Handt, a young German graduate student who had landed the project, had quickly discovered that the Iceman's DNA was extremely degraded. Because DNA chains are very long and delicate, scientists cannot see even an entire chromosome, much less the whole genome, at one stretch. When extracted from fresh tissue, DNA breaks into lengths of anywhere from a few hundred to fifty thousand base pairs. With ancient DNA, breakage was a much bigger problem, since the natural process of decay and other chemical changes have begun to destroy the chains. Pääbo had found that lengths of more than two hundred base pairs did not survive in Egyptian mummies or extinct animals. Handt's results with the Iceman were even more discouraging.

Though not a barrier to continued work, this did mean that it would be difficult to amplify very long segments of DNA. More than 99 percent of human DNA is exactly the same in every individual. Where differences do occur, they are almost always along certain rather small portions of the DNA chain. In order to find differences among individuals, molecular biologists therefore have to locate these segments. Handt had wanted to isolate one or more of these variable sequences from the Iceman and compare it with those of other individuals. But she was not going to be able to get enough *nuclear* DNA out of the sample to locate and study any particular gene. That was unfortunate, since any statement she could end up making on the Iceman's origin or ethnic identity would have been stronger if backed up by nuclear DNA evidence. The fewer sites along the man's DNA she could check, the less she would ultimately be able to say about who he was.

Handt had, however, identified several short segments of mtDNA. Because the rate of evolution of mtDNA is so slow, it was virtually certain that the Iceman's exact sequence would still be present among some modern populations. Its exact function is irrelevant for the study of genealogies; the important thing is that it varies slightly in different people. The task now was to compare the sequence of base pairs in one particular segment with the same segment in other individuals from various population groups, including some from the Alpine region in which he was found.

Handt's findings were straightforward. The sequence failed to show up in the mtDNA of 57 sub-Saharan Africans, 143 Siberians, or 419 Native Americans. Neither was it found in 16 individuals from the Ötztal.[1] However, Handt did find it once among 72 Swiss and three times among 228 people from the Mediterranean region. It occurred a bit more frequently among populations from north of the Alps, showing up seven times in 155 people from northern Germany, Denmark, and Iceland and twice among 100 British people.

She analyzed the results in another way as well. Leaving aside the exact matches, she counted the number of base pairs that differed from the Iceman's in each individual's sequence and then found the mean number of differences, called substitutions, for each population group. She assumed that the greater the number of substitutions, the longer the two sequences had been diverging from each other, and the more distant the relation. In this analysis, she found that the populations from the Ötztal and Alpine groups had the lowest means, with 3.38 substitutions each. The sub-Saharans had the highest mean divergence score, with 7.45 substitutions. Based on these results, Handt concluded that the Iceman's sequence was most closely related to the northern European and Alpine populations. Given where the Iceman was discovered and what archaeologists knew about the movement of populations in Europe since then, the conclusion was not surprising. But this was the closest science could get to locating the Iceman on the biological map of the world. The Iceman fit right in with the modern populations in Europe. Without more samples of Neolithic DNA, little more could be ascertained. Of course, the results said nothing about his ethnic group, the language he spoke, how he made his arrowheads, or whether he knew how to smelt copper. Ultimately, it was more of a rare exercise in working with frozen prehistoric DNA than a great insight into prehistoric populations. But that was how science went. Handt and Pääbo quickly published their findings in *Science* and went on to the next project. Their careful words on the Iceman's DNA were not, however, to be the last.

In the late summer of 1993, almost two years after the Iceman's discovery, the Research Institute for Alpine Prehistory invited the

world's mummy experts for a meeting. Archaeologists and anthropologists, radiologists and pathologists, conservators and adminis-
trators came from England and the United States, Germany and
Switzerland, France and Canada, China and Peru, Spain and Italy.
They were specialists on bodies preserved in ice, bogs, and caves, on
mountainsides, in graves, and beneath rocks. The symposium provided an unprecedented opportunity for participants to exchange
information on research as well as on conservation and display.

For the Iceman's guardians, the conference also provided the
chance to demonstrate to their peers that they were doing the right
thing—to dispel, once and for all, the notion that Austrian science
was not up to the challenge posed by the Iceman. A year earlier, at
their first conference on the Iceman, the participants had delivered
their papers in whatever language was most convenient, and the faculty and staff in Spindler's department had dressed in dirndls and
lederhosen, the quaint ethnic Tyrolean costumes, unusual for an
academic event. But this mummy symposium sent a different message. Everyone wore suits and spoke in the international language
of science: English.

Platzer himself led selected participants on a rare tour into the
bowels of his Institute of Anatomy to show off his charge. The curious scientists strained to get a look at the Iceman as he was
wheeled out on his stretcher and unwrapped. If anyone thought the
swaddling routine could be improved upon, they did not say so to
Platzer. Maybe the anatomist's techniques were basic, but they were
still working after almost two years. The 5,300-year-old corpse
looked like he was in stable condition.* But what had the anatomist
learned about the corpse? The discussion over whether the Iceman
was a fake had overshadowed the fact that virtually none of the ten
million dollars that Platzer wanted for the research had been raised.
None of the scientists invited from foreign lands dared ask whether
that meant that the research was not going to get done. But several,

---

*Nine sets of radiocarbon datings were completed. Taken together they revealed
a 31 percent probability that he died between 3352 and 3300 B.C.E., a 36 percent
probability between 3235 and 3175 B.C.E., and a 33 percent probability between
3166 and 3108 B.C.E.[2] For simplicity's sake, the author will continue to cite 3300
B.C.E. as the approximate year of his death.

including Don Brothwell, made no secret of the fact that they had funds available and were just waiting to get samples.

After the visit with the Iceman, the most anticipated event of the conference was Spindler's presentation. He was at the vortex of all inquiries into the man and his equipment. Nearly everyone in his institute had contributed to the project, and he had also collected considerable information and advice from research by Egg, zur Nedden, the botanists, Patzelt, and a host of other researchers. From all these strands of research, Spindler had woven the first integral hypothesis about what had befallen Ötzi. Since the discovery, his other work had practically ground to a halt as he worked night and day to finish the book, *The Man in the Ice,* which was now due out within weeks. The talk he had prepared for the conference was largely excerpted from it, under the tantalizing title "The Iceman's Last Weeks."

The room in the main university building was nearly full as Spindler, speaking carefully in English, launched directly into his talk. The lights were dimmed so that slides could be seen better. He began by endorsing the hypothesis that the Iceman was a wandering herdsman. "This means, and no part of the evidence is inconsistent with this theory, that our man had spent the summer before his death with herds of sheep and goats in the high pastures of the Upper Ötztal," he said, reading from a manuscript and indicating a slide of the modern-day sheep drive past the Similaun lodge.[3] "He may have been with other herdsmen."

As the summer drew to a close, said Spindler, the man rounded up his flock and prepared to drive the animals home to his village south of the Hauslabjoch in what is today the Vinschgau. The evidence for his home being south of the main Alpine ridge in Italy came mainly from the botanists. Among all the different woods and other plant material the man had carried with him—from the embers in the birch-bark container to the wood in his bow—nothing identified so far was restricted enough in its growth to pinpoint precisely where the man had come from. But since many of the woods he used grew much closer to the south than to the north, the botanists told Spindler that it was more likely that he had made his home there.

"Everything seems to indicate that he reached his native village in the Val Venosta [Vinschgau] area safely," Spindler said. "The inhabitants were in the middle of their harvest, and at this time of year everyone in a farming community is extremely busy." Ötzi immediately pitched in to help with the tasks. Perhaps he had to choose what sheep to slaughter, conserve the meat, or prepare skins. If, on the other hand, the sheep needed to be sheared—archaeologists were not sure whether people were using the wool of their sheep at this point in history in the Alps—then he might have done that. Perhaps it was when he was helping to bring in the harvest that the few grains of einkorn got caught in his fur clothing. Spindler continued:

> At some point during these days the incident, which we have termed as the "disaster," must have occurred. In any case there was a violent confrontation which lead [sic] to the man being physically injured and to pieces of his equipment being abandoned or damaged. It is justified to theorize on the causes of the disaster, but it is not possible to prove anything. During his absence of several months from his village, there may have been changes in the situation of his family. The "disaster" need not necessarily have been triggered off dramatically by jealousy: there may have been a confrontation in connection with the hierarchal [sic] order (a struggle for power). Another possible cause for his personal "disaster" might have been connected with his own misbehaviour, the loss of sheep or goats or an infringement of the communal rules.

Spindler acknowledged that many scenarios were possible, but the one he settled on was particularly brutal. A massacre had occurred in the Iceman's village, and he had somehow managed to escape it alive. That such things happened in prehistory was demonstrated, he said, by the discovery in Germany of a mass grave that dated to the Neolithic period. Archaeologists had excavated thirty-four skulls from the grave, including those of children, women, and older men, and they had concluded that the people had been murdered and buried together. Given that not even children had been spared in that massacre, Spindler surmised that the people who attacked the Iceman's village would have been particularly enraged if a man had been able to escape, and they would have pursued him. The Iceman, Spindler suggested, was fleeing. By the time he died on the Hauslabjoch, he might already have been on the lam for days or even weeks.

Though he had made it out of his village alive, neither he nor his equipment was in good shape. Spindler posited the "disaster" as the cause of virtually all the damage he and Markus Egg had found so puzzling about the man's equipment. It was during this "violent confrontation" that a previous longbow was either broken or lost, which required him to begin making a replacement. The confrontation also explained the condition of the quiver and its contents. Spindler hypothesized that, during the fight, the man had shot off all but two of his arrows, and the remaining two were broken.

The quiver's closure and the carrying strap were torn off and the support rod along the outside was broken during the confrontation, he said. Spindler emphasized that part of the quiver's closure as well as the broken middle section of the rod were recovered near the corpse, rather than with the quiver. This, he said, demonstrated that the quiver had been damaged before it was set down on the rocks. He assumed that the man had kept this broken piece on his person with the intention of repairing the quiver when the opportunity arose.

Far more decisive in the man's fate than the damaged equipment, however, were his extensive injuries. Citing the results of zur Nedden's radiological examinations, Spindler reported that the altercation left the Hauslabjoch man with several extremely painful broken ribs on his right side. Despite this serious injury, which may well have left a less robust modern man flat on his back, the Iceman had managed to grab his copper ax and backpack, as well as a bit of dried meat and some embers from one of the village's hearths, before he fled. As he packed some maple leaves around the ember, a few fragments of the newly harvested wheat found their way into the birchbark container, too.

But the man did not go straight from his village to his death on the Hauslabjoch, Spindler said. For by the time he died, he had been well on his way toward replacing his lost or damaged equipment. His first concern must have been to replace his bow and arrows. He knew where to find a stand of yews, and he went straight there. Spindler's conclusion, based on the work of an experimental archaeologist, was that the Iceman did use his ax.

To get the appropriate length of wood, he first felled and then split a nearly eight-inch-diameter yew, presumably using his ax.

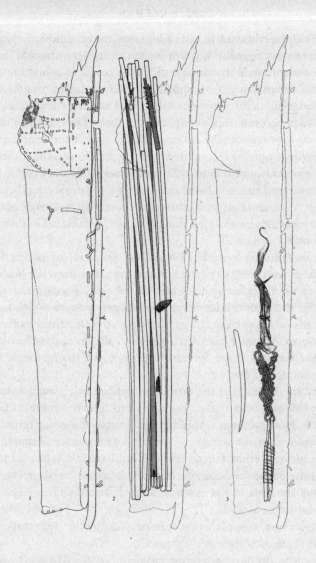

The quiver and its contents before it was emptied. Note the bundled string, the antler point (bent at one end), and the bundle of bone points probably intended for use in the arrows. The ends of the broken arrow in the center of the bar are in alignment, while the break near the top of the bag has shifted slightly. ROMAN-GERMANIC CENTRAL MUSEUM, JULIA RIBBECK

Based on experiments by archaeologists using different types of tools and working with different woods, Spindler estimated it took the Iceman about forty minutes to fell the tree and another hour to split it. Perhaps using the flint blade he had carried in his pouch, he then had to work the bow out of the wood and then smooth it. One bow maker accomplished similar tasks in about five and a half hours.

"If we now transfer the results from the experimental archaeologists to the rough bow from the Hauslabjoch and add the additional work of making a bow from split logs, it becomes clear that a complete bow could be produced in a day at the most," Spindler said, adding, "The fact that a Neolithic man certainly had more practice working with these tools has not even been considered in these calculations."

He also needed to replace his arrows. For this, he hastened to a wayfaring bush. He cut twelve straight branches from the bush and stripped off their bark and a number of tiny shoots growing off them. In the ends of each he cut a small groove into which the arrowheads were to be fitted. Spindler suggested that from each of the four pieces of antler bundled together with bast, the man could have fashioned perhaps five arrowheads, more than enough to fit the shafts he had cut.

Spindler figured that the production of just one arrow, including the arrowhead, might take two hours and fifteen minutes. Had he finished all twelve, that would have meant twenty-seven hours. But these twelve arrows were only perhaps one quarter finished. Still, under normal circumstances, Spindler estimated that the man might easily have spent the better part of two days getting his new equipment to the stage it was in when he died, and then one day to get from the lower altitude to the Hauslabjoch. Based on the archaeological evidence alone, then, it seemed clear that he had survived for at least three days after the "disaster."

However, circumstances were far from normal. He was badly injured. Every breath sent stabs of pain rippling around his torso. Surely he was not able to carry out such strenuous tasks as felling a tree and carving out the branch at a normal pace. The picture Spindler painted of the Iceman looked dire indeed. Weak, laboring under shortness of breath and excruciating pain and possibly even being pursued, the man was heading toward the high main Alpine ridge at an inauspicious time of year, when snowstorms could disorient even the most seasoned and one big snowfall could make a saddle impassable for the rest of the winter. Yet he chose to seek out those pastures where, just days before, he had blithely watched over his sheep. Why? Because, Spindler assured his listeners, it was the territory he knew best. "Due to the approach of winter, he must have been hoping to find a hiding place in the summer pasturing areas after shaking off his pursuers," Spindler suggested.

This is where the careful tallying of the time required to make the tools and get to the site came in. The X rays showed no sign that the broken ribs had already begun to heal. A preliminary interpretation of the X rays also revealed that relative to the left one, the joint of the upper right arm was slightly decalcified. Zur Nedden had told Spindler that this could have occurred from the man holding his arm in a stable position, just as one does when trying to minimize the pain from broken ribs. The decalcification would show up after about two weeks of inactivity in the arm. Spindler thus concluded that the injuries had happened two weeks before the man's death. There was, thus, plenty of time for him to have gotten the raw materials for his new weapons, begun work on them, and hiked to the Hauslabjoch from the Vinschgau.

Around two weeks after the disaster, then, the man was approaching the pass that connected the Schnalstal with the Ötztal.

It is not known whether he knew that his last hour had come when he had reached the chasm below the Hauslabjoch and only 262 feet from the summit ridge. In any case, the trench offered some protection from the weather conditions, which were obviously an immediate threat to the man. . . . [He] was in a condition of exhaustion. . . . He layed [sic] his axe, bow and [backpack] on the rock ledge, squatted down and ate the last of his food supplies—a piece of dried ibex meat.

The remains of this snack were two pieces of ibex neck bone that had turned up in Lippert's dig. But this minor nourishment could not have done much for him. The only other food he carried was the bluish berry, now identified as the edible, if extremely sour, fruit of the sloe, or blackthorn, bush. Horst Seidler had told Spindler that the man had not had an ounce of fat too much on his frame when he died. Possibly, Spindler suggested, he was even starving.

Spindler closed his talk with a stirring account of the doomed Iceman's last minutes.

> He knew that sleep meant death. To keep himself warm and awake he trudged a few paces up and down. His quiver fell to the ground, five yards away from the rock ledge. He must have staggered forward, completely exhausted and frozen, he then tripped on a rock after taking five steps and could not get back onto his feet. His cap fell off, so that he was now bare-headed. With his last ounce of strength he turned himself onto his left side, the least painful position for his injured rib cage. Then he fell into the sleep from which he was to awaken no more. Snow covered his body.

The last slide clicked off, and the lights went up. The large room was quiet as Spindler collected up his papers and returned to his seat in the front row. No question or discussion time had been scheduled, and no one had been designated to respond to the paper. As the participants filed out into the corridors for a break, a few exchanged questioning looks. One archaeologist raised his eyebrows in disbelief and, almost imperceptibly, shook his head. This was not your typical conference talk.

Outside the corridors of academia, the media had a very different response to Spindler's story. Ötzi was unveiled as a fugitive. That was a big story. The media that could afford it were willing to pay. Weeks before the conference, the German weekly news magazine *Stern* had run an elaborate three-part series on the Iceman, mainly excerpted from Spindler's forthcoming book. The deal, cut not by Sengthaler but by a lawyer, brought the university $130,000. The *Stern* article contained by far the most vivid depiction of the man's life and death to date, and with the magazine's millions of readers it was sure to corner public opinion on the find. It also unveiled for the first time the details of the man's unusual clothing. Over the next several weeks, the story took off.

The article was the perfect teaser for Spindler's book. Called the only "authorized" story of the Hauslabjoch Man, the book provided a full account of the disaster theory and was soon selling rapidly across German-speaking Europe.[4] Bertelsmann, the publisher, paid $400,000 for the title, 20 percent of which went to an agent the university had retained to handle business with the media. The two contracts together finally put the account of the Research Institute for Alpine Prehistory in the black. Still, the earnings came to just a fraction of the ten-million-dollar goal.

Spindler was able to seize the Iceman bullhorn again for the first time since the information embargo had gone into place. Like Heim's and Nosko's tale of forgery, the disaster theory was appetizing to the public. It had violence, escape, distress, desperate preparations, a struggle to survive, and finally, calamitous death. In Spindler's intimation that adultery might have caused the fight, there was even a whiff of sex.

But for many scientists on the project, the disaster theory came as a complete surprise. Most researchers outside Spindler's department were unprepared for a disaster hypothesis and knew nothing of the broken ribs or the restored clothing until the news appeared in the media. While many had channeled their research results to Spindler or Platzer or shared detailed background information from their disciplines with them, very little information and even fewer results had been transmitted back to them. Key researchers such as Annaluisa Pedrotti, Markus Egg, Horst Seidler, and Don Brothwell had only the dimmest idea of what the others were doing, or even that they existed. When a researcher first learned of important results in a comprehensive theory presented in the popular press, he or she was hard-pressed to influence it directly.

Meanwhile, the botanists Oeggl and Bortenschlager, who possessed some of the most promising archaeological material, had distanced themselves from the project leadership. Already alienated by the marketing plan as well as the lack of any overall research objectives, Oeggl had grown increasingly annoyed with what he perceived as a tendency by Spindler to view the botanists as hirelings whose results could be plugged into the Iceman death scenario of the moment. The botanists were among the very few who had prepared detailed outlines of their ambitious research project, and many of their colleagues knew the kinds of results they might eventually receive from them.

Though the formal marketing concept had fallen flat, the project was designed to funnel all results to Spindler, for his use in his books, articles, and speeches. The botanists were concerned that their results might be misused or misconstrued. They also wanted credit for their work. If they had interesting results, they wanted to present them. As a result, communications between the Institute of Botany and Spindler's prehistory department had virtually ceased.

The key to the reconstruction of the man's clothing had been the little tab of fur found tucked inside the man's shoe. Roswitha Goedecker-Ciolek had quickly realized that a second such tab was still sewn onto the edge of one of the other garments. One loose tab in the shoe and a second sewn onto the garment could indicate only the prehistoric version of the elastic stirrups sewn onto the ankles of snow pants to keep them tucked into boots.

Until that point, Goedecker-Ciolek had not known for sure which side of the clothing was up and which was down. But once she realized that these little tabs marked the bottom of some kind of leg wear, everything fell into place. Egg and Goedecker-Ciolek decided to call the Iceman's unusual leg wear "leggings." They were not real trousers but more like waders without feet. The ensemble worked much like a garter belt, straps, and stockings. Ötzi had slipped his foot through one of the tubular fur leggings and pulled it up to the middle of his thigh. He then cinched it tight around his thigh with a leather lace threaded through slits along the top. A strap, of which little now remained, extended from the front of each legging up to his waist, where he probably attached it to a belt. The design was a little sketchy at this point, but Goedecker-Ciolek suspected that one of the long leather pieces among the finds had been the belt. Around the ankle was another leather tie that kept the opening there tight against his leg. Last, he had tucked the little fur tab inside his shoe. The design prevented snow or cold air from creeping up his legs. Both leggings were well-worn and had been mended, especially on the inside of the legs, which probably rubbed together as the man walked. Constructed of many different scraps of fur sewn together very neatly, the leggings were apparently what the Messner group had seen through the water and described as being wrapped around the legs.

After Goedecker-Ciolek figured out the leggings, the two other garments started to make sense, too. The leggings left the man's

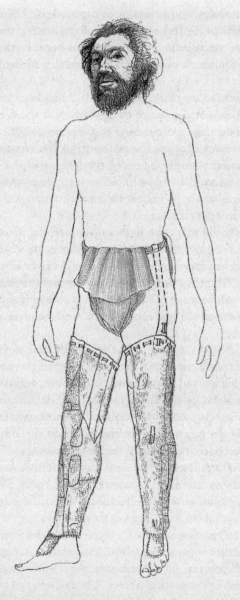

A leather belt around the Iceman's waist held the loincloth and also held straps that attached to the patchwork-style leggings.

upper thighs, loins, and genital area exposed until he tucked in his loincloth. That, Goedecker-Ciolek realized, must have been what the smaller rectangular piece of leather had been. It was constructed of several wide bands of leather sewn together along their vertical edges, using a fine whipstitch of sinew thread. One half of the loincloth was almost complete, but the other had been virtually obliterated, probably in the recovery. A seam near the obliterated end had marked the center of the long rectangular construction. Only a few ragged pieces of leather survived from the second half, which the conservators thought had probably been the part covering the man's rump because it had been exposed to the recovery team. The intact half was better protected because the man was lying atop it while the excavators worked.

If the seam did mark the halfway point in the loincloth, then it had been more than three feet long. Goedecker-Ciolek imagined that the man had taken one end of it, hung it over a belt around his waist at the back, then pulled the cloth through his legs and tucked it over the belt in front. The loincloth was deeply creased lengthwise, which suggested that it had been bunched up to pass between his legs.

The conservators agreed that the fourth garment had to have covered the torso, but its tailoring still escaped them. Spindler had told *Stern* that the piece was most likely a coat, and the magazine's illustrator, guided by the archaeologist, had drawn a beautiful coat of alternating light and dark stripes of fur running vertically down the man's body. Egg had immediately noted the similarity to the stripes carved onto the backs of the statue-menhirs.

But the interpretation was not certain. The conservators had found no obvious remains of any sleeves or collar. Possibly it was just a big fur blanket. The one clue that it had been worn close to the body was that the skin side was stained dark, probably from dirt and sweat, and parts were heavily worn. There were also several repairs, including the presumably hurried one made of grass that they had noticed early on. Along one edge were some strips of fur sewn perpendicular to the vertical stripes. The conservators thought they might have been the remains of a yoke running across the top of the shoulders. Possibly the sleeves could have been attached to this, but since there were no extra pieces of fur, they could not say for sure.

The Iceman wore a striped fur coat. The stippled line indicates sections from which the fur has not been found.

If the garment was a coat, the front closure was very odd. Goedecker-Ciolek expected a coat to close in an obvious and neat way. But the front edges were just the ends of the pelt itself. To the conservators' surprise, the animal teats on the pelt were still intact and dangled at the edge. Since they were aligned symmetrically on both sides of the opening in the front, Egg assumed the tailor had intended to leave them there. The conservators couldn't see how they could be functional. They did not seem to be part of the closure. In fact, they could see no way to keep the coat closed.

It was an enormous garment, so wide that two people could have fit inside, and it reached well past the Iceman's knees. Being fur, it was also quite thick. Possibly a belt would have kept it closed. At first Egg thought the leather fanny pack might have done the job. Ötzi then would have had easy access to the flint tools he needed for making his arrows and bow. But when results from the chemists had come back showing that the black material stuffed inside the pouch was not pitch but a shredded feltlike wad of the true tinder bracket *Fomes fomentarius,* a few hairs, and traces of pyrite, Egg changed his mind. Here, at last, was the kindling the archaeologists had expected. The Iceman would have wanted to keep the kindling dry, and the most effective way to do that was to wear the fanny pack containing it inside his clothes, right next to his skin.

Egg was not entirely comfortable with the coat interpretation. He thought it might be just a large wrap. To signal his caution about the interpretation, he instructed the artist who illustrated the man's clothing for the Roman-Germanic Central Museum to draw in a stippled line, instead of a full line, to suggest only the way the yoke and sleeves of the coat *might* have looked. Whatever it was called, it had clearly been used for warmth. For Egg, one remarkable thing about the clothing was how utterly unusual it all was. Never had any prehistorian predicted leggings. In fine weather the man probably wore nothing but a loincloth. Probably only when he needed extra warmth did he slip the leggings on. The solution to the problem of cold legs had not resulted in a complete rethinking of how to clothe oneself from the waist down; the man had just added on clothes where he was cold.

The outfit was not the light and flexible ensemble one might have expected of today's shepherd. In fact, it was difficult to imagine how

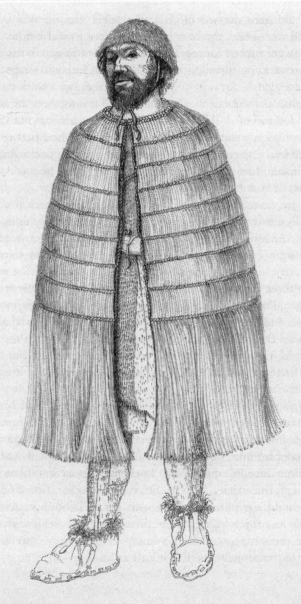

Portrait of the fully outfitted Iceman. The grass cape is a re-creation based on woven grass remains found beneath the corpse on the boulder.

he could have dressed more warmly. He had boots on his feet, stuffed with grass, the best known insulation of the time. Into his boots were tucked fur leggings that reached nearly to his groin. A belt around his waist supported a thick loincloth and straps attached to the leggings. Around his shoulders was either a thick fur coat or cape that was so large that he could wrap it into every crevice of his body. On top of all this was the grass cape, reaching past his knees, an item known to be worn by shepherds in several cultures as rain protection. The ensemble was topped off by a hat of the thickest fur imaginable. Just by keeping it on or taking it off, he could quite effectively adjust his body temperature.

There were still, however, a few puzzles about the clothing: What had become of the remnants of the clothes covering his shoulders? When the Simons stumbled upon the Iceman, there was nothing covering his shoulders and upper back. Naturally, Egg noted that the parts of the corpse that had first melted out of the ice were precisely those from which clothing was missing. Possibly it had decayed rapidly and blown away as soon as it had been exposed.

A second mystery concerned the hat, which was found packed in ice *below* the rock on which the man had lain. The chin strap that had held it on his head was still knotted in the center, but the strap itself had snapped at one point. Egg wondered when it had fallen from the man's head.

Egg's task was not, however, to figure out what had happened in those five thousand years at the Hauslabjoch. Once the restoration of the clothing was complete, which Egg thought would take several more months, he and his collaborators in Mainz would publish a volume detailing their work. Then, as soon as Spindler was ready for them, the artifacts were to be returned to Innsbruck for further study and then, ultimately, to South Tyrol. Though journalists and colleagues in archaeology were still calling him weekly with requests to see the artifacts or hear his interpretation, Egg's direct involvement in the project was drawing to a close.

It is the nature of scientific inquiry that even as data believed to be factual are tentatively set down in print or announced at meetings, new information is being uncovered that calls the old data into question or even chases it into oblivion. Such was the case in the Iceman project as well. Even as Konrad Spindler was hammering the first two years of results into a story involving a fleeing herdsman, his colleagues were slowly but surely coming up with new data that challenged him to refine or change his hypothesis.

Contrary to all expectations, Horst Seidler's team found higher than normal concentrations of copper, manganese, nickel, and arsenic in the man's hair.[5] Given that the main impurity in the Iceman's ax was arsenic, the discovery of that metal on his body was significant. The copper smelted for his ax contained arsenic, so fumes from the smelting process might have carried particles of it into his lungs and subsequently to other parts of his body. The arsenic would not show up after just one visit to a smelting site. It was built into the internal structure of the hair, which meant it had been present during the growth of the hair cells. The implication was that the man had been exposed to contamination from arsenic fumes over some period of time. The results not only seemed to confirm that metallurgy was practiced in his corner of the Alps during his lifetime but also suggested that Ötzi himself was exposed to it.

Not long after the Vienna results came out, a physicist at Oxford University named Geoffrey Grime came up with similar results using an even more sensitive method. Grime found pure copper particles on the surface of the hair and arsenic in the center, an indication that the latter had come through metabolism, from either swallowing or breathing in the element. Tests of animal hair from the man's fur clothing failed to turn up either element, suggesting that their incorporation into the man's hair occurred before he died and not during his storage in the ice. Both teams wanted to test their results by repeating the experiments with more samples. They asked Platzer to make samples from the lungs available to them as soon as possible.

Meanwhile, in the Netherlands, a Dutch leather researcher, Willy Groenman–Van Waateringe, commissioned by Markus Egg, had been determining the species of animals used in the Iceman's clothing by examining the pore pattern, hair type, and the size and thickness of the hides. Her surprising results indicated that Ötzi or his tailor had made very little use of the skins of domesticated animals, such as sheep or goats. Groenman–Van Waateringe found that of the three items of clothing, the loincloth alone was made unquestionably of the skin of a domesticated animal, in this case goat.[6] For the coat and the leggings, the tailor had selected the hide of a red deer, which would have been abundant in the Alps at the time he lived.

Ötzi's hat had been made of the fur of the brown bear, expertly sewn of several triangular-shaped panels. Groenman–Van Waateringe found bear skin again in the soles of the shoes, while the upper parts were made of red-deer skin. The soles and the head are particularly subject to the cold, and bear skin, a particularly thick fur, would have been the warmest material available to him.

Both sets of results presented obvious problems for the guiding assumptions the archaeologists were currently following, especially the herdsman hypothesis. As Lawrence Barfield formulated it, if the man had been a herdsman, why weren't more of his clothes made of the skins of the animals he tended? Why would a herdsman go to the trouble of hunting when he would have had ample animal material available for his clothing?

Moreover, would a herdsman have been involved so closely in metallurgy? Egg wondered whether the copper particles might be explained by the fact that the Iceman would have had to sharpen his ax occasionally, creating copper dust that could easily have gotten into his hair if he rubbed his hands through it. The arsenic in the hair was harder to explain. Since neither the Ötztal nor the Schnalstal had copper deposits, the raw material for the ax must have come from some distance. If Ötzi had been involved in copper processing, what was he doing in a region where he was unlikely to find his raw material? The archaeologists just did not know enough about how Neolithic societies organized their metal production. While they wrestled with these new results, the medical side of the investigation was slowly picking up pace. Platzer had finally received his special titanium tools and was about to allow the first samples to be taken from the corpse's interior. University of Innsbruck surgeons planned to cut tiny holes in the Iceman's chest cavity, insert the titanium endoscope, and then snip out minuscule samples from the lungs, the colon, the liver, and other key organs.

Until this point, the few researchers investigating the corpse itself had had to make do with surface tissue samples or the study of external conditions, such as the man's fascinating tattoos. By photographing the corpse with infrared light, which penetrates objects more deeply than normal light does and reveals the dark pigmentation beneath the dark skin, Norwegian anthropologist Torstein Sjøvold had discovered several new tattoos on the mummified corpse.[7] Ultimately, he identified fourteen sets of tattoos from the man's lower back to his feet, and he urged Platzer to take a skin sample to determine whether the two parallel markings around his left wrist were also tattoos.

Most of the tattoos were sets of lines, arranged vertically, like those on the back. Other sets, like one grouping of seven short lines, were concentrated on the left calf, which included a small cross on the inside anklebone, and on the right knee and calf. A second cross, on the inside of the right knee, also was made at a joint. A Dutch group of investigators that had analyzed a punch from one of the tattoos had not been able to determine the material or the method used, but they believed it was probably soot. Commonly, soot was first rubbed onto the skin, which was then punctured in the desired pattern, pushing a little of the soot into the hole, but the reverse method was also possible.[8]

Sjøvold had quickly realized that the placement of the tattoos very often occurred at points that were particularly prone to aches: the joints, the back, the legs, and the feet. When he learned that zur Nedden's radiological images of the corpse showed arthritis in the man's neck and hip, he was intrigued. Sjøvold suggested that the tattoos might have been intended as some kind of therapy for pain in these regions. At least one Pazyryk mummy had been tattooed along its spine, and one excavator had hypothesized that the marks had some medical significance. Sjøvold wanted to discuss whether the man's tattoos coincided with known acupuncture points. Just as zur Nedden could not determine whether the Iceman really experienced pain, Sjøvold could not say with certainty that the tattoos were a response to it. Neither was he willing to guess whether they would have had any therapeutic effect. Just as in modern Western medicine, belief counts for a great deal, but given that the tattoos would not have been visible under the clothes the Iceman wore, at least not in cold weather, both Sjøvold and the Dutch researchers agreed that they were probably not decorative.

Another research project involved a small bit of surface flesh, about the size of a fingernail, which had gone via Seidler to a small group of chemists and a forensics expert at the University of Vienna that wanted to investigate precisely how the man had been preserved. Under the leadership of Christian Reiter, a professor of forensic medicine, the team had already spent many months studying the chemistry of other naturally preserved corpses. In particular, they were interested in the differences between mummification by desiccation and adipocere formation, the waxy, Styrofoam-like material that characterized many corpses recovered from glaciers. Already they had discovered that these processes were not nearly as uniform as believed. There was more than one path to mummification.

For corpses to convert to adipocere required a storage place that was both humid and anaerobic, such as an oxygen-poor bog or a cold lake. In very wet conditions, where the body became waterlogged, the epidermis just slipped off like a surgical glove. The slightest disturbance in the water around the corpse could cause the epidermis to disintegrate. Thus, a missing epidermis was one indication of storage in cold water. The scientists were anxiously awaiting the results from their first tests on the Iceman's tissues.

In Innsbruck, meanwhile, the botanists were trying to sort out conflicting data. One problem concerned the timing of the Iceman's death. The pollen samples removed from the ice near the body had indicated that the man died in early fall, the same season in which he had been discovered by the Simons. As soon as Bortenschlager announced these results, researchers immediately agreed that they made sense, and they quickly came up with reasons to support it. It was likely, they said, that death came at the end of the summer, for that was when the snow was most shallow. It was also a likely time for the season's first big snowstorm and likely that that snow might not melt again all winter. Such a snow cover would at least protect a cadaver from predators. Mummification, they said, could have taken place under this snow covering.[9] A mid-September death also provided a convenient explanation—the transhumance—for what the man was doing at that altitude. Nothing about the timing thus conflicted with the herdsman idea.

The entire line of reasoning and questioning was backed up initially by Oeggl's finding that the single sloe found at the site had been ripe. But in the summer of 1994, Oeggl had a sudden realization. In the Inn Valley, where the Innsbruck botanists lived, the sloe did, indeed, ripen in mid-September. But in the Schnalstal, where the summer is hotter and longer, it ripened at the end of July. So where had the man picked up that sloe?

The inconsistency troubled Oeggl. Those who took the ice sample assumed that it had formed at the time the body was deposited. But this assumption had always seemed flawed to Oeggl. Ice could melt and refreeze, and certainly the temperature at the Hauslabjoch had fluctuated greatly in those five thousand years, even if the body had managed to stay preserved in ice. They just could not know for sure that the ice taken from the spot had really formed at the same time the Iceman died. Spindler's story about the Iceman's corpse and his belongings ended with the man's death. But Oeggl had long suspected that the man's death was just the beginning of another story that involved the deposition and storage of the find.

The way into that story was via the time-consuming sorting and identification of all those pounds of botanical remains and mud brought up in Lippert's dig. All day long and sometimes well into the night, a botany student or two could be found in the institute's lab, head bent to a microscope pointed at a stew of organic matter and mud. Using tiny tweezers, brushes, and little picks, the botanists in training carefully picked the mass apart, separating the grasses from the hair, the grains of sand, the droppings of animals, feathers, and even tiny twigs. Most of what emerged from the stew was hardly earth-shattering. Already they had filled hundreds of sample dishes. Oeggl was not looking for any one thing in particular but trying to understand the pattern of everything all together. Still, every once in a while, something out of the ordinary turned up.

Three little fragments of wood, each just an inch or two long, had been found separately in the sediments of the trench. There was nothing unusual about them. They looked like a thousand other little pieces of wood that one walked by every day, lying in the gutter, on a path, or on the floor of a forest. But in the spectrum of what the botanists were uncovering, they were unusual. Any wood found in the trench aroused interest because trees did not grow at that altitude. Their presence meant that someone had brought them up there. Most intriguing was that all three were from the wayfaring bush, a wood that had already shown up in some very important artifacts.

One day Oeggl pulled up a chair to have a look. The pieces were so light that his breath almost blew them away when he got too close. He examined their broken edges, looking for little cracks, a particular coloring, or knobs. They were somewhat eroded, as if they had been in water for some time. Each also had one curved side, which was probably the outside edge of the branch they had come from. Perhaps, Oeggl thought, they were part of the same section of the branch. After a little fiddling, he discovered that two bits did indeed match up and belong together. Squeezing them together, he held them against a light and examined the fit. It wasn't perfect, but it was definitely a match. The edges were just slightly eroded.

Carefully, he picked up the third piece. Did it belong in there somewhere? Oeggl tried the third piece first one way, then another, and then another. Miraculously, he found a fit. The three shards came from one branch. And it was a very familiar branch. Again, he pinched them together and looked at the construction from all angles. The pieces formed about a four-inch-long section of a skinny branch, less than a half inch in diameter. The bark had been removed, and both ends were broken. Oeggl could not quite believe his luck. He had just reassembled a piece of a broken arrow shaft.

He knew right where it came from. Though Spindler tended to ignore it, one unfinished arrow shaft in the quiver had been broken off, and its missing end had never been found. This little bit might fit onto it. Oeggl had plans for these pieces, so he was not quite ready to share the discovery with anyone. After all, the importance of these pieces of wood lay not in their reconstruction per se but in what they told him about the deposition and storage of the find as a whole. For years now he had been pondering the story of the discovery and the recovery of the Iceman, going over every step of what was found, who found it, where, and in what condition. This little piece of arrow shaft had sharpened some of his suspicions. But before he could say anything concrete, he wanted a lot more evidence.

In the meantime, he already had results on the origins of the woods found among the Iceman's belongings. As he had already shared with Spindler, the yew appeared to be one key to locating his settlement. Ötzi had presumably acquired the yew wood for the bow some time before his death. Based on information gleaned from papers on experimental archaeology, Spindler hypothesized that he acquired the wood within two weeks of his death.

Unbeknownst to Oeggl, Markus Egg had earlier enlisted a German experimental archaeologist named Harm Paulsen to make and test replicas of several pieces of Ötzi's equipment, including the ax and the bow and arrows. Their hypothesis was that the man had used the equipment he carried with him to make the bow. Using a replica of Ötzi's copper ax, Paulsen easily chopped through a fresh four-inch-diameter yew branch. It took just one minute. Out of curiosity, Paulsen also tried chopping through the same branch with a stone ax, the technology that preceded the copper ax. Though it took the same amount of time, the angle at which he had to strike was more oblique.

After splitting the yew wood, he removed the bark and all the sapwood. Most modern bowyers insisted that the most resilient bows came from wood that had been cut so that both the heartwood—the interior, dead core of the tree—and the sapwood—the softer wood that conducts water and sap—were still present. The heartwood was the muscle of the tree, but the presence of sapwood assured that it would not break under tension. To the archaeologists' surprise, however, all the sapwood in the Iceman's bow had been removed. Many Neolithic bows from Switzerland also lacked their sapwood, and this fact had befuddled bow experts for years.

Paulsen tried to be true to the original. For the whittling, he again used the copper ax, taking short even strokes down the length of the fresh yew branch, a process known as tillering. The ax worked well because he had chosen fresh wood, which was still relatively soft. Paulsen assumed Ötzi had worked it in precisely the same way.

What he could not determine was whether the yew wood in the bow had been "seasoned," a process in which wood is stored for several months or even years to allow it to dry out enough so that the product does not warp. But if the Iceman used his ax to work it, he must have used unseasoned wood, since seasoned wood would have been too dry and hard for the ax. Of course, prehistoric people had followed certain guidelines in making their tools, but perhaps, he thought, the Iceman had not had enough time to get seasoned wood.

But Paulsen learned quickly that the unseasoned heartwood-only bow was very brittle. The first replica he made broke after just sixty shots, and the second after about one hundred and twenty. Paulsen wondered whether an experienced Neolithic archer, which the Iceman must have been, would have tolerated such performance. After all, he was not shooting just at deer. Ötzi wore a hat made of the fur of a bear, not an animal he would have wanted to have in his sights when his bow snapped in two. On the other hand, perhaps there were cultural or economic reasons for his choices. The fact that prehistoric Swiss bowyers also removed the sapwood suggested that this was not a fluke.

While Paulsen pursued his experiments on the yew bow, Oeggl was also investigating yew. How the Iceman came by this particular length of wood Oeggl could only guess. But his consultations with various bow and wood experts around Europe (not including Paulsen), as well as his own botanical researches, had convinced him that not just any yew was right for a bow. A bow might look simple, but building one was far more complicated than just taking any old branch and tying a string to both ends. Oeggl was learning that the Iceman's bow had extraordinary properties.

First, the yew he had selected was particularly dense. Bowyers had told Oeggl that a good yew bow required at least ten year rings per centimeter. Measurements from splinters of the Iceman's bow showed that it had sixteen year rings per centimeter, packed in so closely that counting them with the naked eye was not easy. It was an astonishingly dense packaging of the rings. That kind of build afforded the wood the right combination of rigidity and elasticity it needed to flex and then return to its original shape.

Following this analysis, Oeggl and his students made several trips to South Tyrol to see if they could locate a stand of evergreens with the same year-ring profile. In the millennia since the Iceman had lived, the flora had changed considerably, but Oeggl thought he still might be able to learn something from the existing trees in the region. Finding the yew in the Vinschgau was not as easy as he expected. During the Middle Ages, the yew had been harvested for export far and wide, and they had been largely depleted. Few stands had survived except for those planted on steep ledges of the mountains not accessible to people.

But in the centuries since then, the yew, though still classified as endangered in Europe, had recolonized the valley bottom of the Vinschgau, where the humidity was high enough for them to thrive.

Borings from these yews all showed much less dense concentration of year rings than did the Iceman's bow. There were yews that now grew on the rocky sides of gorges and cliffs as well, but the results were the same. Oeggl felt that he could safely conclude that the Vinschgau would not provide natural conditions that could produce yew wood of the quality the Iceman had used in his bow. However, the wood could still have come from the Vinschgau.

Oeggl believed that the Iceman's bow came from a yew tree that had been cultivated specially to produce the extremely dense and tough heartwood. In order to achieve such wood, prehistoric farmers could have managed their growth by wounding the trees, stripping off branches, and maybe even neglecting to fertilize them so that they were not able to absorb as much sunlight and remained lean. Just as they had cultivated their high-altitude pastures, so, too, did these prehistoric people practice forest management. These trees were perhaps planted by one generation so that the following ones would have the fine wood. When Ötzi set out to get the wood for his new bow—if he, indeed, had done so—he was after a very precise branch.

The management did not stop when the tree was felled. Oeggl was convinced that no bowyer would ever invest time in making a bow with fresh wood. Contrary to Paulsen's approach, Oeggl was adamant that the wood for a successful bow first had to be seasoned. Several bowyers told him that several years could pass before a length of wood was sufficiently dried to be carved into a bow, and that required lots of advance planning. Bow production was its own little industry. A village would not only have to make sure they had enough yew trees under cultivation, but they also had to be maintaining a stockpile of yew rawlings in various stages of drying. Someone had to keep track of how old each rawling was.

When the time came to turn a rawling into a bow, the bowyer was presented with a hardened piece of very dense wood. Such wood, Oeggl inferred from an experiment by one of his students, could not have been cut by Ötzi's copper ax. None of his tools could have cut it.

In fact, Oeggl had noticed something about the copper ax that made him doubt that Ötzi had used it for any practical purpose. The clue was not in the blade but in the wooden handle: It was a beautifully finished handle of yew, whereas most known prehistoric ax handles were made of oak or ash. Oeggl's analysis of the handle further revealed that it was bisected by another branch that now had been cut away. It had entered the handle at an angle parallel to the ax's angle of strike. That greatly weakened the handle. Oeggl predicted that with just a few blows of the ax against a tree or branch, the handle would snap in two at the site of the bisection. He was sure that the Iceman could not have used that ax, not even for shaving down his bow.

That in itself was a revelation. But it was not the only lesson Oeggl took from this finding. Spindler and others had supposed that the ax had been used to make the bow. That, Oeggl realized, was only one instance of a tendency among certain researchers to see the situation at the Hauslabjoch as entirely self-explanatory, as if all the artifacts and the corpse could be interpreted simply in relation to each other. The longbow certainly looked unfinished, and the ax certainly seemed to be designed to cut, but those observations alone did not merit the conclusion that one had made the other. In order to understand the bow or the ax, Oeggl thought they needed to go back and test the relationships they had simply assumed among the artifacts: the ax to the bow, the ibex bones to the last meal, and the embers to the birch-bark container—even, Oeggl thought, the relation of the Iceman to the boulder on which he was found.

CHAPTER 9

EXPANDING MARKETS

I N THE WINTER of 1995, the British science journal *Nature,* which earlier had criticized the slow pace of the Iceman research, learned that several Iceman researchers were calling Ötzi *Homo tirolensis.* In a biting commentary, the editors chastised the scientists for ignoring the conventions of biological nomenclature by assigning the frozen glacier corpse to a new species. "Readers will look in vain for the careful systematic and diagnostic argument that such nomenclature requires," they wrote.[1]

Of course, the editors at *Nature* knew the scientists were using the name lightly, but that was not scientific and could even be misleading. Ötzi could not even have been an ethnic Tyrolean at the time he lived. Not until the Middle Ages did the mountainous region between Innsbruck and Bolzano acquire the name "Tyrol."

Nature's little reprimand angered Platzer, though he himself had never used the term, and he vowed never to publish in the journal. But Horst Seidler, while somewhat embarrassed, was more sympathetic to the journal's point. Human diversity had vexed biologists for centuries, and Seidler was acutely aware of the murderous damage done by ill-conceived classification systems. Until very recently, scientists had tried to group people according to shared characteristics, such as head shape, skin color, nose size, or blood type. Like most American physical anthropologists, Seidler had concluded that such preconceived racial categories were inadequate to account for human diversity. No matter what traits researchers came up with, or how many, individuals always defied the classifications.

Seidler often cited a study by the American researcher Richard Lewontin that showed that 85 percent of all human genetic variation (with some other conditions) was found to exist inside any local population, tribe, or nation. If those local populations, tribes, and nations were grouped together into one of the major races, such as Europeans, then an additional 8 percent of all human genetic variation showed up in the group. Only 7 percent of genetic variation was found between the groups that had been called "major races."[2] Thus, much more variation exists among individuals of any one group than between members of that group and another as a whole. No matter how humans are divided up, the overwhelming majority of diversity exists within any one group. Because of this, only a few American scientists speak of biological (as opposed to social) races, except in the most colloquial sense.

Seidler was especially alert to race issues because of his country's implication in Nazi Germany's racist policies, which led to the murder of more than six million people. In the turbulent years leading up to the rise of Nazism, Germans grew concerned that their society was sick. One explanation offered by anthropologists was that the primordial racial types were interbreeding and that the Nordic race was being debased by so-called lesser types, such as Jews and Gypsies. Under the Third Reich, many German anthropologists joined the Nazi Party and contributed to the development and implementation of the Reich's racist policies. Without exception, anthropology departments at universities in Germany and Austria toed the party line. Among other things, they helped decide who should be sterilized, and they developed and conducted racial evaluations of people whose genetic stock was uncertain.[3] These tests evaluated individuals relative to predetermined "types"—sets of traits supposedly representative of distinct races. But the traits chosen were arbitrary, and few people fit exactly into any one category. A non-Aryan classification often resulted in a person being sent to a concentration or death camp.

Seidler felt a special responsibility to deal with his institute's heinous past, so he wrote extensively on Nazi anthropology and critiqued scientists whom he felt perpetuated the old racial stereotypes. Seidler was also vociferously opposed to Austria's neo-Nazi fringe groups and right-wing politicians, whose strength was growing throughout the 1990s mainly because of their anti-immigrant stance. Seidler's in-your-face style had earned him plenty of enemies in his difficult rise to the country's highest academic position in human biology. Occasionally he even received threatening letters rife with anti-Semitic slurs. "You know, Seidler is Jewish!" one colleague once suggested privately. Seidler said he was not Jewish. His father was, in fact, a member of the Nazi party.

When in the middle of the controversy over whether the Iceman was a castrated Egyptian a Viennese anthropologist named Johann Szilvassy announced that he had definite proof that the mummy was of the "European race," Seidler was furious. Szilvassy, the head of the anthropology department at the Natural History Museum in Vienna, came to his conclusion from measurements he made from X rays of the man's skull.

"The sinuses in the face assume a special relevance among the characteristics of the human skeleton detectable by X ray," Szilvassy told the Austrian newspaper *Die Presse*. "Not only can they be used for the classification of race but with their help one can also carry out studies in variation and heredity."[4] Szilvassy went on to say that the Iceman's large frontal sinus and large nasal cavity were characteristic of Europeans. If he were Egyptian, one might expect him to have small upper jaw cavities, typical of the "African race," he said. If he were from South America or a member of the "Mongoloid" race, one would expect his large frontal sinus to be much smaller. "All that shows that the Stone Age man from Hauslabjoch can only be assigned to the European race," Szilvassy concluded.

Werner Platzer dismissed Szilvassy's comments immediately, noting that the man had never even seen the corpse and had not been invited into the project. But Szilvassy's comments infuriated Seidler, who found them reminiscent of the old racial studies that had survived in German physical anthropology after the war. Seidler had previously seen Szilvassy use categories such as "Alpine race," which were wholly discredited. Anthropologists in the United States, too, laughed uncomfortably when asked about Szilvassy's claims. Craniometry, the science of measuring skulls, still reeked of Nazi anthropology, and most stayed far away from the subject, as confused over the validity of craniometry as they were over the race concept as a whole.

Szilvassy's work was easily dismissed, in part because he was excluded from the project, yet another anthropologist who thought the Iceman's skull might hold clues to the population he was from had been involved in the project from the beginning. Ironically, Seidler himself had proposed asking Wolfram Bernhard, a German from the University of Mainz, to join the project.

Bernhard was considered one of Germany's foremost physical anthropologists, a group Seidler had openly criticized in the past, and he wielded considerable power within the anthropological establishment in the German-speaking world. His research on the Iceman started with the very assumption Szilvassy had made, that similarities in the size and shape of a person's cranium, including the face, frequently expressed genetic or what he called "ethnogenetic" relationships.

Generally, Bernhard thought his studies might be used to understand whether new cultural developments were due to innovation by the local population or to the arrival of a new population bringing new technology. Continuity in the morphologies of the skeletons might indicate local development, while the appearance of quite different traits might indicate that new immigrants had arrived in a region.

During several trips to Innsbruck, Bernhard made dozens of measurements of the Iceman's skull, including the greatest head length and width, the height of the middle of the face, and the width and height of the nose. The next step was to evaluate them against the same measurements taken from contemporary skulls in the Alpine region. For this, he turned to a database of measurements from other Neolithic and Bronze Age skulls. Unfortunately, only eleven measurements could be done on all 144 skulls he was interested in. By contrast, some recent studies have been based on fifty-seven measurements.[5] Still, he continued the investigation. He divided the skulls into three source regions: northern Italy; eastern Switzerland and France; and southern Germany, Austria, and western Hungary. Among the finds included in the northern Italian region were skulls from Remedello. Bernhard was disappointed that no skeletal material at all was available from several Neolithic and Copper Age cultures in northern Austria, southern Germany, and the Czech Republic. These cultures were generally contemporary with the Iceman, and not distant from the Hauslabjoch, so their absence was regrettable.

With the data he had, Bernhard ran two types of computer analysis. The program looked for patterns of traits and came up with a cladogram, a branching diagram that suggested how the skulls might be related. The first showed that the strongest similarity existed between the Iceman's skull and one found in Meilen on Lake Zürich from the Horgen culture, which was carbon-dated to the same period as the Iceman.[6] There were also strong connections to the Cortaillod culture of Switzerland and to skulls from Remedello and Trentino. The second type of analysis gave the skull a 50 percent probability of belonging to the northern Italian group.[7]

Bernhard concluded that the skulls most similar to that of the Iceman were from cultures geographically closest to the Hauslabjoch. He said nothing about the man's origin or genetic family. He concluded nothing about whether the Iceman was more closely related to a modern Tyrolean or a German or an Italian. The results seemed straightforward and were hardly surprising.

But privately, Seidler was not at all happy with the study, and he raised the same complaint he had made about Szilvassy's comments. So much variation existed within any one population, that nothing at all could be said about the ethnic group or origin of a single skull. Several other physical anthropologists in the United States who took a look at the results were also skeptical of the work. While a few American researchers did analyze the morphologies of skeletal remains for clues to ethnic identity, they concentrated their studies on entire populations from one graveyard and one time period.

Among the German physical-anthropology establishment, Bernhard's paper got little attention. Though two different versions were published in the volumes of scientific research on the Iceman, it was never discussed formally at any of the scientific meetings. No one, including Seidler, ever publicly challenged either the methodology or the conclusions.

Summer after summer, for four years now, the archaeological results in the area around the Hauslabjoch had been discouragingly slim. There was no sign of any settlement where Ötzi might have spent his long winters, helped plant the fields in the spring, and perhaps even smelted copper for his tools and slaughtered his animals. Every one of those activities left distinctive marks on the landscape that could survive for millennia. The archaeologists had hiked up every valley, crossed every pass, explored every hilltop, examined nearly every boulder, and still there was no trace of any permanent Neolithic settlement where the Iceman or anyone else could have made a home.

Along the way, however, they had found ample evidence of the Iceman's predecessors in the region, the Mesolithic hunters who had moved through the mountains millennia before his lifetime. At more than a half-dozen sites around the Hauslabjoch, all but one in South Tyrol, archaeologists had detected the faintest traces of Mesolithic hunters' camps. This evidence had lain just a few inches below the surface for some seven thousand years. Typical of the sites was one just south of Vernagt, where colleagues of Annaluisa Pedrotti from the University of Trento found a few tiny flint tools. Even more interesting than the artifacts, however, was the pattern of the camps. Most were near or even on the long transhumance path that stretched from the Vinschgau over a mountain ridge to Vernagt in the Schnalstal, then up to the Hauslabjoch, and into the upper Ötztal. The chain of rest stops lent further support to the glaciologist Patzelt's contention that the Iceman had died just off a prehistoric trail.

The northernmost finds along this route were made just south of Vent, Austria, by a group from Konrad Spindler's department at the university. Sometime in the very distant past, a gigantic boulder had come crashing down from a nearby ridge and rolled to a stop on a gently sloping terrace less than one hundred yards from the modern path between Vent and the Similaun lodge. Such boulders were known to be common campsites for prehistoric, and even modern, people, since they provided shelter from sun, wind, and rain.

This twelve-foot-high boulder seemed particularly suited to the task, since it had large overhanging edges under which a person could crawl to be completely out of the rain or sun. Walter Leitner, the assistant professor in Spindler's department who headed the archaeological team, named it Hohle Stein (hollow stone), because of these impressive hollows.[8] In the team's first probe of the ground around the site, they uncovered the outline of a campfire. Ultimately, the site yielded splinters of flint and rock crystal, a clear quartz that could be fashioned into beautiful tools. They also found burned animal bones and a tiny piece of ocher-red chalk, which was interesting because it was often used in prehistory to draw or mark the sites of the dead.

But the most significant finds were the four blades of caramel-colored flint. Leitner knew the types well, as did all his students. The flints were among the most distinctive markers of the Mesolithic. Flint did not occur naturally in this part of the Alps, so when it turned up, archaeologists knew that someone had to have carried it in, even from hundreds of miles away. If archaeologists could figure out where it was mined, then they would have a clue to the network of trade and communication and perhaps even to the movement of people through a region.

Leitner believed that this type of flint came from south of the site. He also knew that the Iceman's flint, although a different color, was supposed to be from south of the Hauslabjoch. Apparently, that long trail had also been conducting flint into the region.

Given what archaeologists, particularly Annaluisa Pedrotti, had already hypothesized about the Mesolithic period in this region, there was nothing surprising about these additional high-altitude finds. Bagolini and his colleagues had made many high-altitude discoveries of evidence of Mesolithic hunters. But then, around the time agriculture started, the finds at high altitudes stopped. Rather suddenly, or at least it appeared that way in the archaeological record, the finds in Trentino and South Tyrol became clustered at lower altitudes, on the terraces near the valley bottoms, which were prime agricultural lands: relatively flat, well drained, and with good sun exposure, rarities in the Alps. There was also a climatic shift at this time, which some archaeologists thought partially explained how land use had changed. Temperatures rose a little, and trees began growing at higher altitudes. That meant that the game that survived off the shrubs and grasses that grew above the tree line were squeezed out. Hunting might also have overtaxed the available game, and the hunters had to resort to some other way to feed themselves. Whatever the explanation, archaeologists thought it indicated that journeys to high altitudes were no longer profitable enough.

Pedrotti noted yet another shift, around 3300 B.C.E., in the altitude at which archaeological finds tended to turn up.[9] The people in South Tyrol and Trentino appeared to again make use of the upper reaches of the mountains, crossing passes and setting up shelters beneath cliff overhangs and settlements on hilltops. Some archaeologists had suggested that the spurt in population that came about with the beginning of agriculture meant that there was not room enough for everyone to farm on the fertile terraces. Some people might have been forced to move higher up into the mountains, and to make the corresponding adaptations to the harsher environment, where water was less abundant and the snow lasted longer on the fields. Pedrotti was baffled over what kind of agriculture they could have cultivated at such high altitudes. She suspected they might have needed a supplemental way of getting food, perhaps by hunting or herding animals. Importantly, this was the same period from which Sigmar Bortenschlager had evidence that people began burning the high pastures in order to open up grazing land. Living at a higher altitude, they might also have needed to become more mobile, moving between their settlements and the mountain pastures, where they kept their animals.

At one Neolithic site, the archaeologists had found the bones of many sheep and goats. The question was whether they were used primarily for their meat and hides or for their secondary products, such as milk and wool. At another site under a cliff overhang, a ladlelike tool used in casting was found, which suggested that these people were making their own copper.

Pedrotti also noticed that the pottery from the period was not very pretty. It was simple, often without decoration, and she thought the people who made it were probably not very interested in it. A few centuries earlier, when agriculture was getting under way, people were creating beautiful ceramics with finely incised patterns and interesting forms. Pedrotti wondered whether the return to higher altitudes she was hypothesizing was related to the neglect of the pottery. People who were on the move with their animals might not want to lug around pottery. The Iceman had none with him. Instead he had carried the two birch-bark containers. She thought people who lived high in the mountains might have focused their energies on the relatively lighter wooden and birch-bark containers instead of pottery.

The paucity of discoveries from the Neolithic period was disappointing. But the situation had made Pedrotti delve further into cultures contemporary with the Iceman that had lain to the north of the Hauslabjoch. She checked illustrations of artifacts, paid visits to colleagues in Switzerland, Germany, and Austria, and studied all the available archaeological material. What she learned convinced her that the population that lived in the Alps at that time had little to do culturally with the Remedello people on the Po plain. Though she recognized that some loose connection must exist between them because of the similarity in the axes, the environments were very different. They also had little to do with contemporary populations in Switzerland, who built their dwellings on piles next to lakes. And yet there were many similarities between groups of mountain dwellers at this time. Pedrotti still needed to do more checking, but she thought she was onto something.

Several years into the Iceman project, Konrad Spindler commissioned a German geologist named Alexander Binsteiner to find the source of the flint in the Iceman's tools. It was a plum assignment, and Binsteiner, who had ample training in archaeology, seemed suited to the task. The flint in the Iceman's dagger blade was gray and flecked with white, and Binsteiner knew it had not come from quarries north of the Alps.

So, in the spring of 1994, Binsteiner headed for the foothills of the Monti Lessini, which rise out of the Po plain near Verona like an enormous medieval fortress. In those formidable limestone hills lay extensive sources of good-quality flint that had been mined since Paleolithic times. Even as recently as the nineteenth century, the flints for the Austro-Hungarian army's guns were quarried there. The remarkable feature of Monti Lessini flint was the ease with which it could be won out of the limestone in which it had formed. As the hills' porous limestone eroded, fissures, sinkholes, and sometimes large underground caverns formed, and the large nodules of more durable flint settled at their bottom. Monti Lessini flint came in a variety of colors, but the most characteristic was tan, brown, or gray with opaque white speckling.

Binsteiner's plan was to tour the hills along the Adige Valley, a sparsely populated region of farmers and people who still made their living off the stone industry. Every few miles, he stopped to examine a flint outcropping or a road cut for signs of human activity. Success came sooner than he could have dreamed.

Near the tiny town of Ceredo, high in the Lessinian hills, he found exactly what he was looking for. A recent earthmoving project for a street had cut right through one of the fissures in which flint nodules—some as large as basketballs—had weathered out of the limestone. Nearby, Binsteiner came upon an enormous field pocked with odd bowl-shaped cavities in which the flint accumulated. Everywhere he looked he saw half-worked flint blades, splinters, rinds, and other debris from mining activity. This material could not have broken naturally. Humans had clearly been here, working this flint, and the shapes of the pieces he was finding told him that they had been here in the Stone Age.

Not long after his discovery, Binsteiner stopped by the office of Annaluisa Pedrotti and Bernardino Bagolini to show off what he had found. Though Pedrotti had eagerly piped information to Spindler on the northern Italian Neolithic period, little information about the archaeological results ever made it back to Italy from Spindler's department, and she was initially surprised that Spindler had sent someone down to Italy to look for the Iceman's flint. She, too, suspected his flint came from the Monti Lessini region, but when she saw the pieces Binsteiner had retrieved there she advised caution. The stone might be compositionally equivalent to that used in the Iceman's dagger blade, but most of the flakes Binsteiner had in his hands had not been struck in the Stone Age. The Neolithic miner's technique produced flakes that were distinctive. The area around Ceredo had been the site of a lot of mining activity over the centuries, she gently warned her colleague, so there was a lot of flint debris there that was much younger. Since Binsteiner was new to the region, Pedrotti offered to assist him in interpreting what he found. By the time he left her office, she was excited about a possible collaboration. That summer, she, Binsteiner, Spindler, and other Italian and Austrian archaeologists agreed to collaborate the following year on a project to survey and dig around Ceredo. In the protocol of the meeting, during a discussion of the owners of the property on which he found the flint, Binsteiner is quoted as saying that the site's link to the Iceman should be kept quiet in order to avoid plundering. But the next thing the Italians knew, the young geologist was announcing his finding in the press.

Binsteiner wrote in the German newspaper *Süddeutsche Zeitung* that he had located "Ötzi's mine."[10] "In the flint are found the tiniest, millimeter-sized remains of fossilized organisms that once lived in the Jurassic and Cretaceous seas of the Alpine region," he wrote. "The fossils are visible under the microscope and carry a type of 'fingerprint' that is unmistakable even after millions of years. The question of the origin of Ötzi's flints appears answered with all of these facts," Binsteiner concluded.

Binsteiner was so sure of his discovery that he even invited a German film crew to come with him to the site. He walked up to what appeared to be a pile of flint just lying exposed under some trees. He bent down, picked up a piece, and showed it to the camera.

"You see how thick the stuff is lying. This is all mine material. The Stone Age miner considered this stuff to be trash and just threw it away," he said, turning the flake around to show its many facets. He explained how the combination of fossils in the Iceman's tools matched those in some of the flint at this site. "This is how we can say, with almost one hundred percent certainty, that the material from the Iceman originates in this very mine," Binsteiner said. In the film, as the music swelled and the camera panned over the fog-shrouded landscape near Ceredo, the narrator announced that the exact location of the site had to be kept secret in order to protect it. It was an awesome moment in the film, and the secrecy made it all the more powerful.

Back in Innsbruck, Spindler, unaware that Binsteiner's certainty might be premature, was thrilled that Ötzi's mine had been located. Because of the ubiquity of most materials in the Iceman's equipment, the flint provided a rare opportunity to ferret out one of the man's long-distance connections. The Iceman had not used just any flint but the best in the region. Perhaps that explained why the flint tools he had were so small. Hurriedly, arrangements were made to have the article published in a professional mining journal.

Months later, when Pedrotti got a copy of the article, she blanched. Both she and Lawrence Barfield knew about those heaps of debris Binsteiner had stumbled upon. They were the remains of the *nineteenth century* mining works. They had not lain there five thousand years but perhaps a century. Binsteiner had illustrated not Stone Age technology but gun flint.[11]

Before they could respond formally to Spindler, the case quickly took an unexpected turn. Binsteiner had become embroiled in a dispute with Platzer and Spindler over payment for his work. Ironically, he was virtually the only scientist whose research project was being funded almost entirely by the Research Institute for Alpine Prehistory. In a fury over the way he was being treated, Binsteiner quit abruptly.

In the meantime, Barfield, Pedrotti, and Spindler were going ahead with the plans to survey and dig in the Monti Lessini. Barfield's familiarity with the Monti Lessini dated to the early 1980s, when he had first surveyed the area.[12] Monti Lessini flint had been found at sites as far south as central Italy and, more recently, as far north as southern Germany. How the flint traveled, Barfield did not know. Finished tools could simply have been passed from one hand to the next as gifts. The tools could also have reached their final destinations via traders or middlemen who journeyed from one village to the next. Formal trade, however, implied an economy with specialists, and archaeologists generally agreed that such a society had not yet developed in northern Italy when the Monti Lessini was first mined. If it had, Barfield thought, those labor divisions would probably have resulted in a hierarchy that would have shown up in burials and even in the statue-menhirs.

One of the goals of the survey Barfield did in the 1980s was to determine whether Monti Lessini was a place that had been open to all people or whether it had been controlled by one group that worked the flint and traded it to others. As expected, the survey uncovered ample evidence of prehistoric quarrying and mining activity, particularly near a landmark known as the Ponte di Veja, an enormous natural limestone bridge that had formed when a cave collapsed, leaving only the arch at the doorway. Archaeologists often noticed concentrations of finds around landmarks like that bridge, and Barfield suspected that people in the Copper Age might have used the Ponte di Veja as a point of reference, like a gas station sign high on a pole next to the highway. His cursory survey turned up no trace of a permanent settlement, but he was eager to try one more time.

As plans for the new survey were taking shape, Pedrotti learned that Spindler, apparently still unaware that Binsteiner's flint was not prehistoric, had found some unlikely candidates to carry out the excavation of Binsteiner's mine.

Months earlier, a few Austria-based scientists on the Iceman project had established connections with colleagues at Wake Forest University in Winston-Salem, North Carolina. After a little coaxing from Horst Seidler, the well-endowed American university had kicked in about twenty thousand dollars for the privilege of taking part in the Iceman research.[13] The donation was highly unusual. As part of the deal, Werner Platzer was also to get an honorary doctorate for his work on the Iceman and his lifetime achievement in the field of anatomy. In the spring of 1996, Platzer, his wife and daughter, and a small group of scientists from the Iceman project, including Seidler, journeyed to Winston-Salem for the occasion.

For the anatomist, it was a moment to savor. Unlike Spindler, who had become famous through his book and speeches, Platzer had not made himself very accessible to the media or the public. He was seldom recognized publicly as one of the leaders of the project. This kind of recognition, by another university, in the controlled setting of a graduation ceremony, without the relentless scrutiny of the media, fit his style perfectly.

A little over a month after the ceremony, a Wake Forest archaeology professor named Ned Woodall and a large group of undergraduates arrived in the Monti Lessini to excavate the mine that Binsteiner had claimed was prehistoric. The invitation to do the dig had come from Spindler, who had not mentioned that there was some question whether the mine was prehistoric.

The Italians saw Spindler, ostensibly the leader of the excavation, only once at the site, during the filming of the dig for a second BBC documentary on the Iceman. Poised in front of the excavation area, he spoke authoritatively about Monti Lessini flint and its movement across the Alps, though he had not participated in any of the archaeological surveys or digs aimed at illuminating the Iceman's home territory since the discovery. When the filming was done, Spindler got in his car and drove away.

Spindler had become the most recognized archaeologist in the German-speaking world. Even more than four years after the discovery, hardly a week went by when he did not receive an invitation to deliver a talk on the Iceman. He spoke at schools, universities, museums, and other public institutions. He even appeared before industry groups or corporate meetings, both of which paid considerably better than any academic body. In one particularly busy year, Spindler delivered virtually the same lecture more than sixty times.

Though Spindler had expected the research to flourish for many years after the discovery, results were coming in at a trickle now, and he had little concrete idea what some researchers, such as the botanists, were finding out. His audiences did not seem to mind or even to notice. People seemed to like to hear the basics of the Iceman over and over again. The fees for these lectures could be quite lucrative, ranging from several hundred to several thousand dollars. Spindler had also discovered that his appeal was general enough that people would pay him to speak on other topics of archaeological or historical interest. One year he was hired to give several lectures on the classical world during a luxury cruise on the Mediterranean. This was not his field, but the organizers did not care. What mattered was that he was the leader of the Iceman project.

So many offers for speaking engagements came into the institute that Spindler had to share some with his junior colleague, Walter Leitner. Before long, Spindler was driving a new Mercedes and Leitner a new red Alfa Romeo. Since research on the corpse and the artifacts was still under way, South Tyrol had extended the contract with the University of Innsbruck, so there was no foreseeable end to Spindler's privilege.

Spindler's "disaster theory," as he called the tale of the fight and flight, had accordingly taken root and flourished in the popular imagination. Among his academic peers, it fared less well. When his colleagues finally saw the slim archaeological evidence presented in its full form in Spindler's book, most concluded that it was inadequate to support the drama he had written. Crucially, the disaster theory had not turned up in the same form in any peer-reviewed journal of archaeology.

A year after Spindler's introduction of the hypothesis, however, a watered-down version of it appeared in the *Journal of Archaeological Science*. The article, the bulk of which reported on the latest findings of the radiological investigation, endorsed the broad outlines of a "theory of a 'personal disaster with a departure in full flight.' "[14] The authors of the paper included several of the main researchers on the project—zur Nedden, Seidler, Platzer, and Spindler himself. The inclusion on the author list of many of the project's top researchers, though they may have contributed only marginally to an article, was part of the project's policy. In this case, at least two men named as authors disagreed with the disaster hypothesis. Apart from Spindler, none of the authors have mentioned it in their writings since then.

The common theme in most critiques of Spindler's disaster theory was that he had overstepped the bounds of his profession. Speculation was permissible, of course. But instead of assembling all the evidence and then inferring a parsimonious explanation, Spindler heavily interpreted select facts while ignoring others. The story he ended up with was highly contingent, and his interpretations of the evidence highly arbitrary. By what criteria had he decided which damage occurred to the tools before the man had died? Given the radiologists' uncertainties over the timing of the rib breaks, why did they play such a key role in Spindler's account of the man's demise? Were there no other possibilities?

Writing in the respected English journal of archaeology *Antiquity*, Lawrence Barfield dealt with the question of altercation and flight with a telling terseness. "If the injury was the cause of death, then it would seem unlikely that he could have made the climb, especially encumbered by so much equipment. The careful packaging of some of the items would also argue against a hasty flight. A more economical explanation would be that he was already up in the mountains with his sheep when an accident prevented his descent to the valley before the snow came."[15]

In a review for *The Times Literary Supplement*, British archaeologist Paul Bahn criticized Spindler's "regrettable tendency to slide from hypothesis to certainty."[16] Bahn, who had previously criticized the delays in the Iceman project in the pages of *Nature*, was also perplexed by the disaster theory: "It is in his account of the Iceman's death that Spindler reveals himself to be a frustrated novelist, anxious to pass beyond the limits of archaeological interpretation."

Raw criticism was typical of the English academy, where, as in the United States, scholars often made their careers by overturning the theories of their own professors. But the German and Austrian systems were different. Open attacks against the head of the University of Innsbruck's Department of Prehistory were not advisable, even though every manner of criticism and even ridicule was allowable behind closed doors. One who did wager a jab was a journalist named Michael Zick, who questioned Spindler's book's claim to be the only "authorized" story of the find. Authorized by whom? Zick wondered in an article. Ötzi?[17]

Undeterred by the academic criticism, Spindler stood by his version of the Iceman's last weeks, even as he delved into new, but related, projects. He was especially eager to share his expertise with other scientists who found themselves in possession of such treasures. In the fall of 1995, he got his first opportunity to do so. In distant Peru, the five-hundred-year-old frozen corpse of an Incan girl was discovered at 20,700 feet, just below the summit of an ice-covered Andean peak. Sonia Guillén, a Peruvian anthropologist whom Spindler had recently befriended, was involved in the new discovery, and he and Horst Seidler soon signaled their interest in the find to her and prepared to journey to Peru.

Seidler's responsibilities had been expanding, and he was genuinely interested in other frozen mummies. Recently, he had assumed the editorial direction of the publishing of the scientific papers on the Iceman. Nine volumes were planned, including several lines of research by him and his colleagues in Vienna. Before they left for Peru, he tipped off a filmmaker he knew from Germany's Spiegel-TV, which had recently bought exclusive rights to document the Iceman research until his return to Italy.* Seidler be-

---

*Ultimately Spiegel-TV paid the Research Institute for Alpine Prehistory about fifty thousand dollars under two exclusive contracts.

lieved he was doing the man a favor, but he also realized he and Spindler would not be hurt by having a friendly media group along.

Just a few weeks after the discovery, Seidler, Spindler, another Innsbruck scientist, and a team from Spiegel TV arrived at Catholic University in Arequipa, where the mummy was temporarily stored in a top-load freezer.

The girl made a terribly moving figure. Wrapped in a brilliant ocher and white shawl, she was frozen in a tucked position, with her knees pulled toward her chest and her arms wrapped around her belly. Her chin was raised, and her desiccated, sun-bleached face with wide dark holes where the eyes once were held a serene expression. Her right hand clutched tightly at her dress in what Johan Reinhard, the American anthropologist who had discovered her, called a "death grip."[18] He suspected that she had been sacrificed to the gods on the Nevado Ampato, the volcano whose summit loomed about two hundred feet above the spot at which she was found. Other such human offerings were known, but Juanita, as the Peruvians named her in honor of Reinhard, was the only female.

The media were wild over her, and Guillén, Reinhard, and the other Peruvian scientists were busily navigating the shoals of research opportunities, funding, and publicity. By the time the Iceman scientists arrived in Peru, the National Geographic Society had already cornered the market on Juanita; Reinhard had quickly struck a deal with them that solved short-term storage problems and funded an archaeological expedition back to the site. As far as he could see, there had been no other choice. He had known that neither Catholic University in Arequipa nor the government of Peru would be able to foot the bill for an all-out research project on the mummy. Already hundreds of dried mummies in Peruvian museums were slowly disintegrating for lack of funding and interest. It was irrelevant that the experts thought Juanita was special because she was frozen. If the girl had not been discovered by someone with connections to a wealthy media outlet, she might well have faced the same fate as the others. Peru said it could not afford to prioritize archaeological research. But tales of discovery and "primitive" sacrifice played differently in the United States and Europe.

National Geographic had also closed a deal with Reinhard for an exclusive article on the find, as well as for largely exclusive broadcast rights for a film on the subject. This was the type of relationship the Iceman scientists had rejected as too exclusive when National Geographic had approached them with a much more lucrative offer five years earlier. But neither Reinhard nor José Antonio Chávez, the chairman of the archaeology department at Catholic University who was codirector of the project, saw any problem with it. They were relieved to have the prestigious and wealthy organization on their side, and they knew that more money and interest in the project would probably flow their way because of it.

Reinhard was thus surprised that the Iceman scientists had shown up with a journalist, a filmmaker, and a camera team from Spiegel in tow. Despite the Peruvians' association with National Geographic, the Spiegel team pressured Reinhard to let them do their own film on the subject. Spindler, meanwhile, began coaching Reinhard on how best to market Juanita. His relentless message was that they should begin immediately to turn the media's interest in the find into cash for the project. He told Reinhard that his book on the Iceman had earned more than a million dollars, all of which had then been plowed back into the Iceman project.

Both Seidler and Spindler also hammered away at another administrative point. They thought Reinhard and Chávez, the project's codirectors, should devise a contract like the one the University of Innsbruck had required scientists to sign before working on the Iceman project. Despite the opposition it had met with, such a step, they insisted, was the only way to guarantee that control of the project and its commercial exploitation rested with the university.

Finally, both Seidler and Spindler also advised Reinhard to include the names of all head researchers on all scientific publications about Juanita, even if they were not involved directly in the particular research. Reinhard balked at that suggestion. In his view, only those people who made a significant contribution to a paper should have their names on it. He told them that he was not going to take credit for something that he did not do.

Though he thought Spindler's dogged fixation on the mummy's commercialization was unfortunate, Reinhard listened well to the Iceman scientists. Seidler made it known that he would like to do some comparative studies of Juanita's and the Iceman's frozen tissues, and he offered to have her brought to Austria so zur Nedden could do a thorough radiological examination. Clearly, they were speaking from experience, and Reinhard thought they would be valuable advisers on the project. Still, he recognized one big difference between them: Both men had ended up with an Iceman by sheer luck, but this was Reinhard's life work. Juanita was just one very small piece of the puzzle. The Incans were believed to have made a practice of sacrificing children on mountaintops, and Reinhard wanted to find more such bodies before looters did. That was where he hoped to devote his energy.

In the spring of 1994, Dieter zur Nedden's team had rescanned the Iceman's corpse using computed radiography, the newest technology available, and results had been coming out slowly ever since, as he and his colleagues painstakingly examined and discussed the images. The new images revealed that the man's skull was considerably deformed, especially in the face and at the base. The deformations were not visible with the naked eye, but Horst Seidler said he had been able to detect them by trigonometric analysis of the cranium.[19]

For Seidler, the deformed skull was yet another reason why Wolfram Bernhard's ethnogenetic analysis of the Iceman's cranium was incorrect. The deformed skull would not yield true measurements, so any analyses conducted with them were bound to be skewed. Though Seidler had informed Bernhard of the deformations, Bernhard did not mention them in either of two papers he wrote for the first two volumes of Iceman research published by the Research Institute for Alpine Prehistory. To the contrary, he did not believe they were relevant. In fact, he called Seidler's paper on deformations "dilettantish."

Seidler thought the deformations in the cranium were important for other reasons as well. Further study of the CAT scans revealed that the skull was also marbled with countless hairline fractures. They could not have been with the man in his lifetime because he could not have survived them. Seidler reasoned that they must have occurred sometime after the man's death. His first thought was that the pressure of the glacier had borne down on the skull, pinning it against the rock on which the man was lying and reshaping it slightly.

Yet another possibility was that the fractures were the result of freeze-thaw cycles in the ice. The contraction and expansion of bone might well have caused it to crack. Temperature differences could be extreme at the Hauslabjoch, and the shifts could occur quickly. When the Simons discovered the Iceman, his head had been sticking out of the ice, taking the full glare of the sun, while the rest of his body was still embedded in ice. During the day, the ice was slushy, but at night it refroze hard. In the days around his recovery, the temperature of the cranium might have seesawed back and forth over the freezing point. Seidler was beginning to see that ice, or even glacial meltwater, might well have had significant impact on the contents of the trench.

One researcher who had long blamed the glacial ice for a critical instance of damage to the corpse was William A. Murphy, Jr., the American radiologist working with zur Nedden in the analysis of the hundreds of CAT scans and X rays. Murphy had always doubted that the Iceman's rib fractures had occurred before his death. The doctors still had not been able to determine the number of broken ribs, but there were at least five, all in a row, on the man's right side, toward the front. Typically, Murphy saw such injuries only in severe accidents, such as in somebody who had been going eighty miles an hour in a car when it rolled and he or she then slammed into the door or the steering wheel.

People with these injuries could not normally walk. They were in extreme pain. Every breath hurt, so they did not breathe well, and lung secretions were not properly cleared, creating a good place for bacteria to build up and encourage infection. Murphy was just not convinced that someone in such grave condition could have chopped down a tree and carved a bow while running away from persecutors. He was pragmatic when it came to pain. Prehistoric people might have led different lives, but they were still human. He could not think of a good enough reason for the Iceman to climb a mountain in the condition he was in.

Murphy also found it hard to imagine that the kind of trauma Spindler had hypothesized—one or several blows in a fight—would have caused those injuries. Normally, a blow is much more focused and breaks only one or two ribs. A fall seemed a much more likely cause, but even about that Murphy was skeptical. What troubled him was the angle of the breaks. The Iceman's ribs were bent to a nearly right angle, and the right side of his rib cage had collapsed. That was just not normal, unless one considered how the Iceman had been found.

Murphy had analyzed the first photographs of the man in the ice and read the testimony of people who had seen him there. According to this evidence, the man was on his stomach, and the breaks were aligned with what would have been the point of last contact between the ribs and the ground. To Murphy this suggested the breaks might have occurred as pressure was applied from above, forcing the corpse against the rock.

"It's not just the fractures, but the context," Murphy said in one interview.[20] "The thorax is impressed, the soft tissues are compressed, that there's a right angle, that there is weight being placed on the thorax and it is collapsing over time. If you just use the one feature, you're going to go down a merry path and that's what people do—they pull a single fact out of context and off they go."

Zur Nedden knew of Murphy's reservations, but he was still noncommittal. For him, the amount of new information to be gleaned from the images now stood in marked inverse proportion to the amount of effort and time needed to get at it. He was quite sure that no one could determine with certainty when the breaks had occurred. But in the spring of 1996, while at Wake Forest University, he, Seidler, and Platzer heard from a physical anthropologist named David Weaver who believed he could answer the question.

All he had to do, Weaver told the Austrians during a long presentation, was examine the broken ends of the bone under a microscope. When a bone breaks, blood supply to the fracture increases within minutes, and the area swells and turns reddish. The body quickly recruits cells to reabsorb old bone and dig tiny holes on the ends. Then, different cells begin laying down new calcium phosphate at the sites. In an X ray or CAT scan, the first signs of healing at a fracture site show up between five and twelve days after the break. If the break occurred at least forty-eight hours before the man's death, then Weaver would expect to be able to see the tiny holes excavated on the ends of the bone. After Platzer heard the proposal, he was quiet for a moment. "How much bone would you need?" he asked. Weaver replied that he would need between two and three millimeters, plus a bit of the tissue from around the bone. By Platzer's standards, it was a lot, more than anyone had gotten to date. He made no promises to Weaver.

In the spring of 1996, several months after a second trip with Spindler to Peru to consult on the mummy, Seidler learned that Reinhard and the Peruvians were planning to transport Juanita to the United States for a round of radiological investigations at the Johns Hopkins Medical Institute in Baltimore. Carrier Corporation, an American refrigeration firm, had offered to design and manufacture a freezer in which the mummy could be both conserved and displayed, as well as a cooler in which to transport her to the United States. It would even build a second such freezer as a backup. Carrier, which had designed the climate-control system for the Sistine Chapel at the Vatican, said its tally for the freezers would be about $250,000, no small investment, but the Peruvians would get it all free. The entire operation had been organized by National Geographic. In exchange, Juanita would be put on temporary display at the National Geographic Society in Washington, D.C., during which time Carrier specialists would monitor the mummy and the case to make sure the system worked. The society frequently organized exhibits around research projects it financed, and this display would be excellent publicity for Reinhard's upcoming article and the film.

The news shocked Seidler and Spindler. They had expected Juanita to come to Austria for a full round of CAT scans and evaluation. Moreover, both men were opposed to displaying corpses to the public, and the idea infuriated them. Two weeks later, they arrived in Arequipa and promptly invited the rector of Catholic University, Chávez, and the director of Peru's National Institute of Culture, who would have to approve Juanita's export, to lunch at the residence of the Austrian ambassador. There, Seidler pleaded with the men not to allow the corpse to go to the United States. Neither he, Spindler, nor Sonia Guillén* had seen Juanita in months or spoken in detail on where the research stood, yet he claimed that no one had yet done a thorough microbiological check on Juanita,

*Sonia Guillén had left the project after a falling out with its leaders.

so they did not know what was lurking on her skin or in her body. In particular, he was concerned about the possibility that bacteria would thrive during an exhibition. Unless such tests were conducted, he said, researchers would not know how the corpse had fared while it was out of the Peruvians' care. He also cast doubt on the security of the Carrier freezer, implying that a change in the storage conditions might inflict irreversible damage on Juanita.

By the end of his plea for Juanita's well-being, Seidler had worked himself into a frenzy. Even the Austrian ambassador seemed furious at the Peruvians over the plans to take the corpse to the United States. The rector and Chávez listened quietly to Seidler's impassioned argument—after all, they were officially on Austrian territory—but they felt patronized. Though the notoriously finicky National Institute of Culture would have the final say, most Peruvians agreed that the prominent display of this beautiful and moving symbol of the Incan Empire in the American capital was the best possible advertisement for Peru. Like Tyrol, the country was eager for tourists, and the United States was an important exporter of visitors as well as a creator of global market tastes. The Peruvians were offended by the implicit suggestion that they had no idea what they were doing.

When word of the incident reached Reinhard, he was outraged and perplexed that the Iceman team might be trying to go behind his back with concerns that, if true, were serious. At this point, despite Spindler's and Seidler's exhortations, Reinhard and Chávez had not asked them to sign a contract to work on the project. But faced with this heretical behavior, they changed their minds. In a terse conversation with Seidler, Reinhard demanded that they sign the contract before speaking with him further. Loosely modeled on the Iceman contract, the document was shorter but even more restrictive. It prohibited researchers from so much as discussing the project with outsiders without permission from the directors. They were also required to share their results with the directors. Within days, Seidler, Spindler, and two other researchers signed the contract. Despite everything, the Austrian team still wanted to be in on the project.

In the meantime, the mummy was screened for microbiology on its surface in order to establish a baseline against possible changes in the girl's tissues. Reinhard was assured that no scientific basis existed for fearing that Juanita was on the verge of decay. In early May, the National Institute of Culture finally gave its approval for the export, and soon afterward Juanita was loaded into Carrier Corporation's cooler and taken to Johns Hopkins. The results of the CAT scans were astonishing. The girl's skull was fractured. Using normal surgical-steel equipment, researchers took biopsies from the skin and passed them on for other investigations.

Hours after the examination, Juanita was installed in the National Geographic Society's Explorers Hall. In a demonstration that the exhibit had the backing of Peruvians, a group of immigrants from a village near Nevado Ampato showed up for the opening, as did Peru's president, Alberto Fujimori. Washington's elite filed through the darkened hall to view the sacrificed virgin. Tens of thousands of people lined up to see her.

On the other side of the Atlantic, Seidler and Spindler were fuming. A few days after the exhibit opened, comments Seidler had made to a colleague at Wake Forest University were posted on the Internet. In essence, they said that Juanita's welfare was being sacrificed for the sensationalist profiteering of National Geographic. Then, in an e-mail to Reinhard, he resigned from the project.*

Meanwhile, Spindler, who had spent considerable time contemplating the relationship between the media and science, was not keeping quiet either. In an interview with *Der Spiegel,* he attacked the very idea of the display and accused National Geographic of imperialistic behavior.[21] He also warmed up Seidler's scientific concerns: because of her microbiological condition, the display ran the risk of destroying the mummy. "What is being done there is from my point of view a mixture of Hollywood and Disneyland against a background of trying to achieve successful sales, while science makes a crash landing," Spindler told another reporter.[22]

In a swift response to *Der Spiegel,* Reinhard noted that scientists from several countries, including the Iceman team itself, had agreed that the mummy had been maintained in an excellent state since its

---

*Seidler maintains he resigned from the project before his concerns were aired on the Internet.

discovery and that it had not decayed in that time. He flatly denied that anyone had any grounds to fear for its preservation.

The contract Spindler and Seidler had signed just two months earlier, the very one they had pressed on the Peruvians, was designed precisely to hinder such renegade comments on the project. They had violated the very principles they had required others to sign not for the sake of better mummy research but for publicity. For Reinhard, the Iceman team's credibility had been destroyed.

High on the slopes above Innsbruck, Klaus Oeggl was still working day and night, largely out of touch with the media and the project leaders and financed only by his own department and the grants he had won. No one needed to remind him that some of his colleagues were growing impatient waiting for even preliminary botanical results. Yet Oeggl was stubbornly sticking to his own methodical plan. He was taking his time, checking everything repeatedly, and consulting with various colleagues, including the department head, Bortenschlager, who was entirely supportive of his approach.

He was about to embark on the most exciting research yet. Months earlier, he had received from Platzer a coveted bit of material: forty milligrams of the Iceman's colon contents, part of the Iceman's last meal. The meal came in a very unassuming package. First of all, it was extremely small, about the size of a little fingernail.

Already, there had been exciting news from Don Brothwell's British team, which had also gotten a sample. Among the remains, the Brits had discovered the eggs of the human whipworm, *Trichuris trichiura*. Today, many people who do not live in areas with flush toilets also carry the worm, which can cause unpleasant symptoms, such as stomachache and diarrhea. Infestation occurs by ingesting the eggs, perhaps from a plant or water. In some cases, the illness can be severe, and the infected person may even suffer malnutrition because of it. But the scientists had no way of knowing whether the Iceman had any such complaints.

One spring night, after almost everyone else had left for the day, Oeggl removed the frozen clump from the freezer and got to work. This was probably the only food sample he was ever going to get, and he wanted to wring as much information as possible out of every step of the process. He had spent weeks pondering and discussing how to handle the precious bit in order to avoid contamination and to minimize its destruction. Once certain chemicals were applied, the sample would be altered, and further tests would not be reliable. He decided to cut the sample into four pieces and handle each separately. One piece he kept to look at under the electron microscope, which could magnify the contents up to five thousand times. The other three he would work through very slowly, concentrating first on the large bits of organic matter, if there were any. They were his biggest worry, since they might decay rapidly when exposed to the chemicals. Pollen grains, if they were present, were more resistant and would probably fare better.

The first step was to add a few drops of saline solution to the first sample in order to fatten it up. As it was now, it was highly desiccated, just like the Iceman's body. After a few moments more, Oeggl prepared the sample for the microscope and then took a look. A thick stew of particles met his gaze. At this low level of magnification, only the biggest things were recognizable. He took a few moments to get his bearings, and then he saw them. Here and there, spread evenly throughout the sample, were flakelike particles with distinctive cell patterns. Oeggl examined them closely. They were everywhere, and most were about the same size. They were einkorn, the same type of grain Egg had found among the clothing. If scientists had had any lingering doubts about the Iceman's connection to an agricultural community, then this laid them to rest. Ötzi had eaten einkorn, the most important wheat in prehistory in this part of the world. It was not just food for his animals.

Oeggl was amazed at the good preservation of the particles. The vast majority of the prehistoric organic material he had seen did not look nearly as good as this. Most of the einkorn was in the form of bran, the broken skins of the wheat grains. That suggested that the wheat had been ground up into a very fine meal and probably made into bread. If the einkorn had been eaten whole, boiled, or roasted, then Oeggl would have expected to see larger bits of grain and many grains still intact. Einkorn has low levels of gluten, so the bread it made was probably hard, somewhat like a cracker, and rather tough on the teeth.

Attached to the grains, Oeggl noted tiny black specks, which he recognized as charcoal. They might indicate that the bread had been baked over an open fire. Oeggl could see that the charcoal came from the wood of conifers, which abounded in the region in which the Iceman was found; sadly, the samples were too small to be identifiable to a species level. Lindow Man had also had charred remains of wheat in his gut, and scientists had suggested that they came from bread that had been baked in an oven, on a griddle, or even on a rock.

Interspersed with the einkorn bran, but in a much lower concentration, was other plant-cell material. The tissue types Oeggl identified were common and showed up in a number of edible varieties belonging to plant families such as the rose, the pea, and the goosefoot.[23]

Already Oeggl was amazed at how unambiguous and clear his findings seemed to be. But because of the lack of archaeological evidence from the region, he had very little context for his results. If the studies of Swiss lake dwellings, just over the Alps, were any guide, then the variety in the Iceman's stomach was not unusual. Because late-Neolithic crop yields were low, plants had supplied only part of humans' dietary requirements. People still had to hunt and gather to meet their needs. In the Swiss lake dwellings, archaeologists had discovered stores of dried apples, sloes, raspberries, blackberries, strawberries, and elderberries. People had also collected and stored hazelnuts, acorns, and beechnuts. Other foods such as vegetables and greens must have been eaten as well, but because they were harvested and eaten before their seeds ripened, no trace of them remained in the settlements. Likewise, mushrooms— like the two found on the strings carried by the Iceman—must also have contributed to the diet or pharmacy of the Neolithic people, but they do not survive in the settlements.

Of course, prehistoric people had also eaten meat. Neolithic sites were full of the bones of slaughtered animals, both wild and domesticated, but no trace of them had ever been discovered in the few stomachs investigated. Don Brothwell had been hoping that some bit of flesh would turn up this time and that he might be able to extract the DNA from it to tell what animal it had come from. But so far, his investigators had had no luck.

Oeggl next investigated the pollen. The hard little shells of the pollen grains were very durable, and he expected that they would be in fine shape. How they had ended up in the Iceman's stomach was another story. The Iceman could have breathed them in, or they could have been present on something the man had eaten or drunk. Their importance lay in the fact that they contained a record of his surroundings in the hours before his death. Every pollen grain found would have to be counted, just as Bortenschlager had done with the pollen from the bogs. They would have to examine how the various pollen spread, whether by wind, animal, insect, or water, and even whether they were edible. The spectrum of pollen would also have to be compared with that derived from the site itself and at locations all around the Hauslabjoch. If the man had been walking through a field of crops, Oeggl would expect to find the pollen of various cereals. If he had been lingering on the Austrian side of the mountain, then Oeggl might find a lot of the pollen from pine. If the pollen was distinctive enough, Oeggl might be able to say where the man had spent his last day.

To get a view of the pollen, he would have to get rid of some of the fats and proteins that were packed around the smaller bits in the sample. This was an irreversible step. He had to choose a chemical that would dissolve those fats and proteins but not harm the other material in there; the usual choice was alcohol. Crossing his fingers, he did the procedure and then looked at the sample again, this time under a higher magnification.

He could now see a few of the bizarrely shaped pollen in there, but he decided to repeat the procedure. When he looked through the scope again, dozens of the little pollen floated past his lens. There were seven hundred possible types in the local flora, and he knew them all by heart. They were strange little creations, amazing in their complexity and variety. But something was odd. Everywhere he looked, he saw the same pollen, a type he had never expected. They seemed to be in the majority. Oeggl was alarmed, as this was highly abnormal. Additionally, the sperm, containing the genetic material, were still intact inside each of the pollen grains. Normally, these gametophytes spring out at their first opportunity, and have a maximum life span of six weeks.

Because of the unlikelihood that the sperm could have remained intact, Oeggl immediately suspected that the sample had somehow become contaminated. He had not been present when Platzer's surgeons removed the sample from the colon, but he had to assume it was a clean operation. Could the contamination be coming from his own lab, which was filled with botanical material? Oeggl could not immediately exclude the possibility that some of this pollen was at this very moment wafting around the air in the lab.

Before he could move through the rest of the samples, he had to make a control slide. Using freshly sterilized glasses and sieves, he took some of the saline solution he had been using to rehydrate the samples and prepared it for the scope. By looking at just this solution, he could see if it was the problem. With some apprehension, he peered through the lens. Nothing was there. He adjusted the slide and looked at a different spot. Again, there was nothing. With great care he explored every single corner of the viewer. Everything was clean. Oeggl sat back in his chair and took a deep breath.

Now he was ready for the second sample. In the first little bit, he did not see the pollen. But in the second, he spotted it again. If this bit of the Iceman's last meal was contaminated, it would be a catastrophe. He looked at the third piece of it, and it was there, too. He was beginning to believe that what he was seeing really belonged there.

He had all the equipment sterilized again, and then he took the last sample. He readied the slide, put it under the viewfinder, and then leaned in for a look. It was still there. It could not be contamination. It was really in the man's gut.

This abundant pollen happened to come from a tree that grows only in regions with a particular climate and conditions. It was almost as if the sample was carrying a flag announcing where it had been. If these results could be trusted, then there was little question about where the Iceman had spent his final day. Despite the late hour, Oeggl was tremendously excited. On the way out, he ran into Bortenschlager and asked his boss to come look at the sample again with him. Before he made any rash announcements, he wanted everyone in his institute to look through the scope to confirm that he was seeing what he thought he was seeing. Then, he decided, he was going to have to take a little trip.

CHAPTER 10

"A PROPER FOREFATHER"

K LAUS OEGGL maneuvered the car into the far right lane, switched on his turn signal, slowed down, and then swung into the Schnalstal. The two-lane road rose at a breathtaking angle along a ledge cut into the rocky gorge at the valley's entrance. To Oeggl's left, the chilly Schnals Creek dropped away quickly, tumbling wildly in the opposite direction on its way to the river Adige.

After a few minutes, the gorge opened slightly, revealing the first human settlement. High on a bluff that overhung the valley stood a solitary church, its white steeple gleaming against a backdrop of Alpine peaks. The bluff and the church were the most distinctive landmarks in the valley. The village in which they were situated, and to which Oeggl was driving, was called Katharinaberg.

Leaving the main road, Oeggl made a hairpin turn to the right. This road switched back and forth, higher and higher, creeping along the side of the mountain, finally depositing Oeggl at a small parking lot. Not long ago, this little village was considered one of the most remote places in the Alps. But although the people here still practiced a traditional kind of farming, they were fully integrated into European culture and saw a steady stream of tourists each summer. The first thing Oeggl noticed as he stepped out of the car was the line of recycling bins set up by the community.

The tiny village consisted of just a few dozen houses, all clustered in the wake of the church and its little walled-in yard that jutted, like the prow of a ship, over the valley far below. As he passed by, a few local farmers, wearing the blue smocks that are the uniform of the Tyrolean farmer, nodded to him. Though Oeggl had grown up in Innsbruck, he was still considered a tourist. Everyone knew everybody else here, and they spoke a dialect of German that they could make almost incomprehensible to outsiders. Oeggl climbed up the ancient stone steps to the church and walked through the little cemetery to lean out over the church wall. The site commanded a tremendous view up and down the Schnalstal. It was the perfect spot on which to honor your god or gods. Archaeologists such as Annaluisa Pedrotti believed it had been considered sacred for a long time. Years earlier someone had found a few pieces of ceramic here, but since they were not in context, they couldn't be dated. Archaeologists would have loved to find a statue-menhir here, or evidence of copper smelting, or even the metal itself. When Pedrotti talked about the typical settlements of the late Neolithic or Copper Age, she thought of places exactly like Katharinaberg, which had good access to the pastures above the tree line and to the animals such as ibex, chamois, and deer.

Behind the village rose the pasture and fields that these villagers worked. Along the top of the fields, perhaps half a mile above the church, was a widely spaced row of beautiful old, timbered farmhouses with pitched roofs and geraniums bursting from every window. All the farmhouses were connected by a path that came over the mountain from the Vinschgau and continued on up the valley, eventually joining the path that led from Vernagt over the ridge into Austria. Since the gorge at the entrance to the Schnalstal had been too steep and wet to negotiate, people had come into the valley way up here. This was the ancient route into the Schnalstal, and Oeggl expected it had been used in the Iceman's time.

Since the Iceman's discovery, Oeggl had made dozens of trips into the Schnalstal, exploring the landscape and the vegetation that grew on the impossibly steep slopes. For years he had obsessively gone over the data. But only in the pollen had he found the crucial clue to the Iceman's habitat. He had cross-checked it with the other data countless times, made his colleagues do blind checks of his information, and was sure he had it right.

Twelve hours before his death, the Iceman had been here, in the vicinity of Katharinaberg. He had taken a sip of some water, maybe from one of the many little streams that gushed down the slope, and that water had contained a tiny clump of pollen from a hop hornbeam. Ötzi probably had not noticed it. But it was the red flag Oeggl had long been looking for. All the other woods associated with the Iceman were conceivably available north of where he had been found, but the hop hornbeam grew only to the south, in the very habitat in which Katharinaberg was situated. Katharinaberg might even have been Ötzi's hometown.

The climate in this place was very particular. Below the village, in the gorge, the humidity was high, the perfect environment for trees such as the hazel, yew, maple, ash, lime, and elm, all of which Ötzi had used for his equipment. The ash, chosen for the haft in his dagger, was ubiquitous. Several were growing just below the wall of the church, and Oeggl noticed that they had been trimmed back repeatedly, probably because the people still used the foliage to feed their sheep. No yews or maple grew here nowadays, but Oeggl knew they could survive if someone had wanted to plant them.

Up in the village, the land flattened out somewhat and, since it had a southward tilt, it enjoyed the sun's direct rays. The winters were relatively mild, and the snow melted on this side of the valley first. This was where the farmers had their fields. It was also the natural habitat of the thermophilic mixed-oak forests. On the upper edge of that environment grew trees that needed drier ground, like the Juneberry, the wayfaring bush, the dogwood, as well as the fir, larch, and pine. The Iceman had gotten several woods for his equipment from this habitat, such as the wayfaring-bush branches for his unfinished arrows. The rough-hewn laths the Iceman had used in the backpack frame to keep the bent wood in position were made of larch, which grew frequently in the valley bottoms.

To the untrained eye, the forested hills and wild streams of the valley might appear to be virgin landscape. Because the present climate was virtually the same as it had been in the Iceman's lifetime, the potential vegetation was the same. But these slopes were deeply altered by millennia of human management. Over the centuries, farmers had cut into the upper edge of the forest to create more grazing space, and they had planted and harvested the trees they needed to maintain their houses and provide for their flocks over the winter. Until now, the ideas about where the Iceman had lived and made his home had been just good guesses. Granted, based on the archaeological evidence in South Tyrol, most researchers had tended to believe he had made his home to the south.* But Oeggl's analysis of the finds went beyond what any scientists had done so far. Instead of linking the Iceman to a population, he had narrowed in on his environment, the area most favorable for supporting all the organic material discovered with him.

Oeggl was not nearly ready to close up this project. He still wanted to know what had happened to the man after he set off from this area, headed for the Hauslabjoch. Sometime that day he had eaten his last bit of bread and nibbled on a bit of meat, a tiny fiber and burnt bone particle of which Oeggl had found with the electron microscope. They were probably too small to identify the animal from which they came. Somewhere around here was also a creek that was the source of diatoms, one-celled algae, that Oeggl had also detected under the electron microscope.

Oeggl had never put any stock in Spindler's disaster hypothesis. So far, too little evidence had been presented to suggest any specific cause of death. Nothing in his colon had settled the question either. Oeggl's remaining evidence was to come strictly from the grasses, moss, plants, woods, and other things the Iceman had carried with him into his grave. These artifacts had substantial testimonial power, but months, perhaps years, of grueling lab work might still be required to sift it out.

Dieter zur Nedden had introduced Horst Seidler to stereolithography, a technology that used CAT scans to construct a one-to-one

---

*Willy Groenman–Van Waateringe, however, concluded from analyses of pollen found in the Iceman's clothing that he came from a village to the north of the Hauslabjoch.[1] More recently, James H. Dickson, of the University of Glasgow in Scotland, and his colleagues concluded from a large sample of moss found among the same clothing and identified as the species *Neckera* that he had come from the south.[2] Dickson also identified a tiny moss leaf Oeggl had found in the Iceman's colon as *Neckera complanata*, which Dickson believed had been swallowed accidentally.[3] The relatively large quantity of *Neckera*, which commonly grows on vertical rocks in shady woodlands and is known to have several domestic uses, suggested that the Iceman intentionally carried it with him.

model of the Iceman's skeleton, including the skull. Until now, its application had been solely in medicine, but Seidler realized that it could give a boost to physical anthropologists. It had not been possible to see what the ridges inside the brain case looked like without cutting a skull open, and this, obviously, could not be done with precious artifacts, some of which might be millions of years old. Now, instead of working on the real objects, scientists could slice these more durable, if expensive, models in half to allow interior views of the skulls.

Seidler had shopped the new technology around to some of the best minds in paleoanthropology and had been invited to coauthor a paper with one of them. For the first time in his career, Seidler's graduate students had a selection of projects to work on. All this success had not gone unrecognized. Seidler had been named to the Austrian Academy of Sciences. He had been invited to Russia to see the frozen Scythian mummies there. Even after the debacle with Juanita in Peru, he was getting invitations to visit other mummies around the world. The press called him regularly to discuss other human biological issues, such as genetic research and human evolution. Seidler acknowledged that all of this was due to the Iceman, but he was determined that it was not going to be the research that defined his career.

Seidler saw that for a few key researchers the Iceman project had already become a cul-de-sac on their career paths, a project so prestigious that it seduced a scientist for the rest of his life. A human body from a distant time was an unbelievably alluring object of study. But since the initial euphoria, Seidler had also begun to believe that the science that could be done on the Iceman was limited. The researchers could tease out every kind of fact on this individual himself—how he died, what he ate, his state of health, and so on— but the conclusions had to do only with this individual. He was just one representative of what must have been a very diverse population. In order to generalize about his society, human biologists needed a hundred more samples, and these were not available.

The confrontations over Juanita in Peru had occasioned some deep soul-searching for Seidler. A promising professional relationship had been shattered, and Seidler accepted a good deal of blame for it. He recognized that his interest in Juanita had been not only for the sake of science. He just wanted to have her, he said, to bring her to Austria, to be involved in this exciting discovery. In retrospect, he recognized that some of his actions had been irrational. His own work was marbled with politics. In their efforts to keep Juanita from going to the United States, he and Spindler had tried to mobilize politicians, the press, and the public. They had gone way outside the bounds of the laboratory to try to achieve their ends.

Scientists might have the first word on these mummies and might be able to parlay their expertise into incredible stories about the human condition, but they could not control interpretations. The occasional discoveries of human corpses that had somehow managed to outwit mortality seemed to arouse all manner of curiosity. Science certainly had a role in their interpretation, but it was not the only arbiter. For confirmation, all Seidler had to do was look around at the variety of uses to which the Iceman had been put.

Even six years after his discovery, the Iceman continued to be fertile ground for both public and scientific imagination. In the summer of 1997, an Irishman named Tom Varley built himself a house of dried mud and sticks on a three-acre lot in southern Austria and announced that for five months he was going to live as Ötzi had. He planted a garden and spent his days collecting nuts, berries, roots, and mushrooms and fishing in a river that flowed over his land. "He hunts small animals, but only when absolutely necessary," reported the animal rights–conscious correspondent for *The Guardian,* a British newspaper.[4] He dressed in skins and a grass coat and spent much time around a campfire, *The Guardian* noted.

Varley's endeavors were not solely for his own amusement or edification. His Stone Age life was organized by a company called Science Wonder Productions, which charged visitors a small fee to observe him from outside the enclosure where he worked. At the end of each day, Varley, who described himself as a "nonacademic human anthropologist," took off his skins and retired to twentieth-century accommodations. Each evening, he wrote up his day's experiences for the company's website.

"It's great living like this," he told the paper. "In the Stone Ages you could do what you wanted, you could sleep all day and you had no job to go to. I advise everyone to do it." Varley's interpretation of the licenses of Stone Age life may not have jibed with the picture of the Neolithic period that archaeologists were uncovering. But the fact that he derived inspiration from Ötzi was not uncommon.

What drew him to the Iceman? What drew anyone to a 5,300-year-old corpse? Maybe, as Spindler and others suggested, some just wanted to make a splash in the news, to feel like a hotshot for the day. But there was perhaps a more generous interpretation. Varley and the others who had made uncommon claims about the Iceman were posing the same questions as the scientists. Just as hundreds of scientists were attracted to the Iceman and scrambled to get their research questions to Platzer and Spindler, so, too, were nonscientists excited by the sensational discovery. They yearned to make a connection to the past, a real-life connection, one they could *feel*. They wanted to embody the Iceman himself, by living the way he had or carrying his child. Their poetic answers were not induced scientifically, but that was not their aim. They were asking questions in a way scientists believed they themselves did not. But though the scientists were trained to suppress any such yearnings, the Iceman often served them in the same way.

In the months after the discovery, the media repeatedly pressed Konrad Spindler to describe "how he felt" when he realized the corpse was so old. Without hesitation, he replied time and again that he felt as the great British Egyptologist Howard Carter must have when he discovered the rich tomb of King Tutankhamen. It was a likely response, and the media loved it. But upon reflection, Spindler seemed embarrassed by it, and in later, less susceptible moments, he said it was not true. Spindler must have realized that while Carter had spent a lifetime searching the Nile Valley for royal tombs, he himself had just happened to be the first archaeologist in the world to lay eyes on this frozen mummy. It was just his good luck.

As the years passed, Spindler repeatedly denied any feelings for Ötzi. In an interview with one local newspaper several years after the discovery, Spindler went to great lengths to show how little the Iceman meant to him. Though at the first press conference following the discovery, Spindler had spoken of a "find of the century," he now rejected that. "The concept 'find of the century' does not exist in science; there is only the matter-of-fact reference to the research object," he said. "The archaeologist who waits for a find of the century is a dreamer."[5]

When asked about his feelings for the Iceman, Spindler was shockingly blunt. "I don't love him," he said.

Even in the eyes of some of his closest colleagues, Spindler's efforts to distance himself from his earlier enthusiastic pronouncements seemed strange. It was obvious to everyone that the discovery had changed the course of the archaeologist's life. He had become something of a celebrity. He traveled frequently to other continents, met lots of people, and made considerable money off the Iceman. As the years went by, his situation even prompted envy among some of his colleagues.

Spindler's relationship to the Iceman was far from "matter-of-fact." Out of a corpse and some tools, he had created a dramatic persona for the Iceman—a man on the lam—and he was directly profiting from it. He was personally invested in being the main spokesman for the Iceman. Other scientists, such as Lippert, who wrote about the find were considered competitors rather than colleagues with different opinions. He scorned other accounts of the Iceman project as "unauthorized." While Spindler apparently wanted to be able to view the Iceman objectively, as just a blob on a slide under a microscope, he cared about what was said about the man. Under the banner of serious science, he indulged the public's desire for a good story about the Iceman, while denying both other scientists and other writers access to the find.

While Spindler had opened and then tried to stanch an emotional vein to the Iceman, other researchers expressly used their science to connect people with the Iceman. In mid-1994, molecular biologist Brian Sykes of Oxford University reported that he had identified the Iceman's nearest living relative. Her name was Marie Mosely, and, according to *The Sunday Times,* she "lives quietly in a detached house in Dorset Avenue, Bournemouth.[6] Mosely was originally from the far corner of Europe, in Cork, Ireland. When she learned of her relation to Ötzi, she told *The Sunday Times* that she was going to take a trip to see him. "He was obviously an Irishman who came to grief while travelling across Europe," she told the paper. "It is marvellous to think we are related. I am considering whether to demand he now receives a decent burial."

Obviously, Sykes's conclusions were far from the understated ones discussed by Svante Pääbo and Oliva Handt in *Science*. Sykes, a coauthor of their paper, had taken the Munich lab's results a few steps further. Sykes's announcement that Marie Mosely was the Iceman's nearest relative could also have been claimed for any of those anonymous people Handt had discovered who had a matching sequence, but Sykes's DNA volunteers knew that if their DNA matched, the results might be broadcast far and wide. Marie Mosely's precise relation to the Iceman was unclear in the news reports. Because men do not pass their mtDNA on, Sykes could not say she was a direct descendant of Ötzi but rather that she shared with him a maternal ancestor, perhaps even the Iceman's mother.

The science behind the revelation was not very clear in the public mind, but that hardly mattered. The amazing thing was science's capacity to draw a line between a contemporary person and a very old famous one. Science granted Mosely the feelings many people might have for their family. Marie Mosely of Dorset Avenue, Bournemouth, might have rights to Ötzi. She and other people who shared that DNA sequence might be entitled to some say in the plans to immortalize her exponentially great-uncle in a museum in far-off Bolzano. Had she been contacted yet by a lawyer?

No scientist on the project was more openly captivated by the Iceman's story, and the possibilities of identifying with him, than the Norwegian anthropologist Torstein Sjøvold. Platzer had invited Sjøvold on board and had seen to it that he landed several research projects, including the study of the man's tattoos and his age at death.

While others professed disdain for the press frenzy of the early stages of the story, Sjøvold, who was head of the Osteological Research Laboratory at the University of Stockholm, thrived on it. Like Spindler, he quickly hopped on the Iceman lecture train, garnering the coveted American market because of his command of English. He also wrote about the Iceman for several American journals and even translated Spindler's book into Norwegian.

Sjøvold made repeated climbs to the Hauslabjoch, in part, he realized, to undergo the same experiences the Iceman had. His willingness to fantasize openly about the Iceman distinguished him from most other researchers on the project. The effort certainly enriched his perspective on how the man had lived and what he may have experienced and felt.

In the summer of 1994, all his attention to the Iceman miraculously seemed to pay off. While visiting the site of the find at the Hauslabjoch, he was stepping off the ledge surrounding the trench when he noticed what he took to be a shred of newspaper beneath a rock. In fact, it turned out to be another piece of the birch-bark container, a rectangular piece that measured about five by eight inches.[7] Like several other birch-bark pieces found at the site, the rim was pierced with holes, along three sides in this case. Not long before, Markus Egg had announced that the Iceman had carried with him not one but two birch-bark containers of more or less the same size. Sjøvold correctly assumed that this was part of the one from which large parts were still missing. This was a miraculous find, and Sjøvold was understandably thrilled. It also raised the uncomfortable possibility that the last excavation at the site, two years earlier, had missed other artifacts, since the excavators had not searched outside the trench.

In 1996, Sjøvold and Othmar Gaber, an assistant professor of anatomy in Innsbruck, also revisited the question of Ötzi's age at death. They reexamined the teeth and skull sutures, and also investigated the microscopic structure of a sample of his damaged thighbone. There they found a high number of secondary osteons, concentric arrangements of bone matrix that increase as a person ages. Their surprising conclusion was that Ötzi died in his late forties.[8]

On another occasion, however, Sjøvold's desire to connect with the Hauslabjoch man ended up muddying his statistical analysis. At the first Iceman conference in Innsbruck in the summer of 1992, Sjøvold delivered a paper outlining several different studies then under way. With a few flourishes, he constructed a family tree that turned everyone in the audience into a descendant of the Iceman. It began with a simple calculation.

Each of us has two parents, four grandparents, eight great-grandparents, 16 great-great-grandparents and so on. If the Iceman died 5,100 years ago, and we take a generation to be 30 years, then he died 170 generations ago. The number of ancestors of each of us would then be 2^{170}, which is approximately

15×10^{50}. This figure is extremely large and is approximately 15 with 50 0's. . . . So many people have so far not lived upon the Earth. If one assumes that at present there are approximately 5 billion people on the earth, that represents only a relatively small figure. . . . Therefore our ancestral lines must have crossed repeatedly in this time in order to result in the present population figure from the available population.[9]

No doubt, Sjøvold was right: We are surely densely related. But it was here that his science mutated into fantasy.

[B]ecause of his copper ax [the Iceman] did not belong to the lower class of the population but to a population group which was surely permitted to have a partner and therefore it is highly probable that he had children. Given the increasing population in Europe since then, one can further assume that at least one branch of his descendants may have survived until now, so the probability is very high that after approximately 170 generations he is *still found in every one of us.* This view has enough to it to make it very probable that *we* have before us a proper forefather [emphasis added].[10]

Sjøvold had turned Ötzi into the European world patriarch. The little exercise was easy to follow, and it found a ready home in Spindler's book and in the series published in *Stern.* "Almost every European, if he could trace his family tree back over five thousand years, would bump into Ötzi," the magazine wrote.[11] The idea was nice, perhaps, but also utterly unfounded. Sjøvold's argument was so laden with contingencies and assumptions—that the Iceman had children and that his descendants not only never died off but multiplied prodigiously—that from a scientific point of view it was nonsense.

Sjøvold, Horst Seidler later noted, seemed to confuse relatedness with ancestry. From the perspective of evolutionary biology, every human is related to the Iceman, since everyone is descended from that one primordial organism that announced the start of life on Earth. But, then, we are also related to the giraffe and the June bug. How many people alive today are direct descendants of the Iceman is a question that no scientist can answer.

Sjøvold seemed to be seeking some blood link between the Iceman and us. He used math in his calculation and just enough of the language of science to purchase popular credibility. Yet ultimately what Sjøvold was engaged in was very humanistic. He was validating a desire to feel sympathy with the man who had died alone on the Hauslabjoch by establishing a direct genetic, material, physical, and biological continuity between him and us, the kinds of connections that, again and again, people find matter so much.

By using pseudoscience to establish the Iceman as our ancestor, Sjøvold appeared to give himself a scientific basis for having strong feelings about him. That was not good science, yet no "serious scientist" on the project ever publicly challenged his conclusions.

CHAPTER 11

THE PLACE HE CAME TO LIE

IN JANUARY 1998, six years and four months after his discovery, the Iceman was at last coming home to South Tyrol. In downtown Bolzano, a new museum of archaeology to house the Iceman and his possessions was nearing completion. After years of research and testing, the Italian firm Syremont had designed a freezer that they claimed would preserve the Iceman in conditions that Werner Platzer had deemed were correct, while also allowing the corpse to be displayed. A yearlong trial run on another frozen corpse had nearly convinced Platzer that the new freezer would do the same job as his tried-and-true wrappings and crushed ice.

In the new arrangement, the Iceman would lie on a stretcher in a small walk-in freezer equipped with state-of-the-art security systems and monitors that registered the slightest change in temperature and humidity. Just as in Innsbruck, a backup freezer was on hand. The corpse would be visible to museum visitors through a small window, about one foot square, at eye level for the average adult. The body that for so long had been seen by so very few would now be on display for all to see. The admission price would be just six dollars.

The costs of the museum were enormous—twelve million dollars had been invested in the restoration of the building and in the freezer technology. Upkeep would also be expensive. So far, all the monies had come from the province of South Tyrol, but officials were hoping to recoup some costs through admittance fees and sales of Iceman products.

Over the last few years, as South Tyrol rushed to complete a proper home for its Iceman, it had watched with growing impatience as others profited off the find. In 1996, the Roman-Germanic Central Museum in Mainz had organized a three-day exhibition of the artifacts just before returning the items to Innsbruck. The German government had invested some six hundred thousand dollars in the four years of preservation work, and the brief exhibition was intended to show gratitude to the German public for their tax support. Markus Egg had expected just a few thousand people to show up during the weekend display, but more than sixteen thousand visitors came.

South Tyrol could do nothing to stop that exhibit, which everyone agreed was owed to the museum for its services and expertise. But a year later, provincial officials got wind of a plan that they feared might do real harm to their own museum. In Mettmann, Germany, a new Neanderthal Museum, devoted to evolution, was just about to open a comprehensive display on the Iceman. The exhibit would show not only replicas of his tools made by the experimental archaeologist Harm Paulsen, but also a life-size replica of the Iceman himself. Worse, the exhibit was scheduled to travel to seven cities, including Munich. If the Mettmann exhibit went ahead, how many Germans would come to see the real thing in South Tyrol?

Just before the museum opened, South Tyrol took action. Claiming that it was illegal to make replicas of items classified as historically protected, it threatened to sue the museum for twenty thousand dollars for each day the mummy's likeness was exhibited.[1] The Neanderthal Museum was having none of this protectionism, however. It countered that the reconstruction portrayed the Iceman as research showed he looked when he was alive, fully dressed and with a head of wavy, dark brown, shoulder-length hair, rather than as a mummy emerging from five thousand years in the ice. The Italian law pertained only to copies of the original mummified man, and this re-creation by artists and a plastic surgeon was certainly not that. It was not a mold of the desiccated corpse but a work of interpretation, an effort to imagine how he might have looked on the way to the Hauslabjoch, it contended.

There seemed to be no way around the museum's argument. After a week of negotiations, the province dropped its threats, and the exhibit went forward.[2] Whether the exhibition would hurt South Tyrol's new museum, no one could say. The next challenge was to come from within the ranks of the Iceman project itself.

Just weeks before Ötzi's much-anticipated return to South Tyrol, Konrad Spindler, in an interview with the *Alto Adige,* publicly criticized the exhibition plan and even suggested that the new freezer might not be able to do the job. Saying the display appealed to "really base instincts" and was designed just to lure people in, he asserted that seeing a corpse added nothing to one's understanding of it.[3] He also reheated old charges, repeatedly denied by Johan Reinhard and the Peruvians, that Juanita had suffered "serious damages" despite being conserved in what was supposed to be the "best" possible way.

To those who knew Spindler, the ethics charge was nothing novel. He had previously criticized South Tyrol's plans for the corpse, but in the general rush to finish the museum that opposition had conveniently been overlooked. No one expected him to raise it again, especially on the eve of Ötzi's return. But the suggestion that South Tyrol might be jeopardizing the Iceman's preservation in a lousy freezer was outright offensive. Given Spindler's prominence, his comments portended a divisive debate over ethics, politics, the market, and who knew what else.

Before South Tyrol could organize a response, Spindler further complicated the matter by revealing that fourteen months earlier he had received a threatening letter from a group calling itself the One Tyrol Task Force. The organization warned that it would "bring an end to the plan" if the corpse was put on display in South Tyrol, which it called the "southern part of Tyrol." "According to local custom and village law, he belongs directly on the Hauslabjoch or interred in the nearest cemetery," the letter read.[4] The letter had been turned over to the authorities immediately, but officials in both Innsbruck and Bolzano agreed not to make it public in order not to draw attention to the organization. Security officials had never heard of the group, and no one was apprehended in the case. But given that South Tyrol had been the scene of a number of acts of terrorism by nationalist Tyroleans in the 1970s, every threat was treated seriously.

South Tyrolean officials and several of Spindler's colleagues were dumbfounded that Spindler unilaterally decided to make the letter public. The revelation looked like a deliberate attempt to sabotage or at least humiliate South Tyrol. The South Tyrolean cultural-affairs adviser, Bruno Hosp, decided that Spindler's wanton comments deserved a sharp response. Noting that Werner Platzer had been on the commission overseeing the development of the new conservation system, he dismissed the charges that the corpse might be any worse off in Bolzano than it was in Innsbruck. He then criticized Spindler directly, saying that it was "strange to hear criticism of the display . . . from the mouth of a scientist who himself has used the marketing possibilities to the fullest."

Spindler, he said, was himself "displaying" the Iceman in his frequent lectures and slide shows, even while scorning the public's curiosity about the frozen body. Spindler had shown photographs of the Iceman's naked corpse, yet he was complaining that the Bolzano display would be particularly disrespectful because it would exhibit the Iceman nude. Was the gaze of a scientist more reverent than that of the public?

The ethics of display were clearly a topic for discussion, as were the ethics of the research. Indeed, it had not been a foregone conclusion that the Iceman would end up conserved in a freezer under glacial conditions so as to be always available for research. Those in charge could have opted to just rebury the man in the glacier, as someone had suggested back at the start of the whole project. They could have done what Canadian archaeologists did in the early 1980s when they found several icy graves belonging to sailors from the nineteenth-century Franklin expedition: They had opened the graves, done a little research, and then sealed the graves back up again.[5] Even in an age of virtually boundless faith in science, not all scientists strove to possess their finds. Hosp detected petty jealousy in Spindler's stance on the display. Moreover, he suggested knowingly, Spindler had already had ample chance to profit off the Iceman.

South Tyrol had wanted to make the transport of the body over the Brenner Pass a media event. Millions of potential tourists to South Tyrol, especially from the German-speaking world, might catch a glimpse of the transfer and know that the Iceman was soon to be on display. South Tyrolean officials thus wanted the transport to be accessible to journalists and the public. They had not reckoned on Platzer, too, putting up last-minute resistance.

In the weeks leading up to the return, South Tyrolean officials haggled with Platzer over the details. At first, Platzer was bent on secrecy and insisted that the date of the transfer not be announced publicly. Rumors began to fly. The corpse, it was said, was to be transferred secretly during the night, possibly in a government helicopter. Understandably, the secretive nature of the negotiations made local journalists all the more determined to cover it. South Tyrolean officials quickly realized that they were being painted as the good guys, on the side of the press, after six long years of Innsbruck's top-secret behavior. One South Tyrolean official announced that they would do everything in their power to stop the Austrians from trying to turn the Iceman's transfer into a "night and fog operation."[6]* At the last minute, the two parties finally struck a deal that allowed a number of photographers and camera teams to document the Iceman's removal from the freezer and the preparations for his journey.

Early on January 16, 1998, the transfer finally got under way. In the anatomy department's library, Platzer addressed a crowd of journalists for what was probably the last time. Just a few months earlier, he had retired from his chair at the Institute of Anatomy. He was sixty-eight years old and had served as the institute's head for twenty-eight years. No one doubted that he would be best remembered for the last six. Though his method of conservation had not been as elegant or progressive as those developed by Syremont or Carrier, his commitment to the man's preservation had never wavered.

While his retirement had not necessarily meant that he could no longer be responsible for the conservation and research of the corpse, South Tyrol had someone else in mind. Over the course of

---

*In German, the phrase *"Nacht und Nebel"* refers to a particularly vicious decree issued by Hitler in 1941 according to which certain enemies were to "disappear" without a trace, and no information about their fate was to be provided to their families.[7]

the last year, Bruno Hosp and Horst Seidler had developed a close friendship, and Seidler was to assume leadership of the research. His responsibilities were to continue the preservation of the Iceman, evaluate the work done thus far, and oversee new research. Though Platzer would be retained on an advisory council, he was effectively stripped of his power. His final words to the media, whom he had never trusted much, were uncharacteristically emotional. With great ceremony he showed the journalists a key. "I have carried this key to the Iceman's freezer with me for six years," he announced solemnly.[8]

Outside the anatomy building, a crowd of journalists and passersby had been swelling since dawn. Just before 8 A.M., the doors of the building swung open and the stretcher bearing the wrapped corpse, guided by four men in white coats, was wheeled to a waiting truck. Their faces were grave as they loaded the body into a large white truck, the flanks of which were painted prominently with the new museum's Iceman logo, as well as the seal of the province and a long list of benefactors. Austrian police, a few armed with submachine guns, were planted next to the truck. As the truck took off south for the Brenner Pass and Italy, a helicopter lent by the Interior Ministry closely followed along the route. Under armed guard, the Iceman was finally coming home.

To celebrate the Iceman's return, South Tyrol invited more than two dozen researchers to Bolzano to share with the public what they had found out about the Iceman. Bruno Hosp was one of the conference hosts. Dieter zur Nedden and Horst Seidler arrived together from Innsbruck in zur Nedden's BMW. Werner Platzer and Othmar Gaber, an associate professor of anatomy, showed up, and so did Torstein Sjøvold.

Hans Moser was there and so was Konrad Spindler, of course, with a small contingent of prehistorians from his department. Annaluisa Pedrotti and some of her Italian colleagues drove up from Trento. Klaus Oeggl and Sigmar Bortenschlager arrived a little late. Markus Egg had not had much to do with the artifacts since they had been transferred to Innsbruck two years earlier, but he made the trip from Mainz. He declined to give a talk but agreed to give a tour of the artifacts. Even Luigi Capasso was there, hovering in the background. Though invited, Andreas Lippert did not come, while Hans Nothdurfter kept a low profile. Less than a mile away, the Iceman was tucked away in his new freezer.

On the surface, everything ran smoothly. Outsiders probably did not notice which researchers clustered together during the espresso breaks between talks and who avoided whom. But beneath the gloss of gentility simmered conflict—scientific, political, national, and personal. In the end, neither the careful planning, the assumed stances of indifference, the talk about the international nature of science, nor even the inevitability of the return had made the transfer any easier. The events of the last year, and especially the last weeks, had shattered any lingering illusions that scientific results were at the center of this project. The Iceman was a commodity, and those who possessed him wielded enormous power.

In the Iceman, Bolzano now had its Eiffel Tower: a symbol for the city, as well as a symbol for South Tyrolean autonomy. The Iceman had proved to be a very important test case by which the provincial politicians had demonstrated to their constituents that they could hold off Rome and Innsbruck and Vienna, not to mention the Germans. This province of only 450,000 was quite capable of preserving its own history and prehistory.

Each day of the conference, Helmut and Erika Simon took up their seats in the front row, next to the center aisle, sometimes taking notes on the researchers' talks. Over the years, the couple had eagerly tracked the fortunes of their discovery. But they were nursing bruised egos. They never had accepted the reward offered by South Tyrol, which they referred to as hush money, and they were now preparing to sue the province.[9] The Simons knew that holding out for more money made them look bad, but they insisted that recognition was the real issue. They were hurt that a large memorial erected a few years earlier on the Hauslabjoch had failed to mention them, and they could not forget that the provincial governor had questioned whether they really had been the first to see the Iceman.

Across the center aisle, in the second row, Konrad Spindler sat stone-faced and impassive, rarely speaking with anyone but a few colleagues from his own department. His recent comments had practically made him persona non grata in South Tyrol, and few of the scientists sought his company. While some of his colleagues might have been displeased with his tactics, no one could deny that Spindler's marketing of the Iceman had brought substantial funds into the coffers of the Research Institute for Alpine Prehistory, as well as serious financial rewards for himself.

As an object of scientific study, the corpse had so far proved less productive. Six years of study had produced three volumes of research, the last of which had appeared in 1996. What would become of the six additional planned volumes, no one could say. The multi-disciplinary and international nature of the project seemed to be borne out by a long list of scientists and researchers from at least eight countries and dozens of disciplines. Yet the contents of several of these scientific papers merited scrutiny, and the interaction among these individuals could hardly be called collaborative. With notable exceptions, most research had been done within the narrow confines of particular disciplines without guidance or context from the project leadership. Dubious reports and claims—from the "missing" penis, to the "discovery" of Ötzi's flint mine, to the naming of the Iceman as the world's patriarch—had been allowed to stand and even flourish. Other sensitive results having to do with the Iceman's ethnicity or race entered the scientific literature without comment. The failure on the part of key scientists to acknowledge mistakes for the sake of better science, apparently out of fear of embarrassment, while at the same time deriding public curiosity in the find perpetuated the perceived cleft between science and society.

Tragically, the Iceman presented to the public, by way of Spindler's promotions, was nothing if not a superhero. From the time of the discovery the scientists, with very few exceptions, saw not a research project but a *person with a story*. Ultimately, the disparate body of scientific facts gleaned from the site did not add up to a real person. That they never could was something that no scientist ever admitted.

Despite the hype, the conference contained few new results but a lot of self-congratulatory talk about how many teams of scientists had taken part in the project and how many countries had been involved. The original plan to have two independent groups on each research project was never mentioned. The night before his talk, Platzer told a few colleagues that he was going to "reveal all" in his speech. "All" turned out to be a video with a live narration by Othmar Gaber that showed a number of sample-taking sessions on the Iceman. A few scientists could barely contain their disgust with the presentation. Platzer barely mentioned what research had come out of all this sample taking or who had received what samples. What he seemed most proud of was how little of the Iceman had been removed. "Only one gram, one gram," he said again and again.*

When, however, zur Nedden saw how samples had been removed from the brain—at random, without the best use of his state-of-the-art imaging equipment, and with no apparent regard to the interesting sections—the normally cool doctor exploded. For years he had been waiting to get a sample of the dark spot on the brain where his neurologist colleague had suspected a stroke. "What's the point of taking the samples when you don't know what you're going to do with them?" he asked.

His annoyance illuminated a central mystery about Platzer's conservatorship. Platzer's interest in the Iceman had never extended much beyond the mummy's indefinite preservation. He had repeatedly complained wearily that if he had let scientists get their way with the Iceman, there would not have been anything left of him. His governing idea was that there was not enough of the Iceman to service all those who wanted a piece. Officially, he had maintained that no researcher would be allowed to get a sample larger than one hundred milligrams, which some researchers said was too small for their work. By limiting the availability of the pieces, like the general flow of information, he did not so much serve science as refine and prolong his own control over the corpse.

His ultraconservative approach also suggested a psychological conflict between his two responsibilities. The removal of samples for research subtly "undid" his conservation work. In place of a comprehensive research program with clearly defined research goals, Platzer had initially come up with a *financial* goal. That goal was abandoned, but the apparatus set up to gain exclusivity, which put

---

*Platzer's colleagues reported three months later that ten grams had been taken from the corpse.[10]

Platzer in sole charge of the corpse, had never changed. As it turned out, scientists had had no problem coming up with funds for the research. Projects faltered not because of a lack of money, but because of Platzer's lack of willingness.

Research could be postponed perpetually with Platzer's argument that future researchers would know more and therefore do a better job. What had not been considered openly was whether future scientists would still be interested in the Iceman. While a few researchers applauded Platzer's caution, others complained that it had meant that not even basic inquiries into the Iceman's state of health and cause of death had been done thoroughly. Preservation was important, but what, some wondered, could be learned from him now? What were realistic expectations for the research results? What was the point of keeping him if not to make him available for study?

Several lines of research had been arrested at the halfway mark because of the bottleneck with samples. Though Platzer said nothing was in the stomach, Don Brothwell kept hoping to get a sample of it, to check whether a little scraping might turn something up. Other researchers had hoped that cells from inside the corpse, which were presumably better preserved, might relinquish some nuclear DNA. A grand design was missing, a framework for what science could tell us or at least try to tell us. Even the central question of the rib breaks was still open.

While the Iceman's corpse had not yet yielded the research results that many scientists had initially expected, the archaeological side of the investigation was struggling with the opposite problem. Despite valiant efforts, the archaeologists had not yet uncovered any major new sites near the Hauslabjoch that helped explain the Iceman's world. Annaluisa Pedrotti's enthusiastic research had, however, turned up a number of similar features in the archaeological records at several sites between Trento and southeastern Switzerland, on both sides of the main Alpine ridge. Over the last several years, her belief that the Iceman was not a representative of the Remedello culture or of any other identifiable northern Italian or Austrian Neolithic culture had crystallized. Across the Alps at about the time the Iceman lived, people seemed to have been returning to the higher altitudes, creating and using pastures. Their pottery was plain. All the flint that showed up in the region came from the southern side of the Alps, probably along well-established lines of trade and communication.

Pedrotti's still tentative conclusion was that all these elements were part of a distinctive culture, the Iceman's culture. His people farmed the poor Alpine soils but also kept herds and hunted. They did not have weaving technology but dressed in skins and might have used them in parts of their dwellings too. They took care of their own copper needs. Since herding and hunting required mobility, they used mainly birch bark, or skins, instead of pottery containers. In their flint-poor region, they often had to make do with materials such as bone and antler. Pedrotti knew her idea was in its infancy and that the culture needed to be fleshed out with more finds. But she wanted her colleagues' feedback and input. For Pedrotti, archaeology was about not only a product but a process.

One of the last to speak at the conference was Klaus Oeggl, who, until this day, had been almost unknown to the public at large. In the last year, he had written but not yet published a number of papers. Bit by bit, he had collected evidence that challenged long-held assumptions and undermined speculative ideas about the corpse, his artifacts, and the environment in which they had existed. Though Oeggl was coy about his obviously chilly relationship with Spindler, his presentations left no doubt that he was slowly but surely aiming to expose the archaeologist's disaster hypothesis as pure speculation.

He had entitled his talk "The Iceman's Last Meal," an ironic if unintentional echo of Spindler's notorious talk years earlier on the Iceman's last weeks. After explaining his method, he outlined in detail the contents of those forty milligrams from the man's transverse colon. He lingered on the discussion of the strikingly well-preserved pollen of the hop hornbeam. The excellent preservation of the pollen's gametophytes suggested that they must have been released from the tree just before the man swallowed them. If they had rested too long in the man's stomach or colon, they would have decayed, Oeggl said. The audience shifted in their seats, realizing that Oeggl was setting them up for something.

In the Vinschgau, the hop hornbeam blossoms from March to June. The majority of the other pollen Oeggl found in the man's gut were also from spring-blossoming varieties. Typical autumn-blossoming varieties, on the other hand, were entirely lacking. What that meant, Oeggl said, was that the Iceman had ingested the hop-hornbeam blossoms sometime between March and June and died very soon thereafter. Death had not come in the late summer but at the beginning.

The news touched off questioning looks throughout the audience. A fundamental pillar of the Iceman's story was suddenly crumbling, and it was taking down a lot with it. But Oeggl was sure. When he saw the spring-blossoming varieties in the colon sample, he realized that he already had other corroborating evidence for a death in the spring. It came from that casual experiment one May day years earlier in Kiel, when he had stripped a branch of its maple leaves, which had torn off without their stems. The Iceman's leaves showed the same fracture pattern. Only later did Oeggl realize that at the end of the growing season, in the fall, the leaf's structure was hardy; by the time it changed color and fell, the whole petiole came off with it when it was pulled. In the spring, however, the leaf's vein structure was not toughened up very much. If someone tried stripping a section of a branch, then the leaves themselves would rip, leaving the stems still attached to the branch. The Iceman must have stripped off his maple leaves in the spring, probably just a day or two before he died.

That also explained why his maple leaves were still green. Oeggl had even succeeded in extracting chlorophyll from them. But in South Tyrol, maple leaves were not green in the middle of September but golden, flaming red, and orange, and they fell from the trees at the slightest breath of wind. That alone told him that a death in the fall was most likely impossible.

Oeggl was not one for anecdotes, and he did not share the story of the maple leaves with the conference audience. That he would handle at some point in a future paper, after he had time to run through all the evidence again. He ended his talk by noting that he expected more information about the circumstances of the man's death to emerge from the sediments of the trench.

Then he walked confidently back to his seat next to Bortenschlager. His talk had stirred up the crowd, and soon the questions started to fly. South Tyroleans believed they understood the moun-

tains well, and Oeggl's suggestion that the Iceman had been crossing that pass at the end of spring unsettled them. After all, at that altitude, the end of spring still meant winterlike conditions. All along,
Spindler and others had been saying that the trench was empty of
snow when the Iceman arrived and that he had carefully placed his
belongings on the rocks. But if the present climate was any guide,
then one would expect to find several meters of snow still blanketing
the pass, making it virtually impossible to navigate. The Similaun
lodge did not even open until the middle of June because the snow
was normally too deep for people to make it up there, unless they
were on skis. A spring death also made it difficult to understand how
the Iceman's corpse could have survived, since the summer melt
would presumably have rid the pass of a great deal of snow.

Oeggl paused. There was so much more he could say, so much
more to report, but his results were still not in top form. He needed
more time. Still, he wanted to respond. He swallowed and, in his
deep voice, tried to formulate an answer.

"Gradually we have to take leave of the idea that the spot on
which he was discovered is the same spot on which he died," Oeggl
said slowly, enunciating each word and smiling just a little.

There was a moment of stunned silence. *The Iceman did not die
on that boulder?* The moderator, unaware of the profundity and
mystery of the statement, was wrapping things up. A few people understood that something was changing. The paradigm was shifting.
The young scientist had not given them enough information to see
where he was going. But clearly he knew more than he was saying.

Konrad Spindler had attributed nearly all the damage found in the
equipment and in the corpse to events during the Iceman's lifetime.
According to him, the arrows had been broken and the quiver damaged before the wounded Iceman fled to the Hauslabjoch, where he
set his gear in the bottom of the trench and then died on a nearby
boulder. There he and his possessions had remained, virtually immobile, for more than five thousand years.

Klaus Oeggl had combed through that theory enough times to
know that the story could not have been so simple. When discovered, both arrow shafts with feathers attached, those Spindler said

were broken in the fight, were sticking out of the mouth of the quiver, alongside all the unfinished arrows. The fracture of one of those shafts lay just about even with the spot where the bundle of arrows emerged from the quiver. Moreover, the first X ray of the contents of the quiver, taken before the arrows were moved, showed that the broken ends of the arrows were still largely in alignment. If the arrows had been broken down in the village, then how could the Iceman have managed to tote his quiver up a mountain without the broken segments shuffling to the bottom of the bag, like broken bits of spaghetti at the bottom of a box? As for the broken section of the quiver rod supposedly found near the Iceman's corpse, Oeggl offered a simple solution. With a little stretching of the dried-out leather in the quiver, the middle section of the rod would have fit back between the two end pieces just fine.

From the start, researchers had assumed that the Iceman's corpse and the quiver were found in the positions in which he had set them. This belief was based on the assumption that the man entered an ice- and snow-free trench, and that he and the artifacts had quickly become frozen to the bottom. But if the quiver had not moved from where the Iceman set it, then Patzelt and the others who lifted the quiver off the rocks should have found some trace of the quiver's outer fur beneath it.

Oeggl's novel conclusion was that on at least one previous occasion the sun had turned the ice in the trench to a slushy sea of meltwater that fostered the damage, disintegration, and dispersion of several artifacts. He had mapped out and analyzed thousands of artifact scraps found during Lippert's excavation. In the process, he revealed that these scraps had not been necessarily concentrated on the spots where the artifacts to which they belonged were discovered. Instead, fragments of several damaged artifacts, including parts of the grass cape and the three pieces of the broken arrow shaft, lay scattered throughout the trench. At some point, these artifacts had been swimming in water.

Other researchers' results supported that conclusion. Horst Seidler and Dieter zur Nedden had already suggested that the multiple hairline fractures of the Iceman's cranium might be due to freeze-thaw cycles at the site. Previous episodes of melting might also explain why the shoulder area of Ötzi's clothing was missing. During a previous thaw, the clothing on the shoulders, which were slightly higher than the rest of the corpse, had simply disintegrated and floated away.

Even more conclusive were results of the analysis of the Iceman's tissues by Christian Reiter, a forensic specialist, the chemist Thomas Bereuter, and their colleagues in Vienna. The results had never made it into the media or to the majority of the researchers on the project. They revealed that the man's tissues had been converted to adipocere *before* undergoing desiccation.[11] The team concluded that the corpse had *not* been packed continuously in ice but also had lain in water for at least several months in the course of several seasons.[12] Oeggl himself had not stumbled on the results until a year after they were published in the Research Institute for Alpine Prehistory's third volume of results.

Oeggl believed that little, if anything, was in the place it had been at the time the Iceman had died: not the quiver, not its contents, not the birch-bark container, and not the enigmatic bow. Even the position of the corpse was open to question. Oeggl did not believe that the man had lain down upon that rock to die. Instead, the corpse had come to rest on that site. The Simons had *not* discovered the pristine scene of a 5,300-year-old death, frozen in time, but a typical archaeological site, heavily and repeatedly disturbed.

For more than five thousand years, snow, sleet, rain, and wind had scoured the ridge. For at least the last seven centuries, humans and their herds had crossed it twice a year, and wild animals had come and gone. In the last century, human traffic over the site had increased dramatically. On a good summer day, several dozen people might pass by, and, as Patzelt had noted years earlier, many had stopped for a rest on the ledge just above the corpse, leaving their picnic trash behind. Hikers had regularly tramped across the field of snow that filled the trench in which Ötzi had lain. As the snow and ice melted, people had trod on the slush just above the finds, perhaps even on top of the thin layer of ice that had covered Ötzi's head and ribs.

As any archaeologist should do, Oeggl was now in the process of mapping out the migrations of the artifacts around the trench since the time of their deposition. He hoped that the exercise might ultimately illuminate the circumstances of the man's death. Already his study, particularly of the arrows in the quiver, suggested that the man's deposition had probably not occurred gently.

Oeggl had spent a lot of time pondering the last day of the Iceman's life. Around eight hours before his death, he concluded, the Iceman was in the vicinity of Katharinaberg, where he had a meal that included bread, vegetables, and meat. Except for the bow and arrows, which he was still working on, all his tools were intact and in good working order. At some point, he started on his hike up the steep valley toward the Hauslabjoch. Since it was spring, he would have been approaching a pass that was almost certainly covered in many feet of snow. He might have been trudging not over bare rock, as previously suggested, but through *fresh snow*. Why else had he worn boots? If he had been walking over old packed snow or rock, he probably would have worn moccasins or gone barefoot, as the Nepalese sherpas do. But instead he had considerable insulation around his feet, and had even tucked his pants into his boots. Those boots were designed for determined trudging through snow, even snow deep enough to obscure the landscape, to bury the usual markers under deceptive drifts. Oeggl wondered whether the man had been able to see the rocks on which he and his possessions ultimately came to rest. He might have been breaking a path.

But then something happened, something so forceful that it snapped his two arrows, the arrowhead, and his quiver backing right in half. Oeggl knew that clean breaks like those were caused by enormous mechanical stress. It was an accident, to be sure. It looked like a bad fall, maybe through a precipice of snow that had been shaped by the southerly wind from the Schnalstal and overhung the rocky shallow. But, unlike others, Oeggl was reluctant to speculate further. Already he was at the edge of his evidence. In a few years, he might be able to say more. But this was the limit of his science.

There was nothing wrong with coming up with a good story about what had befallen this Iceman. But if a scientist wrote it, then the work had to be grounded in good science. Many scenarios might be offered to explain what had happened to the Iceman 5,300 years ago. But some stories were better than others. Of this Oeggl was sure.

EPILOGUE

In June 2001, Dr. Paul Gostner, a radiologist at the General Regional Hospital in Bolzano, was examining a new set of X rays of the Iceman's chest cavity when he noticed a shadowy object near the shoulder. That afternoon, he showed the image to Dr. Eduard Egarter Vigl, the South Tyrolean pathologist who had inherited the job of preserving the mummy from Platzer when it was returned to Italy.

"I think it's an arrowhead," Gostner said.

Without ado the two men went to the museum, where the corpse had been on display since 1998, and removed it from the freezer. In the middle of the shoulder blade they found a tiny puncture that had been overlooked in previous forensic investigations. After warming the tissue up with their gloved hands, Egarter was able to insert a metal probe two centimeters into the canal before it hit frozen flesh again. The discovery of an open path leading to the arrowhead confirmed that this was a fresh wound that had not healed by the time the Iceman died.

Though Egarter considered keeping the finding secret until the museum could publish it, he quickly decided to make the sensational discovery public. A month later, he and Horst Seidler called a press conference in Bolzano. The Iceman, they announced, had been fatally shot by an arrow. The angle at which it was lodged in the body suggested that it had been shot from behind and slightly below, tearing through the man's left shoulder blade as it entered his body. New CAT scans revealed a hole in the shoulder blade that was just big enough for the arrowhead. The wound had bled profusely, and even more internal damage would have been done when the man, or someone else, pulled out the arrowshaft, leaving the point inside. If the loss of blood had not killed him, then an infection probably would have. At last, nearly a decade after the Iceman's discovery, the scientists had found a likely cause of death.

The discovery immediately raised questions about why the arrowhead had not been found before. Dieter zur Nedden and William Murphy, the two radiologists who had spent the most time with the thousands of CAT scans and dozens of X rays of the corpse, could not explain their failure to notice the projectile, which, they realized in retrospect, appeared as a fuzzy object even in the very first X rays.

Zur Nedden took full responsibility for missing the arrowhead, but he noted in interviews with the local media that because Platzer had been so protective of the corpse, the time allotted to do the X rays and other radiological imaging had been limited.

Yet Gostner's X rays had also revealed another anomaly in the Innsbruck radiologists' diagnosis. Ironically, the arrowhead had been discovered because Gostner was looking for the precise location of the Iceman's fresh rib fractures so that samples could be removed from the site for testing. South Tyrol's scientific advisory board, set up to oversee new research on the corpse, had decided to investigate the timing of the rib fractures, which played so large a role in Spindler's disaster theory. The new X rays, taken from all sides of the chest cavity, revealed the arrowhead, and confirmed that the Iceman had several healed rib fractures, but they turned up no fresh fractures. Gostner quickly concluded that there were no fresh rib breaks, and Egarter Vigl backed his diagnosis. Murphy has acknowledged that the earlier diagnosis was based not on the discovery of the fracture site itself, but on the angle of the ribs as they appeared in the X rays. Both he and zur Nedden say they will comment on Gostner's finding only after they have studied the images.

The archaeologists and other researchers who had spent the

better part of the decade studying the Iceman were thrilled by the news of the arrowhead. In Trento, Annaluisa Pedrotti was eager to learn how debilitating such an injury would have been.

"In the old Westerns, the American Indians keep running even when they've been shot in the back with an arrow," she noted. Could the Iceman have made it to the top of the pass from the valley after being shot, or was he shot on the spot or very nearby? Was the shot accidental, perhaps the mistake of a fellow hunter? Or was he shot during some kind of conflict? She noted that the shape of the arrowhead inside the corpse is similar, but not identical, to the two found in his quiver. However, because many different kinds of arrowheads were used even within one culture, she thought the type of arrowhead would be unlikely to reveal anything about the person who had shot it.

In Mainz Markus Egg noted that several recent digs at prehistoric sites in Germany and Austria had turned up grisly scenes of massacre. Violence in those prehistoric societies probably was not unusual, and Egg acknowledged that the Iceman could have been involved in some kind of conflict over land or animals.

In Innsbruck, Konrad Spindler quickly claimed that the discovery of the arrowhead supported his disaster theory. Spindler's role in the research had been severely curtailed by the South Tyroleans since his comments about the museum display but he still lectured frequently in Europe on the Iceman. In all those years, however, he had not modified or revisited his theory to accommodate the new results on the damage to the equipment, the season of death and the ambiguous condition of the corpse itself.

Johan Reinhard, the American researcher who studied the Peruvian mummy Juanita and visited the Hauslabjoch in the summer of 2001, recently said he thinks the site – right on the pass and surrounded by two of the highest mountains in the region – is not arbitrary. Other archaeologists said new efforts had to be undertaken to determine whether the Iceman was intentionally buried on the high pass. If, as Pedrotti said, the Iceman died in front of his foe, the ax certainly would have been stolen. If the site is a burial, however, perhaps the Iceman was buried with his ax. In any case, the idea that the Iceman was seeking shelter from a storm and succumbed quietly to hypothermia now seems very unlikely.

Though no full autopsy is planned, Egarter Vigl would like to remove the arrowhead, and examine its pathway to determine whether it cut any arteries, which almost certainly would have led to the man's quick death. Since the Iceman went on display in the museum in March of 1998, Egarter Vigl has proved eager to try out new techniques for preserving and researching the corpse. In September of 2000, the mummy was removed from the display freezer to a sterile room heated to fifty degrees Fahrenheit. Overnight, the ice that covered the surface and filled his insides slowly melted.

Werner Platzer's earlier investigations of the Iceman's innards had been carried out through cuts in the solidly frozen corpse, and the ice crystals inside had made orientation difficult and had hampered the sample-taking. But Egarter Vigl had decided that thawing the corpse would eliminate these problems. In the morning, working under conditions cleaner than those in an operating room, a South Tyrolean urologist, Dr. Armin Pycha, passed a tiny cystoscope up the urethra through the Iceman's penis, all the way to the prostate. Everthing they saw looked intact. As they worked, Dr. Friedrich Tiefenbrunner, an Austrian microbiologist who had guarded the Iceman against contamination since he came out of the glacier, monitored their every move.

The doctors next probed the corpse from the ragged opening in the buttock left by the jackhammer. The endoscope moved through easily, and the loops of the intestines, pale grey and flexible, came into view. The doctors also picked out part of the Iceman's bladder and the peritoneum, the membrane that lines the abdominal cavity. Using Platzer's titanium instruments, they snipped out a bit of the intestine and removed some of the stool inside. They also looked for the appendix, but were unable to find it before noon, the hour at which Egarter wanted to break off the operation and refreeze the Iceman. Later, plaque was removed from several of the Iceman's teeth, and that and several tissue samples were distributed to six teams whose projects had been approved by the new scientific advisory board headed by Seidler.

After the operation, which the museum publicized well in advance, Egarter held a press conference and gave out a video of the mummy's innards. No one in the media missed the point: a new regime was now in charge of the mummy, and the process was going to be transparent. The next day, the Iceman was back on display.

In September of 2001, a few months after the discovery of the arrowhead, South Tyrol once again invited the Iceman researchers to Bolzano for a conference, this time to mark the tenth anniversary of the discovery. Most of the discussion centred on the arrowhead, but a few researchers did present new results, including new information on where Ötzi spent his childhood. Wolfgang Müller, a Swiss researcher, analyzed the isotopic composition of strontium and lead in the man's tooth enamel, which is laid down in a person's youth. Soils, which a person takes up in food and water, leave different trace element signatures depending on the type of rock they come from. Müller found that the Iceman's dental placque seemed to bear the signature of South Tyrolean, rather than North Tyrolean, geography, and he suggested that he had spent his formative years near the Schnalstal. Italian newspapers immediately seized on the news and noted that he was a "Tyrolean."

Konrad Spindler and three acupuncture practitioners published a study that found that nine of the fifteen tattoo groups on the Iceman's body were on or within five millimetres of Chinese acupuncture points.[1] Working with Klaus Oeggl, the physicist Walter Kutschera of the University of Vienna carbon-dated nearly twenty artifacts uncovered at the Hauslabjoch. He found that all the artifacts attributed to the Iceman, including the bow, the ax and the embers from the birch-bark container, indeed dated to the same period as the mummy itself.[2] However, the datings on two fragments of wood recovered during Lippert's excavation fell well outside the Iceman's lifetime. One dated to between 4790 and 4550 B.C.E., the late Mesolithic period, and the other between 790 to 480 B.C.E. The finding confirmed earlier suggestions that other ancient people had visited this site before and after the Iceman's fatal crossing.

After analyzing certain isotopes in the composition of the Iceman's hair, Stephen A. Macko of the University of Virginia suggested in two reports that the Iceman had a primarily vegetarian diet.[3] Months later, Oeggl and James H. Dickson, his collaborator from the University of Glasgow, challenged that interpretation, reminding Macko and his co-authors of the meat, in the form of tiny muscle fibers, in the Iceman's last meal. Dickson and Oeggl also noted, with apparent exasperation, that the papers were written as if the authors were unaware of the microscopic studies of the colon contents.[4] Indeed, some scientists have complained that there still is no comprehensive approach to the study of the Iceman, and no clearinghouse for information – not even a research website.

Yet the museum, which anchors a prominent pedestrian street in downtown Bolzano, has proved a commercial success. The local shops and restaurants sell Ötzi postcards and Man-in-the-Ice-Cream. Outside the museum, people often line up to wait their turn to enter. There is no question that the main attraction is the body itself. For four weeks in 1999, the museum removed the Iceman from display, and daily attendance fell to a dribble. By the end of 2001, one million visitors had filed past his chamber and gazed into his eyes.

In March 2002, Egarter Vigl made another surprising announcement about the death. Months earlier, during a conversation arranged by an Italian television producer, Alois Pirpamer had told Egarter Vigl that he remembered seeing a "knife" in the Iceman's hand as he was digging the corpse out of the ice. People had long commented that the hand was positioned in such a way that suggested it had been grasping something at the time of death, but this was the first time Pirpamer had mentioned a knife in an interview. Egarter immediately suspected that Pirpamer might mean the dagger, which at the time of Pirpamer's digging, had not yet been recovered.

New X-rays then revealed a fresh, half-inch-long gash to the bone in the right palm. The damage from the gash extended even to the bone of the index finger. At a press conference Egarter Vigl said the wound, which he considered serious, was typical of someone holding up a hand in defense. So far, no connection has been established between the wound and the dagger and many archaeologists have expressed doubt about Pirpamer's new detail. But Egarter says he has studied the tape of the recovery and believes that Pirpamer's version is possible.

ACKNOWLEDGMENTS

I am so very grateful to all those researchers who shared their work with me. Five deserve my special thanks: At a time when most scientists on the project were still wary of the media, Hans Nothdurfter considered what would be helpful, and then simply opened up his files to me. Klaus Oeggl, my wonderful botany tutor, showed me the splendors of the Schnalstal and patiently went over everything until I finally got it. Annaluisa Pedrotti, an indefatigable source of information, generously introduced me to the archaeological community in northern Italy, and also to Teroldego wine. Horst Seidler responded to the toughest questions with insight and unusual honesty, and always made me laugh. Dieter zur Nedden, an entertaining interpreter of Tyrolean culture, handled every request calmly and with tolerance, and graciously cleared obstacles along my other paths of inquiry.

I also wish to thank Lawrence Barfield for allowing me to tag along on an excavation and then a survey in northern Italy, Markus Egg for many crucial discussions and viewings of the artifacts, and Werner Platzer for allowing me to see the Iceman in his freezer in Innsbruck. Sigmar Bortenschlager, Stefan Dietrich, Angelika Fleckinger, Sonia Guillén, Oliva Handt, Rainer Hölzl, Anton Koler, Walter Leitner, William A. Murphy, Jr., Svante Pääbo, Gernot

Patzelt, Harm Paulsen, Johan Reinhard, Dieter Schäfer, Tillmann Scholl, and Erika and Helmut Simon also deserve my thanks for sharing their experiences and work.

Thanks, also, to Jane Buikstra, Michael Dietler, Eugene Giles, Doug MacAyeal, Olga Soffer, and Michael Torbenson for useful discussions about their fields of study.

I am forever obliged to: Ray Anderson at the University of Wisconsin–Madison, who pointed me to New York; Bernie Gwertzman at *The New York Times*, who pointed me to Vienna, and then Bratislava, in 1989; Nicholas Wade, also at the *Times*, whose enthusiasm about the Iceman's discovery in 1991 spurred me toward this project; and Jack Repcheck, whose idea this book was in the first place. At many times in the last decade I have called on the wisdom and kindness of George Johnson, to whom I owe a great debt. Thanks, too, to Esther Newberg and David Schmerler at I.C.M. Bob Loomis, my wise and good editor at Random House, was patient even as the deadlines kept slipping by. Benjamin Dreyer, Richard Elman, Carole Lowenstein, Timothy Mennel, Janet Wygal, and Eva Young, all of Random House, also deserve warm thanks.

In the course of this project, I drew daily on the love, advice and talents of my family and friends. Lisa Brawley, my fellow Libra, listened to every new development, and offered penetrating queries and perceptive insights on several drafts of this book, thereby helping me define what it would be. Linda Diamond-Shapiro's outlandish enthusiasm, wit, and discerning ear informed and inspired me at a very critical juncture in this project. Harry Gottlieb's jones for plot helped me turn a mass of research into something readable.

Jonathan Marks's hilarious lectures on the history of anthropology at the University of California–Berkeley set me straight on the concept of biological race, Jürgen Weiner showed me how to retouch a flint dagger at his kitchen table, and both graciously read the manuscript and saved me from many errors and follies. I always looked forward to discussions with Kallie Keith on DNA and other aspects of science, and her detailed comments on portions of the manuscript were indispensable. Debbie DiMaio listened skeptically to all problems, and her prying questions helped me untangle them.

Heather Lynch-Fowler's enthusiastic review of one early draft convinced me I was on the right path. Conversations with Maureen McLane inevitably led to major rewrites, yet I could not have done without her wild and analytical comments. After my dear Ted Fishman's harangue upon reading a few early chapters, I was afraid to show the manuscript to him again, but still benefited regularly from his witticisms and jasmine tea. If Ted was my yin, his wife Sara Stern was my yang. My words cannot do justice to the myriad ways in which she kept me human while writing this book. Thanks, too, to David Roberts and David Wolfsdorf, for commenting on parts of early drafts and for hiking with me up to the Hauslabjoch. The wide-eyed appreciation of Iceman stories by Dare Brawley and Dmitri Gaskin, not to mention the adult-size questions of Jacob Yanowski, inspired me to keep looking for answers. Knowing that Steve Savage, my faithful correspondent in Brooklyn, was sitting there drawing every day as I was sitting here writing every day was a prime motivator. Thanks, also, to Tom Gottlieb for allowing me to see the Iceman in a new light.

Eleonora Bartoli, Ira Bashkow, Sara Bernal, Christof Biba, Eric Caplan, John Chesson, Cynthia Chou, Rod Coover, Dorothee Fischer-Appelt, Claire Fowler, Claudine Frank, Greg Fried, Igor Gasowski, Michael Goldin, Roy Gottlieb, Estelle Green, Bob Green, Sara Green, Christina Hardway, Amy Harvey, Jeanette Hug, Debra Immergut, Seth Leopold, Jonathan Lorenz, John Marks, Caitlin McQuade, Joe McMaster, Deborah Oropallo, Brigitte Ozzello, Carol Palmquist, John Palmquist, Kirsten Palmquist, Dan Peterman, Suzanne Popkin, Philip Robbins, Leslie Roeder, Danny Rosenblatt, Christine Schillinger, Ted Schillinger, Herman Sinaiko, Laura Slatkin, Sam Speers, Connie Spreen, Elizabeth Stephenson, Elsie Stern, Casey and Larry Straus, Jill Sulzberg, Jen Thomas, Stefan Waldschmidt, Melanie Wallace, Steve Washington, Michael Wise, David Yanowski, and Deb Yanowski all contributed to this project in some critical way.

My friends in Europe sustained me during my long research trips, and I thank them all. In Kerkhove, Belgium, Marie-Louise Vanhuysse-Cappelle and Ludwig Vanhuysse, my treasured second set of parents, have made me feel at home since I first arrived there in 1981 as an exchange student.

In Milan, Italy, Laura Filippucci, my pen pal of twenty-five years, and Marco Ventura welcomed me many times with great conversation and delicious meals.

In Vienna, Austria, my *other* second family—Sigune, Otto, Sascha and Philipp Hartmann—have showered me with more hospitality and ideas than I can handle in one lifetime. Thanks, too, to my friends Christine Lixl and Thomas Halbeisen for invaluable discussions about ethnicity and education in Austria.

In Innsbruck, I was lucky to meet the very kind Frau Maria Kuttler, whose apple strudel is unsurpassed.

From elsewhere in Europe, Annelore Engel, Peter Green, and Hester Wax kept me supplied with random news of the Iceman and encouragement.

As a fifth grader at Brookridge Elementary School in Overland Park, Kansas, I had the tremendous fortune of landing in the class of Ms. M. Kay Willy, who introduced me not only to the concept of exponents, but to the Leakeys and "Zinjanthropus," William Blake, and so much more. Her ethics and love for learning inspire me still.

My deepest gratitude is to my brother, John Fowler, and my parents, Joan Barnes Fowler and Jack Fowler, who have never uttered a discouraging word nor wavered for a second in their love. Finally, for his vision, patience, humor and miraculous love, I am happily indebted to Harry Nathan Gottlieb.

NOTES

PROLOGUE: NO ROOM IN THE HELICOPTER

1. "Leiche auf Finailspitze: Ein Krieger von Friedrich mit der leeren Tasche?" *Tiroler Tageszeitung,* 23 September 1991.
2. Konrad Spindler, *Der Mann im Eis: Die Ötztaler Mumie verrät die Geheimnisse der Steinzeit* (Munich: C. Bertelsmann, 1993), 12.

CHAPTER 1: THE FIRST TO SEE IT

1. W. Ambach, E. Ambach, W. Tributsch, R. Henn, and H. Unterdorfer, "Corpses Released from Glacier Ice: Glaciological and Forensic Aspects," *Journal of Wilderness Medicine* 3 (1992), 372.
2. Sölden Gendarmerie Post communication, gp soelden, gz-p-1359-91 (holzknecht).

CHAPTER 2: A DIFFICULT RECOVERY

1. Austria Presse Agentur (APA), "Leichenfund auf Tiroler Gletscher," *Dolomiten,* 21 September 1991.
2. Ezio Danieli, "Un antico guerriero sul camino di Messner," *Alto Adige,* 22 September 1991.

3. Gert Ammann, letter to author, 26 September 1994.

4. Spindler, *Der Mann im Eis,* 12.

5. Rainer Hölzl, Osterreicher Rundfunk (ORF) raw footage, 23 September 1991.

6. Hans Haid, faxed letter to ORF, 23 September 1991.

7. Institut für Gerichtliche Medizin, Universität Innsbruck, transcript, Case 91/619, 23 September 1991.

CHAPTER 3: A GREAT MOMENT FOR SCIENCE

1. Spindler, *Der Mann im Eis,* 56.

2. Reinhold Messner, telephone interview with author, 17 October 1994.

3. Spindler, 56.

4. Bodo Bernhardt, "Zur Frage der Staatsgrenze," in *Der Mann im Eis: Bericht über das Internationale Symposium 1992 in Innsbruck,* vol. 1, ed. Frank Höpfel, Werner Platzer, and Konrad Spindler (Innsbruck: Veröffentlichungen der Universität Innsbruck 187, 1992), 68.

5. Franz Volgger, *Südtirol Handbuch* (Bozen: Südtiroler Landesregierung, 1994), 25–26.

6. Ibid., 209.

7. Austria Presse Agentur (APA), "Der Tote hat jetzt einen Namen," *Dolomiten,* 30 September 1991.

8. Manfred Neubauer, "Ötzi und die Staatsgrenze: Bericht über die Arbeiten zur Feststellung der Fundstelle in Bezug auf die Staatsgrenze Österreich-Italien am Hauslabjoch," in *Der Mann im Eis: Neue Funde und Ergebnisse,* vol. 2, ed. Konrad Spindler, Elisabeth Rastbichler-Zissernig, Harald Wilfing, Dieter zur Nedden, and Hans Nothdurfter (Vienna: Springer, 1995), 297.

9. Stefan Dietrich, "Die Wissenschaft ist international," *Tiroler Tageszeitung,* 3 October 1991.

CHAPTER 4: ITALY IS WATCHING

1. Lawrence Barfield, Ebba Koller, and Andreas Lippert, *Der Zeuge aus dem Gletscher: Das Rätsel der frühen Alpen-Europäer* (Vienna: Carl Uberreuter, 1992), 106.

2. Robert J. Wenke, *Patterns in Prehistory: Humankind's First Three Million Years* (New York: Oxford University Press, 1990), 262.

3. Colin Renfrew and Paul Bahn, *Archaeology: Theories, Methods, and Practice* (London: Thames and Hudson, 1991), 406.

4. Friedrich Tiefenbrunner, "Bakterien und Pilze, ein Problem für unseren ältesten Tiroler?" in *Der Mann im Eis: Bericht über das Internationale Symposium 1992 in Innsbruck,* vol. 1, 102.

5. R. Dale Guthrie, *Frozen Fauna of the Mammoth Steppe* (Chicago: University of Chicago Press, 1990), 79.

6. Michael Frank, "Mit Spray gegen den Schimmel auf der Mumie," *Süddeutsche Zeitung,* 5–6 October 1991.

7. Dieter zur Nedden and Klaus Wicke, "Der Eismann aus der Sicht der radiologischen und computertomographischen Daten," in *Der Mann im Eis: Bericht über das Internationale Symposium 1992 in Innsbruck,* vol. 1, 131.

8. Elisabeth Zissernig, "Der Mann vom Hauslabjoch. Von der Entdeckung bis zur Bergung," in *Der Mann im Eis: Bericht über das Internationale Symposium 1992 in Innsbruck,* vol. 1, 234–244.

9. Renfrew and Bahn, *Archaeology,* 374.

10. Horst Seidler and others, "Zur Anthropologie des Mannes vom Hauslabjoch: Morphologie und metrische Aspekte," in *Der Mann im Eis: Bericht über das Internationale Symposium 1992 in Innsbruck,* vol. 1, 160.

11. Wolfram Bernhard, "Vergleichende Untersuchungen zur Anthropologie des Mannes vom Hauslabjoch," in *Der Mann im Eis: Bericht über das Internationale Symposium 1992 in Innsbruck,* vol. 1, 177.

12. " 'Der Fund ist ein Wunder,' " *Der Spiegel,* 27 January 1992, 189.

13. Andreas Lippert and Konrad Spindler, "Die Auffindung einer frühbronzezeitlichen Gletschermumie am Hauslabjoch in den Ötztaler Alpen (Gem. Schnals)," *Archäologie Österreichs* 2/2 (1991), 11–17.

14. Georges Bonani and others, "Altersbestimmung von Milligrammproben der Ötztaler Gletscherleiche mit der Beschleunigermassenspektrometrie-Methode (AMS)," in *Der Mann im Eis: Bericht über das Internationale Symposium 1992 in Innsbruck,* vol. 1, 115.

CHAPTER 5: EVIDENCE OF DISTRESS

1. Sigmar Bortenschlager, "The Iceman's Environment," paper presented at the conference on the Man in the Ice, Bolzano, Italy, 22–24, January, 1998, 4.

2. Andrew Sherratt, "Plough and Pastoralism: Aspects of the Sec-

ondary Products Revolution," in *Pattern of the Past: Studies in Honour of David Clarke,* ed. Ian Hodder, Glynn Isaac, and Norman Hammond (Cambridge: Cambridge University Press, 1981), 262.

3. E.J.W. Barber, *Prehistoric Textiles: The Development of Cloth in the Neolithic and Bronze Ages with Special Reference to the Aegean* (Princeton, N.J.: Princeton University Press, 1991), 79.

4. Roswitha Goedecker-Ciolek, "Zur Herstellungstechnik von Kleidung und Ausrüstungsgegenständen," in *Die Gletschermumie vom Ende der Steinzeit aus den Ötztaler Alpen* (Mainz: Römisch-Germanisches Zentralmuseum, 1993), 108.

5. Reinhold Pöder, Ursula Peintner, and Thomas Pümpel, "Mykologische Untersuchungen an den Pilz-Beifunden der Gletschermumie vom Hauslabjoch," in *Der Mann im Eis: Bericht über das Internationale Symposium 1992 in Innsbruck,* vol. 1, 318.

CHAPTER 6: THE MUMMY TO MARKET

1. Werner Platzer, interview by author, Innsbruck, Austria, 9 May 1994.

2. Ethik & Kommunikation, *"Der Mann im Eis": Vom Wissenschaftlichen Sensationsfund zum 'Anliegen der Menschheit,' Integriertes Kommunikations- und Sponsoring-Konzept im Auftrag der Leopold-Franzens-Universität Innsbruck,* August 1992, section 1.9.

3. Goedecker-Ciolek, "Zur Herstellungstechnik," 109.

4. H. C. Broholm and Margrethe Hald, *Costumes of the Bronze Age in Denmark* (Copenhagen: NYT Nordisk Forlag, 1940), 146–56.

CHAPTER 7: A CASTRATED EGYPTIAN

1. Horst Seidler and others, "Some Anthropological Aspects of the Prehistoric Tyrolean Ice Man," *Science* 258, 16 September 1992, 456.

2. Dieter zur Nedden and others, "New Findings on the Tyrolean 'Iceman': Archaeological and CT-Body Analysis Suggest Personal Disaster Before Death," *Journal of Archaeological Science* 21 (1994), 817.

3. E. Ambach, "Paradoxical Undressing in Fatal Hypothermia (Homo tirolensis)," *Lancet* 341, 15 May 1993, 1285.

4. Seidler and others, "Some Anthropological Aspects," 457.

5. Barfield, Koller, and Lippert, *Der Zeuge aus dem Gletscher,* 149.

6. Seidler and others, "Some Anthropological Aspects," 457, n. 1.

7. Lawrence H. Barfield, "The Chalcolithic Cemetery at Manerba del Garda," *Antiquity* 57 (1983), 122.

8. Hans Rotter, "Ethische Aspekte zum Thema," in *Der Mann im Eis: Bericht über das Internationale Symposium 1992 in Innsbruck,* vol. 1, 27.

9. Ibid., 26.

10. Othmar Gaber and others, "Konservierung und Lagerung der Gletschermumie," in *Der Mann im Eis: Bericht über das Internationale Symposium 1992 in Innsbruck,* vol. 1, 96.

11. Francisco J. Ayala, "The Myth of Eve: Molecular Biology and Human Origins," *Science* 270 (1995), 1933.

12. Kary B. Mullis, "The Unusual Origin of the Polymerase Chain Reaction," *Scientific American,* April 1990, 56–65.

13. Allan C. Wilson and Rebecca L. Cann, "The Recent African Genesis of Humans," *Scientific American,* April 1992, 68.

14. John Evangelist Walsh, *Unraveling Piltdown: The Science Fraud of the Century and Its Solution* (New York: Random House, 1996), 69.

15. Michael Heim and Werner Nosko, *Die Ötztal Fälschung: Anatomie einer Archäologischen Groteske* (Hamburg: Rowohlt, 1993), 32.

16. "Lost father 'mistaken for prehistoric iceman,' " *Daily Mail,* 10 January 1992.

17. Spindler, *Der Mann im Eis,* 200.

CHAPTER 8: SPINDLER'S STORY

1. Oliva Handt and others, "Molecular Genetic Analyses of the Tyrolean Ice Man," *Science* 264, 17 June 1994, 1778.

2. Romana Prinoth-Fornwagner and Thomas R. Niklaus, "Der Mann im Eis. Resultate der Radiokarbon-Datierung," in *Der Mann im Eis: Neue Funde und Ergebnisse,* vol. 2, 81.

3. Konrad Spindler, "The Iceman's Last Weeks," paper presented at the International Mummy Symposium, Innsbruck, Austria, 17 September 1993.

4. Frank Höpfel, Werner Platzer, and Konrad Spindler, back book-jacket flap of *Der Mann im Eis: Bericht über das Internationale Symposium 1992 in Innsbruck,* vol. 1.

5. Walter Gössler and others, "Priest, hunter, alpine shepherd, or smelter worker?" in *Der Mann im Eis: Neue Funde und Ergebnisse,* vol. 2, 271.

6. Willy Groenman–van Waateringe, "Analyses of Hides and Skins from the Hauslabjoch," in *Die Gletschermumie vom Ende der Steinzeit aus den Ötztaler Alpen,* 123.

7. Torstein Sjøvold, "Verteilung und Größe der Tätowierungen am Eismann vom Hauslabjoch," in *Der Mann im Eis: Neue Funde und Ergebnisse,* vol. 2, 280.

8. Eddy van der Velden and others, "The Decorated Body of the Man from Hauslabjoch," in *Der Mann im Eis: Neue Funde und Ergebnisse,* vol. 2, 276.

9. E. Ambach, W. Tributsch, and W. Ambach, "Is Mummification Possible in Snow?" *Forensic Science International* 54 (1992), 191.

CHAPTER 9: EXPANDING MARKETS

1. "Naming People Lightly," *Nature* 373, 19 January 1995, 176.

2. R. C. Lewontin, Steven Rose, and Leon J. Kamin, *Not in Our Genes: Biology, Ideology, and Human Nature* (New York: Pantheon, 1984), 126.

3. Robert Proctor, "From *Anthropologie* to *Rassenkunde* in the German Anthropological Tradition," in *Bones, Bodies, Behavior: Essays on Biological Anthropology,* ed. George W. Stocking, Jr. (Madison: University of Wisconsin Press, 1988), 138–79.

4. Heinz Müller, " 'Ötzi,' ein echter Europäer," *Die Presse,* 7 April 1993.

5. W. W. Howells, *Who's Who in Skulls: Ethnic Identification of Crania from Measurements,* Papers of the Peabody Museum of Archaeology and Ethnology, Harvard University, vol. 82 (Cambridge, Mass.: Peabody Museum of Archaeology and Ethnology, Harvard University, 1995), 39.

6. Wolfram Bernhard, "Multivariate statistische Untersuchungen zur Anthropologie des Mannes vom Hauslabjoch," in *Der Mann im Eis: Neue Funde und Ergebnisse,* vol. 2, 226.

7. Ibid., 227.

8. Walter Leitner, "Der 'Hohle Stein'—eine steinzeitliche Jägerstation im hinteren Ötztal, Tirol (Archäologische Sondagen 1992/93)," in *Der Mann im Eis: Neue Funde und Ergebnisse,* vol. 2, 209–13.

9. Bernardino Bagolini and Annaluisa Pedrotti, "Vorgeschichtliche Höhenfunde im Trentino-Südtirol und im Dolomitenraum vom Spätpaläolithikum bis zu den Anfängen der Metallurgie," in *Der Mann im Eis: Bericht über das Internationale Symposium 1992 in Innsbruck,* vol. 1, 362.

10. Alexander Binsteiner, "Ötzis Dolch," *Süddeutsche Zeitung*, 13 October 1994.

11. Alexander Binsteiner, "Silexlagerstätten in den Provinzen Trent und Verona und die Feuerstein-Gruben des 'Mannes im Eis,' " *Der Anschnitt: Zeitschrift für Kunst und Kultur im Bergbau* 46, no. 6 (1994), 208.

12. Lawrence Barfield, "The Exploitation of Flint in the Monti Lessini, Northern Italy," *Stories in Stone*, Lithic Studies Society Occasional Paper no. 4, ed. Nick Ashton and Andrew David (London: Lithic Studies Society, 1994), 74.

13. Research Institute for Alpine Prehistory, Leopold-Franzens University Innsbruck, "Rechnungsabschluss für 1994—Korrektur" (1994 Account—Correction), 23 March 1995, 3.

14. Dieter zur Nedden and others, "New Findings on the Tyrolean 'Iceman,' " 809.

15. Lawrence Barfield, "The Iceman Reviewed," review of *The Man in the Ice,* by Konrad Spindler, *Antiquity* 68 (1994), 20.

16. Paul G. Bahn, "The Iceman Cometh Down the Mountain," review of *The Man in the Ice,* by Konrad Spindler, *The Times Literary Supplement,* 19 August 1994, 32.

17. Michael Zick, "Spekulationen um die Mumie," review of *Der Mann im Eis: Die Ötztaler Mumie verrät die Geheimnisse der Steinzeit,* by Konrad Spindler, *Bild der Wissenschaft* 11 (1993), 85.

18. Johan Reinhard, "Peru's Ice Maidens: Unwrapping the Secrets," *National Geographic,* June 1996, 80.

19. H. Wilfing and others, "Cranial Deformation of the Neolithic Man from the Hauslabjoch," *Collegium Antropologicum* 18, no. 2, December 1994, 280.

20. William A. Murphy, Jr., interview by author, Houston, Tx., 17 February 1997.

21. "Tod am Rande des Kraters," *Der Spiegel* 23 (1996), 176–77, 180.

22. Konrad Spindler, telephone conversation with author, 13 June 1996.

23. Klaus Oeggl, "Die Letzte Mahlzeit des Mannes im Eis," paper presented at the conference on the Man in the Ice, Bolzano, Italy, 22–24 January 1998, 2.

CHAPTER 10: "A PROPER FOREFATHER"

1. Willy Groenman–van Waateringe, "Analyses of Hides and Skins from the Hauslabjoch," in *Die Gletschermumie vom Ende der Steinzeit aus den Ötztaler Alpen,* 119.

2. James H. Dickson and others, "Mosses and the Tyrolean Iceman's Southern Provenance," *Proceedings of the Royal Society of London* B 263 (1996), 569.

3. James H. Dickson, "The Moss from the Tyrolean Iceman's Colon," *Journal of Bryology* 19 (1997), 450–51.

4. Kate Connolly, "Oetzi the Alpine Iceman Cometh, but Only Between Nine and Five," *The Guardian,* 18 August 1997.

5. Stefan Dietrich, "Ötzis Vormund," *Tiroler Tageszeitung Magazin,* 28 October 1995.

6. Lois Rogers, "Ice Man Relative Found in Dorset," *Sunday Times,* 19 June 1994.

7. Torstein Sjøvold, "A Sensational Additional Discovery at the Finding Site of the Iceman at Hauslabjoch, Preliminary Report," *Der Mann im Eis: Neue Funde und Ergebnisse,* vol. 2, 115.

8. Constance Holden, ed., "Ice Man Didn't Die Young," *Science* 272, 28 June 1996, 1875.

9. Torstein Sjøvold, "Einige Statistische Fragestellungen bei der Untersuchung des Mannes vom Hauslabjoch," in *Der Mann im Eis: Bericht über das Internationale Symposium 1992 in Innsbruck,* vol. 1, 193–194.

10. Ibid., 195.

11. "Die Letzten Tage von Ötzi (3): Akupunctur in der Steinzeit," *Stern* 36 (1993), 88.

CHAPTER 11: THE PLACE HE CAME TO LIE

1. Deutsche Presse Agentur (DPA), "Ötzi-Nachbildung darf nicht ins Museum," *Frankfurter Allgemeine Zeitung,* 4 October 1996.

2. Associated Press (AP), "Figur des 'Ötzi' darf ausgestellt werden," *Frankfurter Allgemeine Zeitung,* 11 December 1996.

3. Jutta Kusstatscher, "Experimentierobjekt Ötzi," *Alto Adige,* 6 January 1998.

4. "'Schluss mit der Geschäftemacherei!'" *Die Neue Südtiroler Tageszeitung,* 8 January 1998.

5. D. Notman and O. Beattie, "The Palaeoimaging and Forensic Anthropology of Frozen Sailors from the Franklin Arctic Expedition Mass Disaster (1845–1848): A Detailed Presentation of Two Radiological Surveys," in *The Man in the Ice: Human Mummies: A Global Survey of Their Status and the Techniques of Conservation,* vol. 3, ed. Konrad Spindler and others (New York: Springer, 1996), 95.

6. "Kommt ein Ötzi geflogen . . . " *Die Neue Südtiroler Tageszeitung,* 8 January 1998.

7. William L. Shirer, *The Rise and Fall of the Third Reich: A History of Nazi Germany* (New York: Simon and Schuster, 1959), 957.

8. Marlene Hölzner, "Leichenzug im Blitzlicht," *FF Die Südtiroler Wochenzeitung,* no. 4, 24 January 1998, 14.

9. "Nein zu zehn Mio. 'Schweigegeld,' " *Dolomiten,* 23 January 1998.

10. M. W. Hess, G. Klima, K. Pfaller, K. H. Künzel, and O. Gaber, "Histological Investigations on the Tyrolean Ice Man," *American Journal of Physical Anthropology* 106 (1998), 522.

11. T. L. Bereuter and others, "Post-mortem Alterations of Human Lipids—Part 2: Lipid Composition of a Skin Sample from the Iceman," in *The Man in the Ice: Human Mummies: A Global Survey of their Status and the Techniques of Conservation,* vol. 3, 275.

12. Thomas L. Bereuter, Werner Mikenda, and Christian Reiter, "Iceman's Mummification—Implications from Infrared Spectroscopical and Histological Studies," *Chemistry: A European Journal* 3, no. 7 (1997), 1037.

EPILOGUE

1. L. Dorfer, M. Moser, K. Spindler, and others, "5,200-Year-Old Acupuncture in Central Europe?" *Science* 282, 9 October 1998, 239.

2. W. Kutschera and others, "Radiocarbon Dating of Equipment from the Iceman," in *The Man in the Ice: The Iceman and his Natural Environment: Palaeobotanical Results,* vol. 4, ed. Sigmar Bortenschlager and Klaus Oeggl (Vienna: Springer, 2000), 5.

3. James H. Dickson, Klaus Oeggl, and others, "The Omnivorous Tyrolean Iceman: Colon Contents (Meat, Cereals, Pollen, Moss and Whipworm) and Stable Isotope Analyses," *Phil. Trans. R. Soc. Lond. B* 355, 29 December 2000, 1844.

4. Ibid.

SELECTED BIBLIOGRAPHY

Ambach, E. "Paradoxical Undressing in Fatal Hypothermia (Homo tirolensis)." *Lancet* 341 (15 May 1993): 1285.

―――, W. Tributsch, R. Henn, and W. Ambach, "Austria: '*Homo tirolensis,*' A Mummy Frozen in Time." *Lancet* 339 (1 February 1992): 296–97.

―――, Wolfgang Tributsch, and Rainer Henn. "Fatal Accidents on Glaciers: Forensic, Criminological, and Glaciological Conclusions." *Journal of Forensic Sciences* 36 no. 5 (September 1991): 1469–73.

―――, W. Tributsch, and W. Ambach. "Is Mummification Possible in Snow?" *Forensic Science International* 54 (1992): 191–92.

Ambach, W., E. Ambach, and W. Tributsch. "Austria: Tyrol's Ice-Man." *Lancet* 339 (13 June 1992): 292.

―――, E. Ambach, R. Henn, and H. Unterdorfer. "Corpses Released from Glacier Ice: Glaciological and Forensic Aspects." *Journal of Wilderness Medicine* 3 (1992): 372–76.

Anati, Emmanuel. *Valcamonica Rock Art: A New History for Europe.* Valcamonica, Italy: Edizioni del Centro, 1994.

Arnold, Bettina. "The Past as Propaganda: Totalitarian Archaeology in Nazi Germany." *Antiquity* 64 (1990): 464–78.

Ayala, Francisco J. "The Myth of Eve: Molecular Biology and Human Origins." *Science* 270 (1995), 1930–36.

Bagolini, Bernardino, Elisabetta Mottes, and Umberto Tecchiati. "Richerche di superficia in Val Senales (Bolzano) e aree limitrofe: Premesse e risultati preliminari." *Preistoria Alpina* 28 (1992): 1–55.

Bahn, Paul G. "The Iceman Cometh Down the Mountain." Review of *The Man in the Ice,* by Konrad Spindler. *The Times Literary Supplement.* 19 August 1994: 32.

———. "Last Days of the Iceman." Review of *The Man in the Ice,* by Konrad Spindler. *Archaeology* 48, no. 3 (May/June 1995): 66–70.

———, and Katharine Everett. "Iceman in the Cold Light of Day." *Nature* 362 (4 March 1993): 11–12.

Barber, E.J.W. *Prehistoric Textiles: The Development of Cloth in the Neolithic and Bronze Ages with Special Reference to the Aegean.* Princeton, N.J.: Princeton University Press, 1991.

———. *Women's Work: The First 20,000 Years: Women, Cloth, and Society in Early Times.* New York: W. W. Norton, 1994.

Barfield, Lawrence H. "The Chalcolithic Cemetery at Manerba del Garda." *Antiquity* 52 (1983): 116–23.

———. "The Context of Statue-Menhirs." In *Statue-Stele e Massi Incisi Nell'Europa dell'Eta del Rame.* Edited by Stefania Casini, Raffaele C. De Marinis, and Annaluisa Pedrotti. *Notizie Archaeologiche Bergomensi* 3 (1995): 11–17.

———. "The Exploitation of Flint in the Monti Lessini, Northern Italy." In *Stories in Stone.* Lithic Studies Society Occasional Paper no. 4, edited by Nick Ashton and Andrew David. London: Lithic Studies Society, 1994: 71–82.

———. "The Iceman Reviewed." Review of *The Man in the Ice,* by Konrad Spindler. *Antiquity* 68 (1994): 10–26.

———. *Northern Italy Before Rome.* London: Thames and Hudson, 1971.

———, Ebba Koller, and Andreas Lippert. *Der Zeuge aus dem Gletscher: Das Rätsel der frühen Alpen-Europäer.* Vienna: Carl Uberreuter, 1992.

Baroni, Carlo, and Giuseppe Orombelli. "The Alpine 'Iceman' and Holocene Climatic Change." *Quaternary Research* 46 (1996): 78–83.

Bereuter, Thomas L. "Dead, Drowned and Dehydrated." *Chemistry in Britain* 35, no. 4. (April 1999): 25–28.

———, Werner Mikenda, and Christian Reiter. "Iceman's Mummification—Implications from Infrared Spectroscopical and Histological Studies." *Chemistry: A European Journal* 3, no. 7 (1997): 1032–38.

Bernhard, W. "Anthropological Studies on the Mummy from the Ötztal Alps." *Collegium Antropologicum* 18, no. 2 (December 1994): 241–67.

Biagi, Paolo, and Renato Nisbet. "Ursprung der Landwirtschaft in Norditalien." *Zeitschrift für Archäologie* 21 (1987): 11–24.

Binsteiner, Alexander. "Silexlagerstätten in den Provinzen Trent und Verona und die Feuerstein-Gruben des 'Mannes im Eis.'" *Der Anschnitt: Zeitschrift für Kunst und Kultur im Bergbau* 46, no. 6 (1994): 207–9.

———. "Die Silexlagerstätten des Mittleren Alpenbogens: Ein Vorbericht." *Archäologisches Korrespondenzblatt* 23 (1993): 439–52.

Broholm, H. C., and Margrethe Hald. *Costumes of the Bronze Age in Denmark.* Copenhagen: NYT Nordisk Forlag, 1940.

Brothwell, Don. *The Bog Man and the Archaeology of People.* Cambridge: Harvard University Press, 1987.

Clark, J.G.D. "Neolithic Bows from Somerset, England, and the Prehistory of Archery in North-western Europe." In *Proceedings of the Prehistoric Society* 29 (December 1963): 50–98.

Cole, John W., and Eric R. Wolf. *The Hidden Frontier: Ecology and Ethnicity in an Alpine Valley.* New York: Academic Press, 1974.

Cunliffe, Barry. *The Oxford Illustrated Prehistory of Europe.* Oxford: Oxford University Press, 1994.

De Marinis, Raffaele C., and Giuseppe Brillante. *La Mummia del Similaun. Ötzi. L'Uomo Venuto dal Ghiaccio.* Venice: Marsilio, 1998.

Dickson, J. H. "The Moss from the Tyrolean Iceman's Colon." *Journal of Bryology* 19 (1997): 449–51.

Dickson, James H., Sigmar Bortenschlager, Klaus Oeggl, Ronald Porley, and Andrew McMullen. "Mosses and the Tyrolean Iceman's Southern Provenance." *Proceedings of the Royal Society of London* B (1996) 263: 567–71.

Die Ersten Bauern: Pfahlbaufunde Europas. Forschungsberichte zur Ausstellung im Schweizerischen Landesmuseum und zum Erlebnispark/Ausstellung Pfahlbauland in Zürich. 28 April to 30 September 1990. Vol. 1: Schweiz. Vol. 2: Einführung, Balkan und angrenzende Regionen der Schweiz. Zürich: Schweizerisches Landesmuseum, 1990.

Die Gletschermumie aus der Kupferzeit: Neue Forschungsergebnisse zum Mann aus dem Eis. Schriften des Südtiroler Archäologiemuseums. Bolzano, Italy: Folio Verlag, 1999.

Downs, Elinor F., and Jerold M. Lowenstein. "Identification of Archaeological Blood Proteins: A Cautionary Note." *Journal of Archaeological Science* 22 (1995): 11–16.

Egg, Markus, Roswitha Goedecker-Ciolek, Willy Groenman–Van Waateringe, and Konrad Spindler. *Die Gletschermumie vom Ende der Steinzeit aus den Ötztaler Alpen.* Sonderdruck from *Jahrbuch des Römisch-Germanisches Zentralmuseum* 39 (1992). Mainz, Germany: Römisch-Germanisches Zentral Museum, 1993.

Feder, Kenneth L. *Frauds, Myths, and Mysteries: Science and Pseudoscience in Archaeology.* Mountain View, Calif.: Mayfield Publishing Company, 1990.

Fleckinger, Angelika, and Hubert Steiner. *Der Mann aus dem Eis.* Bolzano, Italy: Folio Verlag, 1998.

Gibbons, Michael, and Björn Wittrock, eds. *Science as a Commodity: Threats to the Open Community of Scholars.* Essex: Longman, 1985.

Gleirscher, Paul. Review of *Der Mann im Eis: Die Ötztaler Mumie verrät die Geheimnisse der Steinzeit,* by Konrad Spindler. *Der Schlern* 68, no. 4 (1994): 244–48.

———. Review of *Der Mann im Eis: Bericht über das Internationale Symposium 1992, Innsbruck,* vol. 1., edited by F. Höpfel and others. *Der Schlern* 67, no. 3 (1993): 247–49.

Glob, P. V. *The Bog People: Iron-Age Man Preserved.* Ithaca, N.Y.: Cornell University Press, 1969.

Gould, Stephen Jay. *The Mismeasure of Man.* New York: W. W. Norton, 1981.

Graupe, Friedrich, and Max Scherer. *Der Mann aus dem Eis: Die archäologische Sensation des Jahrhunderts.* Vienna: Orac, 1991.

Graves-Brown, Paul, Siân Jones, and Clive Gamble, ed. *Cultural Identity and Archaeology: The Construction of European Communities.* London: Routlĕdge, 1996.

Haid, Hans. *Aufbruch in die Einsamkeit: 5000 Jahre Überleben in den Alpen.* Rosenheim: Rosenheimer Verlagshaus, 1992.

———. *Mythos und Kult in den Alpen: Älteste, Altes und Aktuelles über Kultstätten und Bergheiligtümer im Alpenraum.* Bad Sauerbrunn: Edition Tau, 1992.

Hald, Margrethe. *Ancient Danish Textiles from Bogs and Burials: A Comparative Study of Costume and Iron Age Textiles.* Archaeological-Historical Series, vol. 21. Copenhagen: National Museum of Denmark, 1980.

Handt, Oliva, and others. "Molecular Genetic Analyses of the Tyrolean Ice Man." *Science* 264 (17 June 1994): 1775–78.

Härke, Heinrich. "All Quiet on the Western Front? Paradigms, Methods and Approaches in West German Archaeology." In *Archaeological Theory in Europe: The Last Three Decades,* edited by Ian Hodder. London: Routledge, 1991.

———. " 'The Hun is a Methodical Chap': Reflections on the German

Tradition of Pre- and Proto-History." In *Theory in Archaeology: A World Perspective,* edited by P. Ucko. London: Routledge, 1995.

Harlan, Jack R. *Crops and Man.* Madison, Wis.: American Society of Agronomy, 1992.

Heim, Michael, and Werner Nosko. *Die Ötztal Fälschung: Anatomie einer Archäologischen Groteske.* Hamburg: Rowohlt, 1993.

Hess, M. W., G. Klima, K. Pfaller, K. H. Künzel, and O. Gaber. "Histological Investigations on the Tyrolean Ice Man." *American Journal of Physical Anthropology* 106 (1998): 521–32.

Hickisch, Burkhard, and Renate Spieckermann. *Ich war Ötzi: Die Botschaft aus dem Eis.* Munich: Herbig, 1994.

Holden, Constance. "Ice Man Didn't Die Young." *Science* 272 (28 June 1996): 1875.

Höpfel, Frank, Werner Platzer, and Konrad Spindler. *Der Mann im Eis: Bericht über das Internationale Symposium 1992, Innsbruck,* vol. 1. Veröffentlichungen der Universität Innsbruck 187. Innsbruck: Universität Innsbruck, 1992.

Howells, W. W. *Who's Who in Skulls: Ethnic Identification of Crania from Measurements.* Papers of the Peabody Museum of Archaeology and Ethnology, Harvard University, vol. 82. Cambridge, Mass.: Peabody Museum of Archaeology and Ethnology, Harvard University, 1995.

Johler, Reinhard, Ludwig Paulmichl, and Barbara Plankensteiner, eds. *Südtirol im Auge der Ethnographen.* Vienna: Der Prokurist, 1991.

Jolly, Clifford J., and Fred Plog. *Physical Anthropology and Archaeology.* New York: Alfred A. Knopf, 1986.

Kooyman, B., M. E. Newman, and H. Ceri. "Verifying the Reliability of Blood Residue Analysis on Archaeological Tools." *Journal of Archaeological Science* 19, no. 3 (May 1992): 265–70.

Lewontin, R. C., Steven Rose, and Leon J. Kamin. *Not in Our Genes: Biology, Ideology, and Human Nature.* New York: Pantheon, 1984.

Lippert, Andreas, and Konrad Spindler. "Die Auffindung einer frühbronzezeitlichen Gletschermumie am Hauslabjoch in den Ötztaler Alpen (Gem. Schnals)." *Archäologie Österreichs* 2, no. 2 (1991): 11–17.

Loy, Tom. "Blood on the axe." *New Scientist* 2151 (1998): 40–43.

———. "On the dating of Prehistoric Organic Residues." *The Artefact* 16 (1993): 46–49.

———. "Identifying Species of Origin from Prehistoric Blood Residues." *Science* 266 (14 October 1994): 298–300.

Lubec, G., M. Weninger, and S. R. Anderson. "Racemization and Oxidation Studies of Hair Protein in the *Homo tirolensis.*" *FASEB Journal* 8 (November 1994): 1166–69.

Lunz, Reimo. *Vor- und Frühgeschichte Südtirols.* Vol. 1 Steinzeit. Trento, Italy: Manfrini R. Arti Grafiche Vallagarina, 1986.

Lutz, Catherine A., and Jane L. Collins. *Reading National Geographic.* Chicago: The University of Chicago Press, 1993.

Macko, S. A., G. Lubec, M. Teschler-Nicola, V. Andrusevich, and M. H. Engel. "The Ice Man's Diet as Reflected by the Stable Nitrogen and Carbon Isotopic Composition of His Hair." *FASEB Journal* 13, no. 3 (March 1999): 559–62.

Marks, Jonathan. *Human Biodiversity: Genes, Race, and History.* New York: Aldine de Gruyter, 1995.

McEwen, Edward, Robert L. Miller, and Christopher A. Bergman. "Early Bow Design and Construction." *Scientific American* (June 1991): 76–82.

Mittermaier, Karl. *Südtirol: Geschichte, Politik und Gesellschaft.* Vienna: Österreichischer Bundesverlag Gesellschaft, 1986.

Molnar, Stephen. *Human Variation: Races, Types, and Ethnic Groups.* Englewood Cliffs, N.J.: Prentice-Hall, 1983.

Mullis, Kary B. "The Unusual Origin of the Polymerase Chain Reaction." *Scientific American* (April 1990): 56–65.

"Naming People Lightly." *Nature* 373 (19 January 1995): 176.

Nuland, Sherwin B. *How We Die: Reflections on Life's Final Chapter.* New York: Alfred A. Knopf, 1994.

Oeggl, Klaus. "Die Letzte Mahlzeit des Mannes im Eis" (paper presented at the conference on the Man in the Ice, Bolzano, Italy, 22–24 January 1998).

———. "The Diet of the Iceman." In *The Man in the Ice: The Iceman and His Natural Environment,* vol. 4. Veröffentlichungen des Forschungsinstituts für Alpine Vorzeit der Universität Innsbruck 4, edited by Sigmar Bortenschlager and others. Vienna: Springer. Forthcoming.

———. "Woher Kam der Eismann?" *Atti della XXXIII Riunione Scientifica dell'I. I. P. P.* Trento, Italy, 1997. (in press)

———, and Werner Schoch. "Neolithic plant remains discovered together with a mummified corpse ('Homo tyrolensis') in the Tyrolean Alps." In *Res Archaeobotanicae,* edited by H. Kroll and R. Pasternak. Kiel: Oetker-Voges Verlag: 1995: 229–38.

———. "Dendrological Analyses of Artefacts and Other Remains." In *The Man in the Ice: The Iceman and His Natural Environment,* vol. 4. Veröffertlichungen des Forschungsinstituts für Alpine Vorzeit der Universität Innsbruck 4, edited by Sigmar Bortenschlager and others. Vienna: Springer. Forthcoming.

Pabst, Maria A., and Ferdinand Hofer. "Deposits of Different Origin in the Lungs of the 5,300-Year-Old Tyrolean Iceman." *American Journal of Physical Anthropology* 107 (1998): 1–12.

Patzelt, Gernot. "Neues Vom Ötztaler Eismann." *Oesterreichischer Alpenverein (OEAV) Mitteilungen* 47, no. 2 (March/April 1992): 23–24.

Pedrotti, Annaluisa. "Bevölkerungs- und Besiedlungsbild des Spätneolithikums in Trentino-Südtirol" (paper presented at the conference on the Man in the Ice, Bolzaro, Italy, 22–24 January 1998).

———. *Uomini di Pietra: I Ritrovamenti di Arco e il Fenomeno Delle Statue Stele nell'Arco Alpino*. Trento, Italy: Provincia Autonomo di Trento. Servizio Beni Culturali, 1993.

Peintner, U., R. Pöder, and T. Pümpel. "The Iceman's Fungi." *Mycological Research* 102 (10) (1998): 1153–62.

Proctor, Robert. "From *Anthropologie* to *Rassenkunde* in the German Anthropological Tradition." In *Bones, Bodies, Behavior: Essays on Biological Anthropology,* edited by George W. Stocking, Jr. Madison: University of Wisconsin Press, 1988: 138–79.

———. *Racial Hygiene: Medicine under the Nazis*. Cambridge: Harvard University Press, 1988.

———. *Value-Free Science?: Purity and Power in Modern Knowledge*. Cambridge: Harvard University Press, 1991.

Reinhard, Johan. "Peru's Ice Maidens: Unwrapping the Secrets." *National Geographic* (June 1996): 36–43.

Remington, S. James. "Identifying Species of Origin from Prehistoric Blood Residues." *Science* 266 (14 October 1994): 298–300.

Renfrew, Colin, and Paul G. Bahn. *Archaeology: Theories, Methods, and Practice*. London: Thames and Hudson, 1991.

———, and Ruth Whitehouse. "The Copper Age of Peninsular Italy and the Aegean." *Annual of the British School of Archaeology at Athens* 69 (1974): 343–90.

Renfrew, Jane M. *Palaeoethnobotany: The Prehistoric Food Plants of the Near East and Europe*. New York: Columbia University Press, 1973.

Riedmann, Josef. *Geschichte Tirols*. Munich: R. Oldenbourg, 1983.

Roberts, David. "The Iceman." *National Geographic* 183, no. 6 (June 1993): 36–67.

Rollo, Franco, Stefano Sassaroli, and Massimo Ubaldi. "Molecular Phylogeny of the Fungi of the Iceman's Grass Clothing." *Current Genetics* 28 (1995): 289–97. Erratum. *Current Genetics* 29 (1996): 410.

Rubin, Arnold, ed. *Marks of Civilization: Artistic Transformations of the Human Body*. Los Angeles: Museum of Cultural History, University of California, 1988.

Scholl, Tillman. *Der Mann aus dem Eis*. Videotape, 97 minutes. Hamburg: Spiegel TV, 1998.

Seidler, Horst, Wolfram Bernhard, Maria Teschler-Nicola, Werner Platzer, Dieter zur Nedden, Rainer Henn, Andreas Oberhauser, Torstein Sjøvold. "Some Anthropological Aspects of the Prehistoric Tyrolean Ice Man." *Science* 258 (16 September 1992): 455–7.

Settegast, Mary. *Plato Prehistorian: 10,000 to 5000 B.C. in Myth and Archaeology*. Cambridge: The Rotenberg Press, 1986.

Sharp, Robert P. *Glaciers*. Eugene: University of Oregon Press, 1960.

Sherratt, Andrew. "Plough and Pastoralism: Aspects of the Secondary Products Revolution." In *Pattern of the Past: Studies in Honour of David Clarke*, edited by Ian Hodder, Glynn Isaac, and Norman Hammond. Cambridge: Cambridge University Press, 1981.

Shirer, William L. *The Rise and Fall of the Third Reich: A History of Nazi Germany*. New York: Simon and Schuster, 1959.

Sjøvold, T. "The Stone Age Man from the Austrian-Italian Alps. Discovery, Description and Current Research." *Collegium Antropologicum* 16 (1992) 1: 1–12.

Spindler, Konrad. *Der Mann im Eis: Die Ötztaler Mumie verrät die Geheimnisse der Steinzeit*. Munich: C. Bertelsmann, 1993.

———. *The Man in the Ice: The Discovery of a 5,000-Year-Old Body Reveals the Secrets of the Stone Age*. Translated by Ewald Osers. New York: Harmony Books, 1994.

———, Elisabeth Rastbichler-Zissernig, H. Wilfing, D. zur Nedden, and H. Nothdurfter, eds. *The Man in the Ice. Human Mummies: A Global Survey of their Status and the Techniques of Conservation*, vol. 3. 1996. Veröffentlichungen des Forschungsinstituts für Alpine Vorzeit der Universität Innsbruck 3, edited by H. Moser, W. Platzer, H. Seidler, and K. Spindler. Vienna: Springer, 1995.

———. *Der Mann im Eis: Neue Funde und Ergebnisse*, vol 2. Veröffentlichungen des Forschungsinstituts für Alpine Vorzeit der Universität Innsbruck 2, edited by H. Moser, W. Platzer, H. Seidler, and K. Spindler. Vienna: Springer, 1995.

Stead, I. M., J. B. Bourke, and Don Brothwell. *Lindow Man: The Body in the Bog*. Ithaca, N. Y.: Cornell University Press, 1986.

Taylor, Timothy. *The Prehistory of Sex: Four Million Years of Human Sexual Culture*. New York: Bantam Books, 1996.

Trigger, Bruce. "The Past as Power: Anthropology and the North American Indian." In *Who Owns the Past? Papers from the Annual Symposium of the Australian Academy of the Humanities*, edited by

Isabel McBryde. Melbourne, Australia: Oxford University Press, 1985.

Turner, R. C., and R. G. Scaife. *Bog Bodies: New Discoveries and New Perspectives*. London: British Museum Press, 1995.

Tylecote, R. F. *The Early History of Metallurgy in Europe*. London: Longman, 1987.

———. *A History of Metallurgy*. Avon: The Bath Press (The Institute of Materials), 1992.

Tyndall, John. *The Glaciers of the Alps, Being a Narrative of Excursions and Ascents, an Account of the Origin and Phenomena of Glaciers, and an Exposition of the Physical Principles to Which they are Related*. London: John Murray, 1860.

Veit, Ulrich. "Ethnic Concepts in German Prehistory: A Case Study on the Relationship between Cultural Identity and Archaeological Objectivity." Translated by Stephen Shennan. In *Archaeological Approaches to Cultural Identity*, edited by Stephen Shennan. London: Unwin Hyman, 1989.

Vial, A. E. Lockington. *Alpine Glaciers*. London: The Batchworth Press, 1952.

Volgger, Franz. *Südtirol Handbuch*. Bolzano, Italy: Südtiroler Landesregierung, 1994.

Von Haesler, Arndt, Antti Sajantila, and Svante Pääbo. "The Genetical Archaeology of the Human Genome." *Nature Genetics* 14 (October 1995): 135–40.

Walsh, John Evangelist. *Unraveling Piltdown: The Science Fraud of the Century and Its Solution*. New York: Random House, 1996.

Ward, Martha C. *The Hidden Life of Tirol*. Prospect Heights, Ill.: Waveland Press, 1993.

Wenke, Robert J. *Patterns in Prehistory: Humankind's First Three Million Years*. New York: Oxford University Press, 1990.

Wilfing, H. and others. "Cranial Deformation of the Neolithic Man from the Hauslabjoch." *Collegium Antropologicum* 18, no. 2 (December 1994): 269–82.

———. "Untersuchungen an Haarresten des Mannes vom Hauslabjoch." *Naturwissenschaftliche Rundschau* 46, no. 7 (1993): 257–60.

Wilson, Allan C., and Rebecca L. Cann. "The Recent African Genesis of Humans." *Scientific American* (April 1992): 68–73.

Zick, Michael. "Spekulationen um die Mumie." Review of *Der Mann im Eis*, by Konrad Spindler. *Bild der Wissenschaft* 11 (1993): 84–5.

Zohary, Daniel, and Maria Hopf. *Domestication of Plants in the Old*

World: The Origin and Spread of Cultivated Plants in West Asia, Europe, and the Nile Valley. Oxford: Clarendon Press, 1993.

zur Nedden, Dieter, Klaus Wicke, Rudolf Knapp, Horst Seidler, Harald Wilfing, Gerhard Weber, Konrad Spindler, William A. Murphy, Jr., Gertrud Hauser, and Werner Platzer. "New Findings on the Tyrolean 'Iceman': Archaeological and CT-Body Analysis Suggest Personal Disaster Before Death." *Journal of Archaeological Science* 21 (1994): 809–17.

zur Nedden, Dieter and others. "Skull of a 5,300-year-old Mummy: Reproduction and Investigation with CT-guided Stereolithography." *Radiology* 193 (1994): 269–72.

INDEX

Grateful acknowledgment is made to the following for permission to reprint unpublished and previously published material:

Alto Adige: Excerpt from an article by Ezio Danieli from the September 22, 1991, issue of *Alto Adige*. Reprinted by permission of *Alto Adige*.

Antiquity and Lawrence Barfield: Excerpt from "The Iceman Reviewed," by Lawrence Barfield (*Antiquity,* vol. 68, p. 20). Reprinted by permission of *Antiquity* and Lawrence Barfield.

Austria Presse Agentur and Dolomiten: Excerpt from "Leichenfund auf Tiroler Gletscher," from September 21, 1991. Reprinted by permission of *Austria Presse Agentur* and *Dolomiten*.

Sigmar Bortenschlager: Excerpt from a letter from Sigmar Bortenschlager to Hans Moser. Reprinted by permission of Sigmar Bortenschlager.

Ivo Greiter: Excerpt from a letter from Ivo Greiter to Bayerischer Rundfunk (Bavarian Broadcasting). Reprinted by permission of Greiter Pegger Kofler & Partner.

Hans Haid: Excerpt from a letter from Hans Haid to ORF. Reprinted by permission of Hans Haid.

Michael Heim: Excerpt from a letter from Michael Heim to the law firm of Greiter Pegger Kofler. Reprinted by permission of Michael Heim.

The Lancet: Excerpt from a letter entitled "Paradoxical Undressing in Fatal Hypothermia (Homo tirolensis)," by E. Ambach, in *The Lancet,* vol. 341, p. 1285, May 15, 1993. Copyright © 1993 by The Lancet Ltd. Reprinted by permission of *The Lancet*.

Landesgendarmeriekommando für Tirol: Excerpt from a gendarmerie report dated September 19, 1991. Reprinted by permission of Landesgendarmeriekommando für Tirol.

Hans Moser: Quotes from the forensic protocol on the Iceman. Reprinted by permission of Hans Moser, Rector, University of Innsbruck.

Werner Platzer: Excerpt from a letter from Werner Platzer to Helmut Stampfer. Reprinted by permission of em. o. Univ. Prof. Dr. Dr. n. c. Werner Platzer.

Springer Verlag and Konrad Spindler: Excerpts from "Iceman's Last Weeks," by Konrad Spindler, from *Human Mummies: A Global Survey of Their Status and the Techniques of Conservation,* edited by Konrad Spindler and H. Wilfing (Springer Verlag, 1996). Reprinted by permission of Springer Verlag and Konrad Spindler.